D0793821

MOZART'S PIANO CONCERTOS

DRAMATIC DIALOGUE IN THE AGE OF ENLIGHTENMENT

MOZART'S PIANO CONCERTOS

DRAMATIC DIALOGUE IN THE AGE OF ENLIGHTENMENT

Simon P. Keefe

THE BOYDELL PRESS

First published 2001
The Boydell Press, Woodbridge

ISBN 0 85115 834 X

The Boydell Press is an imprint of Boydell & Brewer Ltd
PO Box 9, Woodbridge, Suffolk IP12 3DF, UK
and of Boydell & Brewer Inc.
PO Box 41026, Rochester, NY 14604–4126, USA
website: http://www.boydell.co.uk

A catalogue record for this book is available
from the British Library

Library of Congress Cataloging-in-Publication Data
Keefe, Simon P., 1968–
Mozart's piano concertos: dramatic dialogue in the Age of Enlightenment/Simon P. Keefe.
p. c.m.
Includes bibliographical references (p.) and index.
ISBN 0–85115–834–X (alk. paper)
1. Mozart, Wolfgang Amadeus, 1756–1791. Concertos, piano, orchestra. I. Title.
ML410.M9 K25 2001
784.2′62′092 – dc21 2001025775

This publication is printed on acid-free paper

Typeset by Joshua Associates Ltd, Oxford
Printed in Great Britain by
St Edmundsbury Press Ltd, Bury St Edmunds, Suffolk

For Celia and Abraham

Contents

Acknowledgements

A book-length study invariably incurs many debts of a personal and professional kind. Two individuals in particular helped to shape the style and content of this monograph. John Daverio gave focus to my earliest ideas on dialogue in Mozart's piano concertos at Boston University in 1992 with his customary sensitivity and insight. Similarly, Elaine Sisman supervised my subsequent doctoral thesis at Columbia University in a skilful and erudite fashion. Latterly, Cliff Eisen has offered much appreciated advice and sage counsel on a number of issues connected to this book and to other Mozart-related topics.

Other academics and friends have offered welcome support. Colleagues at Christ Church, Oxford (1997–9), and at the School of Music at The Queen's University of Belfast (1999–), have created excellent working environments from which I have greatly benefited; I extend particular thanks to Chris Corrigan at Queen's University for frequent technical assistance. Three friends over the last decade – Julian Treves, Michael von der Linn and Robert Tucker – have taken a particularly active interest in my research and receive my gratitude.

Family members have provided my most enduring source of support. My parents, Terry and Sheila Keefe, sister Rosanna Keefe and in-laws, Robert and Virginia Hurwitz, have offered unstinting help and encouragement. In addition, my father has cast expert eyes over countless French translations, offering meticulous advice on matters of detail and style. Above all, my wife, Celia Hurwitz-Keefe, has combined loving encouragement and intellectual support in an extraordinary way. Not only has she read every word of this volume, improving the overall style and substance immeasurably, but she has also tolerated my mildly obsessive working habits in a completely understanding and good-natured fashion. It is to Celia and to our young son Abraham – who is already engaging in his own kind of imitative dialogue with us – that this book is dedicated, with heartfelt love and appreciation.

I am grateful to the following for permission to reprint versions of my previously published work, revised to incorporate significant amounts of new material: Oxford University Press for 'Koch's Commentary on the Late-Eighteenth-Century Concerto: Dialogue, Drama and Solo/Orchestra Relations', *Music & Letters* 79/3 (1998), pp. 368–85 (Chapter One), and 'Dramatic Dialogue in Mozart's Viennese Piano Concertos: A Study of Competition and Cooperation in Three First Movements', *The Musical Quarterly* 83/2 (1999), pp. 169–204 (Chapter Three); Bärenreiter-Verlag, Kassel for 'Antoine

Reicha's *Dialogue*: the Emergence of a Theoretical Concept', *Acta Musicologica* 72/1 (2000), pp. 43–62 (Chapter Two); OPA (Overseas Publishers Association), N.V., with permission from Gordon and Breach Publishers for 'The Stylistic Significance of the First Movement of Mozart's Piano Concerto No. 24 in C Minor, K. 491: A Dialogic Apotheosis', *Journal of Musicological Research* 18/3 (1999), pp. 225–61 (Chapter Four).

Simon P. Keefe
The Queen's University of Belfast
12 October 2000

Introduction

Mozart's piano concertos are among the most popular works in the Western canon, a status reflected by the huge volume of secondary literature that exists for almost every aspect of this repertory. One vital component of these concertos, however, has not yet received attention in a book-length study: the interactive relationship between the piano and the orchestra. Given that the works date from the Age of Enlightenment, an era that openly debated the individual's relation to society and continually espoused the virtues of collaboration and communication, interactive relations between the pianist and the orchestra in Mozart's concertos carry rich historical, cultural and contextual significance. As interaction is also fundamental to the structural alternation of piano and orchestral forces, a careful study of it sheds light on the inner workings of musical forms and textures in the concertos as well.

The study at hand situates relations between Mozart's piano and orchestra in historical and cultural contexts, and is rooted in critical discourse of the period. In the late eighteenth century, music theorists and aestheticians were preoccupied with the possibility that music might convey meaning in an analogous fashion to language. Although an integration of text and music was seen to bring greatly valued specificity of meaning to vocal works, leading them to acquire a higher aesthetic position than instrumental music, the potential of instrumental music to achieve a similar specificity was not overlooked. Eager to demonstrate the aesthetic value of instrumental works, writers frequently focused linguistic analogies around the concept of dialogue, a popular metaphor for instrumental interaction. The most revealing and meticulous writings on the concerto in Mozart's time, undertaken by Heinrich Christoph Koch, identify dialogue between the piano and the orchestra as the vital component of dynamic solo/orchestra relations in the late-eighteenth-century concerto.

Although Koch's invocation of dialogue in the context of highly charged interaction between the soloist and the orchestra has found considerable resonance in twentieth-century critical writings on Mozart's piano concertos, its hermeneutic potential for this repertoire has yet to be fully realised. Indeed, as a metaphor for solo/orchestra relations, for example, it remains unsystematically applied. Cuthbert Girdlestone intelligently defines 'varieties of dialogue' in Mozart's piano concertos as '[t]he orchestral link, the echo, the answer, [and] phrases that alternate between solo and tutti' but does not draw upon these definitions specifically in his analyses.[1] Joseph Kerman describes dialogue as the piano and orchestra's repetition of each other's musical material, but provides little else by way of a technical explanation.[2] Other critics are content either to leave dialogue undefined, or to use the term in such a way as to allow it to refer to very general piano/orchestra interaction. Along these lines, Donald F. Tovey locates a piano/orchestra dialogue across the entire development section of K. 488/i; Kurt von Fischer describes the general interaction between the piano and the orchestra in K. 450 as a 'bright, playful dialogue' ('bunt spielerischen Dialogs'); Nicholas Till comments that 'it is not fanciful to hear in Mozart's piano concertos . . . a progressive dialogue between the individual and expressive voice of the soloist and the wider "community" of the orchestra'; and William Kinderman mentions 'the dramatic character of the dialogue between orchestra and soloist' when clearly referring to the general interaction of the two forces during the movement.[3]

From an historical perspective, the idea of dialogue in Mozart's piano concertos carries more specific musical connotations than previously recognised. As we shall see, dialogue had firmly established itself as a theoretical concept applicable to late-eighteenth-century instrumental music by the end of the classical period. Although recent writers have recognised the relevance of historical sources for defining dialogue in chamber music, they have not extended their argument to the concerto genre. Several have characterised dialogue as the concise interplay of short motifs;[4] another, linking the 'dialogue principle' (*Gesprächsprinzip*) to discourse in analysing the logic of motivic and thematic processes in Mozart's and Haydn's string quartets, considers the analogy between ordered thoughts and spoken discourse historically appropriate in musical as well as non-musical contexts.[5] Equally, writers have distinguished intelligently between 'dialogue' and 'concertant' in chamber music, identifying the latter as either the changing soloistic prominence of

[1] Cuthbert Girdlestone, *Mozart and His Piano Concertos* (New York: Dover, 1964 [first published in French as *W.A. Mozart et ses concertos pour piano*, Paris, 1939]), p. 64.

[2] Joseph Kerman, 'Mozart's Piano Concertos and Their Audience', in *On Mozart*, ed. James M. Morris (Cambridge: Cambridge University Press, 1994), p. 154.

[3] Donald F. Tovey, *Essays in Musical Analysis: Concertos and Choral Works*, 7th ed. (London: Oxford University Press, 1981 [first published, 1935–9]), p. 172; Kurt von Fischer, 'Das Dramatische in Mozarts Klavierkonzerten 1784 mit besonderer Berücksichtigung des ersten Satzes von KV 453', *Mozart-Jahrbuch 1986*, p. 72; Nicholas Till, *Mozart and the Enlightenment: Truth, Virtue and Beauty in Mozart's Operas* (New York: Norton, 1992), p. 177; William Kinderman, 'Dramatic Development and Narrative Design in the First Movement of Mozart's Concerto in C Minor, K. 491', in *Mozart's Piano Concertos: Text, Context, Interpretation*, ed. Neal Zaslaw (Ann Arbor: University of Michigan Press, 1996), p. 285.

[4] See Ulrich Mazurowicz, *Das Streichduett in Wien von 1760 bis zum Tode Joseph Haydns* (Tutzing: Hans Schneider, 1982), pp. 130–3; Hubert Unverricht, *Geschichte des Streichtrios* (Tutzing: Hans Schneider, 1969), p. 213; Roland Würtz, *Dialogué: Vorrevolutionäre Kammermusik in Mannheim und Paris* (Wilhelmshaven: Noetzel, 1990), p. 82.

[5] Nicole Schwindt-Gross, *Drama und Diskurs: Zur Beziehung zwischen Satztechnik und motivischem Prozess am Beispiel der durchbrochenen Arbeit in der Streichquartetten Mozarts und Haydns* (Laaber: Laaber-Verlag, 1989), pp. 119–22.

instruments or the exchange of full phrases or periods (for example, 4– and 8–bar units).[6]

In any case, Mozart's piano concertos require a different perspective on dialogue than classical chamber music. The frequent exchange of concise motives, for example, has less of a role in a genre that preserves a fundamental soloist/orchestra hierarchy rather than aspiring to a form of equality among interlocutors, as did classical chamber music. Furthermore, the context in which late-eighteenth-century writers situate dialogue and piano/orchestra relations in the concerto – one of drama – is dissimilar to the conversational context in which they situate interaction in chamber music, thus demanding a formal rather than an informal definition and application of dialogue.

A study that sets Mozart's piano concertos not only in the specific dramatic framework of his operas, but also in the broader milieu of late-eighteenth-century spoken drama is long overdue. When Koch describes solo/orchestra relations in the late-eighteenth-century concerto, for example, he invokes the processive nature of spoken drama. Resonating as it does with other historical sources, Koch's attention to spoken drama inspires in this study a dramatic perspective on dialogue in Mozart's piano concertos not limited exclusively to opera. Widening an historical and contextual foundation to include comparisons of theoretical writings on musical and dramatic dialogue, musical and dramatic processes in specific concertos and plays, and the objectives of contemporary composers and dramatists, encourages the listener to hear these well-known works with fresh ears that more closely resemble those of Mozart's musically and dramatically attuned contemporaries. Equally, by extending the venerable tradition of drawing parallels between Mozart's operas and concertos to dialogue, we are afforded a new perspective on Mozart's stylistic development.

The context of classical dramatic criticism and practice in which Mozart's concerto dialogue is situated includes several of the most important theoretical tracts and spoken plays in the history of European theatre. Recent research by scholars such as Nicholas Till, Georg Knepler and Paolo Gallarati has established a basic kinship between facets of Mozart's operas and musical thought and the nascent theoretical work of Classical dramatic writers.[7] Moreover, Mozart, a self-professed devotee of the theatre who claimed in 1781 that it was his 'sole amusement', would have had the opportunity to see plays such as *Minna von Barnhelm*, *Emilia Galotti* and *Clavigo* in Vienna in the 1780s, even though performances of such great, ostensibly 'classical' plays were relatively rare in the city at this time.[8] In any case, parallels I identify between dialogic

[6] Mazurowicz, *Das Streichduett*, pp. 130–3; Unverricht, *Geschichte des Streichtrios*, p. 213; Würtz, *Dialogué*, p. 82.

[7] See Till, *Mozart and the Enlightenment*, *passim*; Georg Knepler, *Wolfgang Amadé Mozart*, trans. J. Bradford Robinson (Cambridge: Cambridge University Press, 1994), *passim*; Paolo Gallarati, 'Mozart and Eighteenth-Century Comedy', in *Opera Buffa in Mozart's Vienna*, eds. Mary Hunter and James Webster (Cambridge: Cambridge University Press, 1997), pp. 98–111.

[8] The context of Mozart's remark on the theatre – in a letter to Leopold on 26 May, 1781 – is as

procedures in Mozart's piano concertos and in contemporary Classical plays represent more than a mere musical-dramatic *Zeitgeist.* Mozart's concertos are infused not only with the spirit but also with the dialogic prowess of Classical drama, suggesting a tighter bond between dramatic and musical 'classicism' than has hitherto been recognised.[9]

Part I of this study considers the aesthetic and theoretical contexts of dialogue in Mozart's piano concertos; Part II continues with an analysis of the dramatic properties and stylistic ramifications of his concerto dialogue. Chapter One examines Koch's remarks on the expressive qualities of the concerto in the *Versuch einer Anleitung zur Composition* (1782–93) and the *Musikalisches Lexikon* (1802), explaining how they construct an eloquent defence of the genre against its detractors (especially Johann Georg Sulzer). Koch's invocations of dramatic dialogue, at once informed by contemporary musical and dramatic criticism and vital to a highly original view of dynamic solo/orchestra relations, represent an especially rich foundation for investigating dialogue in Mozart's piano concertos.

Chapter Two turns to the historical construction of dialogue as a theoretical concept, focussing on the comprehensive and learned understanding of Antoine Reicha. Clarifying generalised eighteenth-century notions of dialogue and standardizing dialogic conventions, Reicha's theoretical writings provide a solid basis – in an analogous fashion to Koch's aesthetic remarks – for explaining the characteristics and formal functions of dramatic dialogue in Mozart's concertos.

Chapters Three, Four, Five and Six pursue different, although closely related lines of investigation into dialogue and piano/orchestra relations in Mozart's concertos. Chapter Three traces the piano and orchestra's integration of competitive and co-operative behaviour into the first movements of K. 449, 450 and 482, informed by theoretical discussion of late-eighteenth-century musical and dramatic dialogue. The relational development in these movements

follows: 'If only there were even a tolerably good theatre in Salzburg! For in Vienna my sole amusement is the theatre.' See Emily Anderson ed. and trans., *The Letters of Mozart and His Family* (New York: Norton, 1985 [3rd edition]), p. 736. For a complete list of performances of operas and plays at the Vienna *Burgtheater* in 1783–92, see Dorothea Link, *The National Court Theatre in Mozart's Vienna: Sources and Documents, 1783–1792* (Oxford: Clarendon Press, 1998), pp. 5–190.

[9] Although 'dialogic' is used as the adjectival form of 'dialogue' in this study, no reference to Mikhail M. Bakhtin's understanding of the term is intended. The historical, critical and analytical relevance of Bakhtin's influential theories to Mozart's piano concertos lies outside the scope of the present investigation. Their applicability to late-eighteenth- and early-nineteenth-century instrumental music has recently been explored in George Edwards, 'The Nonsense of an Ending: Closure in Haydn's String Quartets', *Musical Quarterly* 75 (1992), pp. 227–54; and Jayme Stayer, 'Bringing Bakhtin to Beethoven: The Ninth Symphony and the Limits of Formalism', *The Beethoven Journal* 10/2 (1995), pp. 53–9. Four of Bakhtin's important essays are compiled in *The Dialogic Imagination*, ed. Michael Holquist, trans. Caryl Emerson and Michael Holquist (Austin: University of Texas Press, 1981).

is compared to that in scenes from contemporary classical plays. Chapter Four compares dialogic organization in the opening movement of Mozart's extraordinary K. 491 to similar organizations in corresponding movements of Mozart's preceding piano concertos (K. 271–488). While there are precedents for both the distinctive dialogic processes of K. 491/i (the striking confrontation between the piano and the orchestra in the development section, for example) and for its general pattern of relational development (intimate dialogue in the solo exposition and recapitulation sections contrasting with less tightly-knit exchange in the development), this movement goes further than its predecessors both in its symmetrical arrangements of dialogue and in its *tour de force* of dialogic ingenuity in the recapitulation. Interpreting Mozart's departure from his standard pattern of relational development in the final three concertos (K. 503, 537 and 595) as an attempt, after the remarkable sophistication of K. 491/i, at dialogic renewal, I reinforce K. 491's position as a climactic work among Mozart's concertos. Chapter Five, developing stylistic conclusions from Chapters Three and Four, correlates dialogic confrontation and co-operation in the first and second movements of the concertos with corresponding behaviour in arias, duets and ensembles from Mozart's operas *Idomeneo*, *Entführung*, *Figaro* and *Don Giovanni*. Establishing Mozart's inter-generic approach, in which conceptions of dialogue in one genre inform analogous conceptions in the other, I underline the pivotal dramatic significance of the first movements of K. 449 and 491 to the stylistic development of confrontation in *both* his concerto and operatic repertoires. Finally, Chapter Six re-engages Mozart's concertos with late-eighteenth-century dramatic criticism, determining the potential of complete cycles to fulfil analogous functions to spoken plays. I explain how resolutions to first-movement confrontations are reinforced in later movements; how specific dialogic procedures recur from first to second movements; and how finales act as dialogic culminations to entire three-movement cycles. Identifying similarities between the theoretical objectives of late-eighteenth-century concertos and classical plays – active audience engagement, edifying effects and broad appeal for listeners and spectators of varying aptitudes – I reveal that processes of dramatic dialogue across Mozart's concerto cycles were as significant a medium of enlightenment in the late eighteenth century as were classical plays and Mozart's own operas.

Inevitably, this study of dramatic dialogue and solo/orchestra relations in Mozart's piano concertos leaves many stones unturned. I do not explore, for example, the extent to which an understanding of dramatic dialogue is affected by controversial issues of performance practice.[10] While 'col basso' indications in Mozart's autograph scores suggest that late-eighteenth-century pianists

[10] For a recent, informative overview of issues of performance practice in Mozart's piano concertos see David Grayson, *Mozart: Piano Concertos Nos. 20 and 21* (Cambridge: Cambridge University Press, 1998), pp. 93–117. For an introduction to the issue in Mozart's output in general see Robin Stowell, 'Performance Practice' in *The Mozart Compendium: A Guide to Mozart's Life and Music*, ed. H. C. Robbins Landon (London: Thames and Hudson, 1990), pp. 372–83.

would often have doubled the bass line in passages in which s/he is not featured as a soloist, thus fulfilling a largely supportive role, the practice itself remains highly contentious.[11] Since the basso continuo would engage in very limited interaction with the orchestra in any case, the ramifications of the technique for analysing piano/orchestra relations are not addressed here. Equally, the extent to which practices of improvised embellishment can and should elaborate piano/orchestra dialogue lies beyond the scope of this investigation. Furthermore, only extant cadenzas by Mozart are considered in interpretations of dialogue and piano/orchestra relations; other cadenzas, irrespective of their musical and stylistic worth, are not considered.

In addition to issues of performance practice, several of Mozart's early concertos do not feature in this study. Whatever their merits, the seven concertos arranged from sonatas and sonata movements by Raupach, Honauer, Schobert, Eckard, C.P.E. Bach (K. 37, 39, 40, 41) and J.C. Bach (K. 107), and the first three 'original' piano concertos (K. 175, 238, 246), lack the interactional subtlety and sophistication of Mozart's later works.[12] The concertos K. 242 and 365 would require an approach to dialogue and piano/orchestra relations grounded in inter-soloist as well as solo/orchestra interaction – on account of the scoring for three and two piano soloists respectively – and are also excluded. The eighteen remaining works (K. 271, 413, 414, 415, 449, 450, 451, 453, 456, 459, 466, 467, 482, 488, 491, 503, 537, 595) provide the material for this historical-analytical investigation. It is in these enduring masterpieces – perhaps more than in any other sequence of instrumental works ever composed – that Mozart remained most true to the spirit of the Enlightenment.

[11] For a comprehensive study of the 'col basso' issue, see Linda Faye Ferguson, 'Col basso and Generalbass in Mozart's Keyboard Concertos: Notation, Performance, Theory and Practice' (Ph.D. diss., Princeton University, 1983), and 'The Classical Keyboard Concerto: Some Thoughts on Authentic Performance', *Early Music* 12 (1984), pp. 437–45. For a dismissal of the 'col basso' as detrimental to the 'drama' of the soloist's entry at the beginning of the solo exposition, see Charles Rosen, *The Classical Style: Haydn, Mozart, Beethoven* (London: Faber, 1971; New York: Norton, 1971), pp. 189–94. See also Rosen, 'Review of *Mozart's Piano Concertos: Text, Context, Interpretation*, edited by Neal Zaslaw', *Journal of the American Musicological Society* 51 (1998), pp. 381–4.

[12] For an examination of K. 37, 39, 40, 41 and 107 (Nos. 1–3) see Edwin J. Simon, 'Sonata into Concerto: A Study of Mozart's First Seven Concertos', *Acta Musicologica* 31 (1959), pp. 170–85.

PART I

THEORIES AND CONTEXTS

1

Heinrich Christoph Koch's Commentary on the Late-Eighteenth-Century Concerto

Towards an Understanding of Dialogue, Drama and Solo/Orchestra Relations in Mozart's Piano Concertos

It has long been recognised that Heinrich Christoph Koch's writings on first-movement concerto form in the *Versuch einer Anleitung zur Composition* and *Musikalisches Lexikon* are the most detailed and illuminating of the classical period.[1] Koch's accounts, which divide alternating ritornello and solo sections into main periods (*Hauptperioden*) and identify an underlying harmonic pattern characteristic of an incipient sonata movement, have been particularly influential as regards recent thinking on late-eighteenth-century concerto form.[2] His comments on the expressive qualities of the concerto, however, while frequently cited by critics, have not yet received their historical or contextual due.[3] In these

[1] Heinrich Christoph Koch, *Versuch einer Anleitung zur Composition*, Leipzig, 1782–93 (repr., Hildesheim, 1969), trans. Nancy Kovaleff Baker as *Introductory Essay on Composition: The Mechanical Rules of Melody, Sections 3 and 4* (New Haven: Yale University Press, 1983), pp. 207–13; and *Musikalisches Lexikon* (Frankfurt, 1802; reprint, Hildesheim: Georg Olms, 1964), cols. 349–55. The historical importance of Koch's discussion of first-movement concerto form was first brought to the attention of the musicological community at large by Jane R. Stevens in 'An 18th-Century Description of Concerto First-Movement Form', *Journal of the American Musicological Society* 24 (1971), pp. 85–95; and 'Theme, Harmony, and Texture in Classic-Romantic Descriptions of Concerto First-Movement Form', *Journal of the American Musicological Society* 27 (1974), pp. 25–60.

[2] Most recently Karol Berger has offered thoughtful and provocative interpretations of first-movement form in Mozart's concertos informed by Koch's periodic structure and emphasis upon punctuation. See 'Toward a History of Hearing: The Classic Concerto, A Sample Case', *Convention in Eighteenth- and Nineteenth-Century Music: Essays in Honor of Leonard Ratner*, ed. Wye J. Allanbrook, Janet M. Levy and William P. Mahrt (Stuyvesant, New York: Pendragon, 1992), pp. 405–29; and 'The First-movement Punctuation Form in Mozart's Piano Concertos', *Mozart's Piano Concertos: Text, Context, Interpretation*, ed. Neal Zaslaw (Ann Arbor: University of Michigan Press, 1996), pp. 239–59. Berger also discusses punctuation in the middle movements of Mozart's piano concertos. See 'The Second-Movement Punctuation Form in Mozart's Piano Concertos: The Andantino of K. 449', *Mozart-Jahrbuch 1991*, pp. 168–72. Koch's explanations of first-movement concerto form differ slightly in the *Versuch* and the *Lexikon*. See Stevens, 'Theme, Harmony, and Texture', p. 41; and Shelley Davis, 'H. C. Koch, the Classic Concerto, and the Sonata-Form Retransition', *Journal of Musicology* 2 (1983), pp. 45–61, esp. pp. 45–9.

[3] Nancy Kovaleff Baker has carried out ground-breaking work on Koch's aesthetic views. See, for example, 'From *Teil* to *Tonstück*: The Significance of the *Versuch einer Anleitung zur Composition*

passages, Koch constructs an eloquent defence of the concerto against its detractors through elegant invocations of dramatic dialogue. An interpretation of the relationship between the soloist and the orchestra that draws on dialogue is, at once, richly imaginative and exceedingly well-informed by contemporary musical and dramatic criticism. As we shall see, Koch's account solidifies the concerto's dramatic credentials and at the same time suggests new avenues of investigation into what is arguably the central dramatic component of the late-eighteenth-century concerto, namely the interaction between the soloist and the orchestra.

Koch's discussion of the relationship between the soloist and the orchestra appears in a passage from the *Versuch* (repeated in the *Lexikon*) immediately preceding his formal exegesis. In contrast to the sonata, in which '[t]he expression of feeling by the solo player is like a monologue in passionate tones', Koch describes the concerto as a 'passionate dialogue [*leidenschaftliche Unterhaltung*] between the concerto player and the accompanying orchestra'. He situates this dialogue in the context of spoken drama: 'In short, by a concerto I imagine something similar to the tragedy of the ancients, where the actor expressed his feelings not towards the pit, but to the chorus.'[4]

Such comments on the concerto are remarkable in that they depart from the prevailing tradition of concerto criticism. In the second half of the eighteenth century a number of prominent theorists found fault with the concerto, linking its reliance upon virtuosic effects with an apparent absence of character (a fatal flaw in the eyes of some).[5] In 1766, for example, the English critic John Gregory

by Heinrich Christoph Koch', Unpublished dissertation, Yale University, 1975; 'Heinrich Koch and the Theory of Melody', *Journal of Music Theory* 20 (1976), pp. 1–48; 'The Aesthetic Theories of Heinrich Christoph Koch', *International Review of the Aesthetics and Sociology of Music* 8 (1977), pp. 183–209; and 'Heinrich Koch's Description of the Symphony', *Studi Musicali* 9 (1980), pp. 303–16.

[4] *Introductory Essay*, p. 209, *Musikalisches Lexikon*, col. 354. (In the *Lexikon*, the reference to the sonata is omitted.) Nancy Kovaleff Baker translates 'leidenschaftliche Unterhaltung' as 'passionate dialogue' while Jane Stevens, quoting the same passage from Koch's *Versuch*, translates it as 'emotional relationship'. See Stevens, 'An 18th-Century Description', p. 94. Given that Koch directly contrasts the sonata's 'Monolog in leidenschaftlichen Tönen' ('monologue in passionate tones' [*Introductory Essay*, p. 209]) with the concerto's 'leidenschaftliche Unterhaltung', the more appropriate translation is Baker's 'passionate dialogue'. Definitions of 'Unterhaltung' (conversation) and 'Gespräch' (dialogue) in German dictionaries contemporary with Koch's *Versuch* and *Lexikon* make it clear that the two terms are used more or less interchangeably, even though the functions of dramatic and conversational exchange are understood as very different. See, for example, Johann Christoph Adelung, *Grammatisch-kritisches Wörterbuch der hochdeutschen Mundart* (Vienna, 1808); Joachim Heinrich Campe, *Wörterbuch der deutschen Sprache* (Braunschweig, 1808–11); and Theodor Heinsius, *Wörterbuch der deutschen Sprache* (Hannover, 1818–22). It is therefore not inappropriate for Baker to translate 'leidenschaftliche Unterhaltung' as 'passionate dialogue' rather than as 'passionate conversation', since Koch explicitly situates concerto dialogue in a dramatic context, and in English we generally refer to dramatic dialogues not dramatic conversations.

[5] Such as Charles Batteux in *Les Beaux-Arts Réduits à un même Principe* (1746) (Paris: Aux Amateurs de Livres, 1989), p. 240. 'La plus mauvaise de toutes les musiques est celle qui n'a point de caractère'. For a thorough, probing study of 'caractère' in eighteenth-century France, see Jane

drew attention to the 'thinness and meagreness of the parts'. He continued: 'It is not easy to characterise the stile of most of these pieces. In truth they have no character or meaning at all. – The Authors of them are little concerned what Subject they choose, their single view being to excite the surprise and admiration of their hearers.'[6] Others, while not quite as severe as Gregory, nonetheless struck a similar tone. In the *Allgemeine Theorie* (1771–4), Sulzer and Kirnberger asserted:

> In fact, the concerto has no fixed character; therefore no one can say what it is supposed to represent or what we are to take from it. At the most basic level, it is nothing but a practice session for composers and players, and a totally indeterminate aural amusement, aimed at nothing more.[7]

Along similar lines, Daniel Gottlob Türk pointed out in 1789 that '[c]ustomarily in this type of instrumental composition, concern is more for the facility of the player than for any particular character'.[8] Although Türk did not indicate that the concerto was incapable of possessing character, he did, like Gregory and Sulzer/Kirnberger before him, suggest a direct link between virtuosity and the absence of specific character.[9]

By invoking spoken drama (the Greek tragedy) and dialogue, Koch lent the concerto new-found *gravitas*. Greek tragedies were universally venerated by eighteenth-century dramatists and opera composers, and used as yardsticks

R. Stevens, 'The Meanings and Uses of *Caractère* in Eighteenth-century France', *French Musical Thought, 1600–1800*, ed. Georgia J. Cowart (Ann Arbor: UMI Research Press, 1989), pp. 24–52. Stevens concludes that 'In musical writings . . . *caractère* seems consistently to refer either to an actual human character or type, or to a human analogue for the music itself' (*ibid.*, p. 40).

[6] John Gregory, 'Discourse III', from his *A Comparative View of the State and Faculties of Man, with those of the Animal World* (London: J. Dodsley, 1766, 2nd edn), pp. 100–1.

[7] 'Concert', in *Allgemeine Theorie der schönen Künste*, ed. Johann Georg Sulzer (Leipzig, 1771–74; reprint Hildesheim: Georg Olms, 1969), 4 vols., vol. 1, p. 573: 'Das Concert hat eigentlich keinen bestimmten Charakter; denn niemand kann sagen, was es vorstellen soll, oder was man damit ausrichten will. Im Grund ist es nichts, als eine Uebung für Setzer und Spieler, und eine ganze unbestimmte, weiter auf nichts abzielende Ergötzung des Ohres'. According to Howard Serwer, Sulzer and Kirnberger collaborated on the music articles up to and including 'Modulation'; Kirnberger and Schulz co-wrote the articles from 'Preludieren' up to S; and Schulz alone was responsible for the articles from S onwards. See Howard Serwer, 'Sulzer, Johann Georg', *New Grove Dictionary of Music and Musicians*, ed. Stanley Sadie (London: Macmillan, 1980), 20 vols., vol. 18, pp. 365–6.

[8] See Daniel Gottlob Türk, *Klavierschule, oder Anweisung zum Klavierspielen für Lehrer und Lernende* (Leipzig: Schwickert, 1789), trans. by Raymond H. Haggh as *School of Clavier Playing* (Lincoln, Nebraska: University of Nebraska Press, 1982), p. 386.

[9] It seems unlikely that the differences in opinion between Koch and his predecessors came about as a result of the theorists encountering different repertories. In the *Versuch* (1782–93) Koch tells us that his model of an orchestra actively engaged in dramatic dialogue with the soloist is inspired by C. P. E. Bach's concertos (*Introductory Essay*, pp. 211–12); and the numerous references to C. P. E. Bach's music in Sulzer's *Allgemeine Theorie* (1771–74) make it highly likely that its contributors had also encountered his concertos. Furthermore, it is probable that Koch only came into direct contact with Mozart's concertos only after the completion of the *Versuch* (1793). It is not until the *Musikalisches Lexikon* (1802) that Koch cited Mozart's rather than C. P. E. Bach's concertos as his paradigm (*Musikalisches Lexikon*, col. 854).

against which to measure artistic success. Dialogue was also held in high esteem both as a literary form and as an artistic, creative and social virtue. The resurgent interest in the dialogue genre in the late seventeenth and eighteenth centuries reflected both an humanistic desire to associate literary and philosophical works with a Platonic model and a firm belief that dialogue was an important intellectual asset capable of probing complex ethical issues.[10] Spoken conversation was especially prized as a social virtue in the eighteenth century. In France, *salons* offered their guests an equal right to interact with one another regardless of social position, and also provided an important forum for writers and musicians to present and discuss new works.[11] In addition, dialogue and conversation were identified by many prominent writers as important creative stimulants. Goethe, for example, used the image of conversation in the preface to his translation of Diderot's *Le Neveu de Rameau* (the implied interlocutor is Diderot) to describe the way in which he (Goethe) overcomes creative sterility. And David Hume remarked decisively that 'Liberty and Facility of Thought and Expression . . . can only be acquir'd by Conversation'.[12]

The general significance of invoking dialogue and drama in the context of the late-eighteenth-century concerto, however, goes only a short way towards explaining why Koch drew these analogies at this time. The ensuing investigation probes Koch's motivations more closely, examining his invocations of dialogue and drama separately in order to show the specific significance that each lends to his argument. Finally, I explain why Mozart's piano concertos provide a particularly rich source for analysing dramatic dialogue in an historical fashion.

Dialogue in the Late-Eighteenth-Century Concerto

Koch's invocation of dialogue in the context of the concerto can be traced back to the extremely popular eighteenth-century metaphor of music as language. Statements such as '[m]usic is a type of speaking',[13] '[m]elody does not merely imitate, it speaks',[14] and '[m]usic is a language', moreover a 'natural language'[15]

[10] The dialogue form was used by such important writers as Berkeley, Bushe, Condillac, Diderot, Dryden, Fielding, Hume, Mandeville, Rousseau, Shaftesbury and Voltaire.

[11] See Jürgen Habermas, *The Structural Transformation of the Public Sphere: An Inquiry into a Category of Bourgeois Society*, trans. Thomas Burger (Cambridge, Mass.: MIT Press, 1989), pp. 33–4.

[12] See Jocelyne Kolb, 'Presenting the Unpresentable: Goethe's Translation of *Le Neveu de Rameau*', *Goethe Yearbook* 3 (1986), pp. 151–2; and David Hume, *Essays: Moral, Political and Literary*, ed. Eugene F. Miller (Indianapolis, Indiana: Liberty Classics, 1985), p. 534.

[13] Noel-Antoine Pluche, 'The Spectacle of Nature' (1746), in *Music and Culture in Eighteenth-Century Europe: A Source Book*, ed. Enrico Fubini, trans. Bonnie J. Blackburn (Chicago: University of Chicago Press, 1994), p. 79.

[14] Jean-Jacques Rousseau, 'Essay on the Origins of Language' (1781), in *Music and Culture*, ed. Fubini, p. 97.

[15] Friedrich Melchior Grimm, 'Poème lyrique' (1765), in *Music and Culture*, ed. Fubini, p. 121.

appeared repeatedly. Parallels between music and rhetoric were also common in the eighteenth century, as were more general comparisons between music and coherent speech.[16]

Along these lines, critics particularly embraced an analogy between vocal music and language believing that such comparisons emphasised vocal music's ability to impart specific meaning. For *instrumental* music, however, the story was very different. In England, Charles Burney remarked that the composer of 'chamber music' (including quartets, concertos and symphonies) 'has less exercise for reflection and intellect . . . than in a connected composition for the church or stage'.[17] In France, where Fontenelle's famous remark 'Sonate, que me veux-tu?' epitomised the low esteem in which non-texted music was held, d'Alembert commented that 'purely instrumental music . . . speaks neither to the mind nor to the soul'.[18] The situation was similar in Germany where critics and aestheticians condemned instrumental music for its inability to 'communicate a moral message as effectively as words and tones combined'.[19] Even Johann Nikolaus Forkel, a great champion of instrumental music's rhetorical potential, offered a value-laden distinction between the chamber style (*Kammerschreibart*) which was designed for private use and entertainment, and the theatrical style (*Theaterschreibart*) which was, by contrast, capable of expressing moral feelings.[20]

Whereas vocal music was praised for the 'specificity and intelligibility of content which only words could bring',[21] instrumental music's communicative potential was uncertain. Indeed, attempts to make instrumental music 'speak' more directly were in progress by the middle of the eighteenth century. The poet

[16] See, for example, Charles Batteux's assessment that the coherent and orderly presentation of expressions in music should be comparable to a coherent speech in *Les Beaux-Arts réduits à un même Principe* (1746), ed. Jean-Rémy Mantion (Paris: Aux Amateurs de Livres, 1989), pp. 239–42. For extended discussions of music and rhetoric in the eighteenth century, see Mark Evan Bonds, *Wordless Rhetoric: Musical Form and the Metaphor of the Oration* (Cambridge, Mass.: Harvard University Press, 1991); and Elaine R. Sisman, *Haydn and the Classical Variation*, (Cambridge, Mass.: Harvard University Press, 1993). For a general discussion of the long-standing analogy in secondary literature between language and Classic music, see V. Kofi Agawu, *Playing with Signs: A Semiotic Interpretation of Classic Music* (Princeton: Princeton University Press, 1991), pp. 6–10. Downing A. Thomas has recently offered an interesting account of eighteenth-century reasoning about music as it relates to searches for the origins of language; see *Music and the Origins of Language: Theories from the French Enlightenment* (Cambridge: Cambridge University Press, 1995).

[17] Charles Burney, *A General History of Music: From the Earliest Ages to the Present Period* (1789) (New York: Harcourt, 1935), 2 vols., vol. 1, p. 10.

[18] 'On the Freedom of Music' (1759), in *Music and Culture*, ed. Fubini, p. 90. For a succinct account of the situation in France, see Maria Rika Maniates, '"Sonate, que me veux-tu?" The Enigma of French Musical Aesthetics in the 18th Century', *Current Musicology* 9 (1969), pp. 117–40.

[19] Bellamy Hosler, *Changing Aesthetic Views of Instrumental Music in 18th-Century Germany* (Ann Arbor: UMI Research Press, 1981), p. 113.

[20] Johann Nikolaus Forkel, *Allgemeine Geschichte der Musik* (Leipzig, 1788–1801), 2 vols., vol. 1, p. 44.

[21] Hosler, *Changing Aesthetic Views*, p. 43.

H. W. van Gerstenberg, for example, set two texts (based on *Hamlet* and on the death of Socrates) to C. P. E. Bach's Fantasia from the Sonata in F minor H. 75 (W. 63/6).[22] As Eugene Helm explains, Gerstenberg's texts were part of a more general fashion, among north European poets and music theorists such as Klopstock, Lessing, Gellert, Forkel and Mattheson, for contemplating the boundary between word and tone, 'the zone where . . . word begins to usurp the pre-eminent position of tone, or vice versa'.[23]

Dialogue entered the realm of instrumental music in the context of 'the *redende Prinzip*, or principle of expressive musical discourse for instruments'.[24] The most famous work embodying this aesthetic is C. P. E. Bach's trio *Melancholicus und Sanguineus* H. 79 (W. 161/1), subtitled 'a Conversation between a Cheerful Man and a Melancholy Man'.[25] In his Preface to the work, C. P. E. Bach explains that the conversation is carried out by instruments rather than by words and voices. He goes on to outline the content of the conversation, aligning verbal expressions with particular musical gestures in his piece. An open fifth and ascending phrase-ending, for example, signify a question, that is 'whether the Sanguineus and the Melancholicus are in agreement'.[26] In the Sanguineus's answer, 'the different tempo [marked Presto as opposed to Allegretto], as well as the overall content . . . shows clearly enough that he is of a very different disposition'.[27] At one point during a brief chromatic ascent, however, the Sanguineus 'purposefully loses . . . some of his liveliness, in order to tempt the Melancholicus'.[28] Even a brief silence constitutes a question: 'The Sanguineus breaks off inquiring whether the Melancholicus would like to continue from where he [the Sanguineus] left off.'[29]

Ludwig Finscher has pointed out that C. P. E. Bach's sonata is, in fact, just one of a number of 'dialogue-type' (*gesprächshaft*) pieces written in the eighteenth century.[30] In any case, the invocation of dialogue in sonatas extended beyond a programmatic work such as *Melancholicus und Sanguineus*. In the

[22] See Eugene Helm, 'The "Hamlet" Fantasy and the Literary Element in C. P. E. Bach's Music', *Musical Quarterly* 58 (1972), pp. 277–96.

[23] Ibid., p. 278.

[24] Ibid., p. 295.

[25] Sonata I for Two Violins and Basso Continuo in C Minor, Wq. 161. In *Zwey Trios* (Nuremberg, 1751; reprint, New York: Performers Facsimiles, 1986).

[26] C. P. E. Bach, 'Vorbericht' to *Zwey Trios*, designated as (a): '[E]ine Frage, ob der Sanguineus mit dem Melancholicus hierinne einig sey'. For a recent discussion of dramatic confrontation in this work, see Richard Will, 'When God Met the Sinner, and Other Dramatic Confrontations in Eighteenth-Century Instrumental Music', *Music & Letters* 78 (1997), pp. 175–209.

[27] Ibid., (b): 'die Verschiedenheit des Zeitmasses sowohl, als durch den ganzen Inhalt . . . deutlich genug zu erkennen, dass er ganz anderes Sinnes sey'.

[28] Ibid., (c): 'Hier verliert der Sanguineus mit Fleiss etwas von seiner Munterkeit, um den Melancholicus desto eher zu locken'.

[29] Ibid., (f): 'Der Sanguineus bricht hier fragend ab, ob der andere das noch fehlende fortsetzen wolle?'

[30] Ludwig Finscher, *Studien zur Geschichte des Streichquartetts 1: Die Entstehung des klassichen Streichquartetts: von den Vorformen zur Grundlegung durch Joseph Haydns* (Kassel: Bärenreiter, 1974), pp. 285–6.

Allgemeine Theorie, for example, Johann Abraham Peter Schulz described C. P. E. Bach's sonatas for two 'concertante' instruments with accompanying bass as 'passionate dialogues with tones' (*leidenschaftliche Tongespräche*).[31] In the same article, Schulz also proposed dialogue as one of three stylistic options for a composer of sonatas:

> In a sonata, the composer can aim at expressing either a monologue in tones of sadness, of lamentation, or affection, or of pleasure and of cheerfulness; or he can try to sustain in sentiment-laden tones a dialogue [*Gespräch*] among similar or contrasting characters; or he may merely depict passionate, violent, contradictory, or mild and placid emotions, pleasantly flowing on.[32]

We can infer from Schulz's account, moreover, that most of C. P. E. Bach's keyboard sonatas fit into the dialogue category: '[they] are so eloquent [*sprechend*] that we think not in terms of tones, but rather comprehensible voices which, in our stimulated imagination and perception, converse'.[33]

As is often pointed out, dialogue was also applied to the late-eighteenth-century quartet. Many Parisian 'Quatuors Concertant' were called dialogues for commercial and aesthetic reasons.[34] According to Finscher, the trend for describing the string quartet in conversational terms began in 1773 with the preface to Johann Friedrich Reichardt's *Vermischte Musikalien*. By 1800, the analogy between the string quartet and conversation was widespread. Goethe's famous remark that we hear 'four intelligent people conversing among themselves' was, therefore, part of an established tradition that extended well into the nineteenth century.[35]

Thus, Koch's invocation of dialogue in the concerto was certainly part of a trend for invoking dialogue in discussions of late-eighteenth-century instrumental music. In the specific context of concerto criticism, however, Koch's remarks take on added significance, engaging with contentious issues

[31] 'Sonate', in *Allgemeine Theorie*, ed. Sulzer, vol. 4, p. 425: 'Die Sonaten . . . von zwei concertirenden Hauptstimmen, die von einem Bass begleitet werden, sind wahrhafte leidenschaftliche Tongespräche'.

[32] *Allgemeine Theorie*, vol. 4, p. 425. Given in Koch, *Introductory Essay*, pp. 202–3.

[33] *Allgemeine Theorie*, vol. 4, p. 425: 'Die mehresten derselben sind so sprechend, dass man nicht Töne, sondern eine verständliche Sprache zu vernehmen glaubt, die unsere Einbildung und Empfindungen in Bewegung setzt, und unterhält'.

[34] Maniates points out that works were labelled conversations or dialogues in order to strengthen their connections to passionate speech and the imitation of the emotions. See her '"Sonate, que me veux-tu?"' p. 130. Janet Muriel Levy remarks that dialogue and conversation labels were designed 'to catch the eye of the prospective buyer . . . Whether intense or trivial, 'dialogue' was a catchword of the period'; see her 'The "Quatuor Concertant" in Paris in the Latter Half of the Eighteenth century', unpublished Ph. D. diss., Stanford University, 1971, p. 67.

[35] Finscher, *Geschichte des Streichquartetts 1*, pp. 287–8. For further discussion of conversation in the string quartet broadened to include the audience as well as the performers, see Gretchen A. Wheelock, *Haydn's Ingenious Jesting with Art: Contexts of Musical Wit and Humor* (New York: Schirmer, 1992), pp. 90–115. See also Barbara R. Hanning, 'Conversation and Musical Style in the Late Eighteenth-century Parisian Salon', *Eighteenth-Century Studies* 22 (1988/9), pp. 512–28.

such as the concerto's virtuosic dimension and its aesthetic and expressive qualities.

Comments from the *Allgemeine Theorie* on the dubious nature of virtuosity in the concerto provided Koch with the starting point for his bold defence of the genre.[36] In addition to Sulzer and Kirnberger's remarks discussed earlier, Kirnberger and Schulz suggested that the listener, in spite of indulging in such pleasures as wondering at the virtuosity of the soloist, rarely shared the enjoyment felt by the solo player. Listening to a concerto offered the same non-aesthetic pleasure, Kirnberger and Schulz argued, as watching someone perform an extremely difficult act such as a tightrope walk.[37] This kind of condemnation of the concerto was, in fact, very common in the late eighteenth century and was invariably associated with the lack of musical and intellectual substance in virtuosic works. Forkel found the concertos of F. S. Sander devoid of 'real musical thought, not even something that resembled one from a distance' on account of all the 'running, jumping and hopping'.[38] Johann Karl Friedrich Triest argued that concertos were the 'special proving ground for virtuosity' and 'hardly one in a hundred can claim to possess any inner artistic value'.[39] And William Jackson, illustrating the ill effects of virtuosity, counselled that the concerto soloist 'no doubt ought to be able to run from the bottom to the top of the keys, in semitones; but let him be satisfied with having the power, without exerting it, for the effect of the passage is to the last detestable!'[40]

Koch was as eager as the *Allgemeine Theorie* contributors and others to condemn the 'acrobatics' (*Kunstsprünge*) often required of a soloist, claiming that they propagated bad musical taste.[41] He made clear, however, that this was not the fault of the concerto *per se*, but simply of those who abused it.[42] While

[36] Nancy Kovaleff Baker's writings (cited in note 3 above) make clear that all of Koch's aesthetic ideas are deeply indebted to Sulzer's *Allgemeine Theorie*. For a tangible manifestation of Sulzer and Kirnberger's influence on Koch compare the contributions of both writers in *Aesthetics and the Art of Musical Composition in the German Enlightenment: Selected Writings of Johann Georg Sulzer and Heinrich Christoph Koch*, ed. and trans. Nancy Kovaleff Baker and Thomas Christensen (Cambridge: Cambridge University Press, 1995).

[37] 'Musik', in *Allgemeine Theorie*, ed. Sulzer, vol. 3, p. 432.

[38] See *Musikalischer Almanach* 3 (1784), pp. 19–20, given in Mary Sue Morrow, *German Music Criticism in the Late Eighteenth Century: Aesthetic Issues in Instrumental Music* (Cambridge: Cambridge University Press, 1997), p. 114.

[39] See Johann Karl Friedrich Triest, 'Remarks on the Development of the Art of Music in Germany in the 18th century', trans. Susan Gillespie, in *Haydn and His World*, ed. Elaine Sisman (Princeton: Princeton University Press, 1997), p. 370.

[40] William Jackson of Exeter, *Observations on the Present State of Music in London* (London, 1791), pp. 20–1.

[41] Koch, *Musikalisches Lexikon*, col. 352. He also remarked in the *Versuch*: 'Good taste does not require you never to show off your skill. Only use it with taste, and beware of seeking approval merely through virtuosity, else you resemble the buffoon, who gets applause for mere mechanical skill.' See *Aesthetics and the Art of Musical Composition*, p. 154.

[42] Erich Reimer discusses Koch's criticism of virtuosity in the concerto in 'Die Polemik gegen das Virtuosenkonzert im 18. Jahrhundert: Zur Vorgeschichte einer Gattung der Trivialmusik',

Koch was willing to defer to Sulzer's 'judgements concerning the other kinds of composition' in the *Allgemeine Theorie*,[43] he could not accept Sulzer's attack on the concerto. Koch asked rhetorically: 'But is . . . [Sulzer's] verdict perhaps too harsh? Should not . . . [his] judgement be directed towards only such concertos as are condemned by discerning concerto players themselves?'[44] Koch's fundamental belief that the concerto could be more than 'mere pleasure for the ear' but, at the same time, 'must be judged from an entirely different point of view than the sonata',[45] led him to the following description of dialogue, now quoted in full:

> [C]onsider a well-worked out concerto in which, during the solo, the accompanying voices are not merely there to sound this or that missing interval of the chord between the soprano and bass. There is a **passionate dialogue** [*leidenschafliche Unterhaltung*] between the concerto player and the accompanying orchestra. He expresses his feelings to the orchestra, and it signals him through short interspersed phrases sometimes approval, sometimes acceptance of his expression, as it were. Now in the allegro it tries to stimulate his noble feelings still more; now it commiserates, now it comforts him in the adagio.[46]

In addition to direct references to Sulzer's *Allgemeine Theorie*, Koch's passage also contained covert references to this work. Koch would certainly have been aware, for example, that Schulz and Kirnberger also drew an analogy between the concerto and dialogue, although their tone was somewhat condescending: the concerto was, they pointed out, 'a sprightly, not unpleasant noise, or artful and amusing . . . gossip [*Geschwätz*]'.[47] In addition, Koch would have recognised that his 'passionate dialogue' (*leidenschaftliche Unterhaltung*) bore a striking resemblance to one of Schulz's comments on the trio: '[g]ood trios . . . are rare and would be still rarer if the composer portrayed, in tones, a complete passionate dialogue [*leidenschaftliches Gespräch*] between similar or opposing characters'.[48] In short, Koch cleverly alluded to the *Allgemeine Theorie* at precisely the moment at which – by presenting a thoroughly positive

Archiv für Musikwissenschaft 30 (1973), pp. 235–44. Reimer finds a social motivation underlying Koch's polemic and that of Johann Adolph Scheibe in 1739: both were strongly opposed to the detached virtuosity associated with aristocratic musical culture in the eighteenth century (ibid., pp. 241–4).

[43] Koch, *Introductory Essay*, p. 208.

[44] Ibid., p. 208.

[45] Ibid., p. 209.

[46] Koch, *Introductory Essay*, p. 209 (emphasis mine).

[47] *Allgemeine Theorie*, ed. Sulzer, vol. 3, pp. 431–2: '[E]in lebhaftes und nicht unangenehmes Geräusch, oder ein artiges und unterhaltendes . . . Geschwätz'.

[48] 'Trio', in *Allgemeine Theorie*, ed. Sulzer, vol. 4, p. 599: 'Gute Trios . . . sind aber selten, und würden noch seltener sein, wenn der Tonsetzer sich vorsetzte, ein vollkommen leidenschaftliches Gespräch unter gleichen, oder gegen einander abstechenden Charakteren in Tönen zu schildern'. This quotation follows shortly after the passage quoted by Koch in *Introductory Essay*, p. 206. Reimer recognises that Koch, in his writings on the concerto, draws on positive descriptions of the sonata from the *Allgemeine Theorie*. See Reimer, 'Die Polemik', pp. 239–41. However, Reimer does not mention connections between Koch's 'leidenschaftliche Unterhaltung' and invocations of dialogue in the *Allgemeine Theorie*.

interpretation of dialogue in the concerto – he most obviously distanced himself from its low opinion of the genre.

But there is much more to Koch's invocation of dialogue in the concerto than cunning rhetoric. Above all, dialogue is the vital component in Koch's highly original view of solo/orchestra relations in the concerto. In order to understand its full significance, we must turn to his invocation of drama.

Drama in the Late-Eighteenth-Century Concerto

Koch was not the first theorist to situate instrumental dialogue in a dramatic context. In 1785, Bernard Germain, Comte de Lacépède, offered a lengthy analogy between the symphony and drama. Lacépède stated, for example, that the composer should 'consider them [symphonies] as just three great acts in a play, to think that he was working on a tragedy, or a comedy or a pastoral'.[49] In the ensuing discussion, he differentiated between prominent and less prominent speakers (*interlocuteurs*) in the context of the dramatic dialogue:

> In order to distinguish, as it were, between different interlocutors, we would choose the most prominent instruments in the orchestra, those whose nature best matched the characters we had imagined. We would use them to create a kind of dialogue accompanied by the rest of the orchestra; sometimes a single instrument would, as it were, speak and we would have a kind of monologue; sometimes by joining together they would form a kind of scene with several characters.[50]

Likewise, Koch's invocation of drama in the concerto was closely linked to the active role played by orchestral instruments. As we have seen, Koch believed that 'the accompanying voices are not merely there to sound this or that missing interval of the chord between the concerto player and the accompanying orchestra' but rather to engage in a 'passionate dialogue'. Koch continued on this theme when drawing his analogy between the concerto and Greek tragedy:

> In short, by a concerto I imagine something similar to the tragedy of the ancients, where the actor expressed his feelings not towards the pit, but to the chorus. The chorus was involved most closely with the action and was at the same time justified in participating in the expression of feelings.[51]

[49] Bernard Germain, Comte de Lacépède, 'Des Symphonies, Des Concertos etc.', in *La poëtique de la musique* (Paris, 1785), 2 vols., p. 331: 'Mais ensuite il faudroit qu'il ne les considérat que comme trois grands actes d'une piece de théâtre, qu'il crût travailler à une tragédie, à une comédie, ou à une pastorale'.

[50] Lacépède, *La poëtique de la musique*, pp. 332–3: 'Pour qu'on put en quelques sorte y distinguer différents interlocuteurs, on choisiroit dans l'orchestre les instruments les plus saillants, et dont la nature conviendroit le mieux au caractères qu'on auroit feints; on s'en serviroit pour former des espèces de dialogues accompagnés par tout le reste de l'orchestre; tantôt un seul instrument parleroit, pour ainsi dire, et l'on verroit une sorte de monologue; et tantôt en se réunissant ils formeroient des espèces de scènes à plusieurs personnages'.

[51] Koch, *Introductory Essay*, p. 209. This passage is repeated in *Musikalisches Lexikon*, col. 354.

Koch's description of the orchestra's prominent role in a concerto's 'action' brings his account into line with approximately contemporary descriptions of the orchestra's elevated role in operas and plays. According to Mme de Staël (1814), Gluck, on at least one occasion in *Iphigénie en Tauride*, identified the orchestra, not the singer, as the principal truth-bearer.[52] André-Ernest-Modeste Grétry's formula for an ideal theater (1796–7) involved orchestral instruments expressing accurately the 'moral details' of the action on stage.[53] And Adam Smith (1795) attributed the 'correctness of the best vocal Music . . . to the guidance of the instrumental' pointing out that the orchestra 'interrupts' in order to 'enforce [an] . . . effect', establish a mood, or rein in the voice when 'it is upon the point of wandering away from them'.[54] A parallel between Koch's commentary on the concerto and a remark made by Gotthold Lessing in the *Hamburgische Dramaturgie* of 1769 is especially revealing: 'Since the orchestra in our dramas in a measure fills the place of the ancient choruses, connoisseurs have long desired that the music played before and between and after the acts, should be more in accord with the substance of these acts.'[55] Not only did Koch draw an analogy similar to Lessing's for the role of the orchestra (that is, as equivalent to the ancient chorus), but he also demanded a similar kind of lively orchestral participation in the 'action'.

In the *Encyclopédie Méthodique: Musique* (1791–1818), Pierre-Louis Ginguené made it clear that the kind of dynamic relations between the solo singer and orchestra outlined above, could have manifested themselves – as did Koch's relations between the concerto forces – in the form of a dialogue. Ginguené's definition of dialogue proceeded from the assumption that orchestral dialogue was more highly nuanced than literal, poetic dialogue because of the greater number of 'speakers' on whom a composer could call. The composer putting music to a drama, then, 'can correct the faults of a poor poetic dialogue, with a good musical dialogue'.[56] He must supply 'intermediate feelings' (*sentiments*

[52] See Mme. de Staël, 'Of the Fine Arts in Germany' (from *De l'Allemagne*), in *Music and Aesthetics in the Eighteenth and Early-Nineteenth Centuries*, ed. Peter le Huray and James Day (Cambridge: Cambridge University Press, 1981), p. 301.

[53] André-Ernest-Modeste Grétry, *Mémoires, ou Essais sur la Musique*, 3 vols. (Paris, 1796–97; new edn., Brussels, 1829), vol. 3, p. 23. '[I]t is only from a thousand nuances between soft and loud, from a thousand ornaments, tiny notes, trills, broken chords, pizzicatos and arpeggios, that the composer can convey the truth of moral details which form the essence of an ordinary action [on stage]'. Translation adapted from David Charlton, *Grétry and the Growth of Opéra-comique* (Cambridge: Cambridge University Press, 1986), p. 12.

[54] Adam Smith, 'Of the Nature of that Imitation which takes place in what are called the Imitative Arts' (1795), in *Essays on Philosophical Subjects*, ed. W. P. D. Wightman and J. C. Bryce (Oxford: Clarendon Press, 1980), p. 203.

[55] Gotthold E. Lessing, *Hamburgische Dramaturgie* (1769), trans., Helen Zimmern as *Hamburg Dramaturgy* (New York: Dover, 1962), p. 70. For a detailed account of Haydn's symphonic music written for the stage and parallels between specific dramatic plots and symphonic movements, see Elaine R. Sisman, 'Haydn's Theater Symphonies', *Journal of the American Musicological Society* 43 (1990), pp. 292–352.

[56] 'Dialogue', *Encyclopédie Méthodique: Musique*, ed. Nicholas Etienne Framery, Pierre-Louis Ginguené and Jérôme-Joseph de Momigny (Paris: Panckoucke, 1791–1818; reprint, New

intermédiaires) missed by the characters on stage and have his orchestra express sentiments that characters cannot.[57]

As argued earlier, Koch may have intended his specific invocation of Greek tragedy to negate the 'abuse' that the concerto had suffered, and consequently to elevate its aesthetic standing. Given the similarity between Koch's 'leidenschaftliche Unterhaltung' and passages in the *Allgemeine Theorie*, it is not overly zealous to suggest that his analogy between the accompanying orchestra of the concerto and the Greek Chorus also contained a clever rhetorical twist. In his article 'Drama', Sulzer pointed out that 'The theatre [of the Ancients] was . . . never empty, as the Chorus was always present'.[58] Since Koch recognised an increasingly prominent role for the orchestra in the concerto, as a result of which, we must assume, the *concerto* was never 'empty', we might detect another cunning play on Sulzer's, Schulz's and Kirnberger's negative statements about the genre.

Above all, Koch's invocation of drama highlighted dynamic relations between the soloist and the orchestra. Since the orchestra participated closely in the dramatic action, stimulating, commiserating, or comforting at different times during the course of the piece, relations between soloist and orchestra evolved as the work progressed. With this new conception of processive interaction, Koch differentiated the dialogue in which the soloist and orchestra engage from literal conversation. To be sure, eighteenth-century writers recognised that a delicate balance between over-participation and under-participation had to be maintained in conversation in order to avoid negatively affecting relations with others.[59] Of equal concern were relations among participants in general.[60] But conversationalists argued from the perspective of a greatly valued equality of participation – something that the concerto could never hope fully to attain. Furthermore, ideal conversations of the late eighteenth century were intended to promote static, rather than dynamic, relationships among participants. Writings on relational decorum were specifically designed to promote the *status quo*, an objective neatly summarised by the Earl of Shaftesbury as 'Privilege of Turn'.[61] Koch's concerto dialogue, in contrast, suggested consider-

York: Da Capo Press, 1971), 2 vols, vol. 1, p. 422. '[L]e compositeur . . . peut corriger, par un bon dialogue musical, les défauts d'un mauvais dialogue poétique'. (Momigny was an editor for the second volume only.)

[57] Ibid., vol. 1, p. 422.

[58] See *Allgemeine Theorie*, vol. 1, p. 706: 'Die Schaubühne wurde bey ihnen nie leer, weil der Chor immer zugegen war'.

[59] While encouraging a person's full participation, Baron von Knigge, for example states: 'Let others also speak and contribute their share towards the general conversation. There are people who without perceiving it, monopolize everywhere the conversation'. See Knigge, *Über den Umgang mit Menschen*, trans. by P. Will as *Practical Philosophy of Social Life, or the Art of Conversing with Men* (London, 1799), p. 20.

[60] See, for example, William Traugott Krug, *Allgemeines Handwörterbuch der philosophischen Wissenschaften, nebst ihrer Literatur und Geschichte* (Leipzig: Brockhaus, 1827), p. 532; and Johann Georg Walch *Philosophisches Lexikon* (Leipzig, 1775; reprint, Hildesheim: Georg Olms, 1968), 2 vols., vol. 1, p. 638.

[61] Anthony Ashley Cooper, 3rd Earl of Shaftesbury, *Characteristics of Men, Manners, Opinions, Times* (London, 1711; reprint, Hildesheim: Georg Olms, 1978), 3 vols., vol. 1, p. 76.

ably more energy, vivacity and changeability in relations between participants – in a word *drama* – than its conversational counterpart.

Dialogue, Drama and Solo/Orchestra Relations in Mozart's Piano Concertos

Koch was neither the first writer to draw an analogy between the classical concerto and drama – in 1778 Karl Ludwig Junker admired the concerto for the 'plot' and 'action' it possessed[62] – nor the first to situate instrumental dialogue in a dramatic context (see Lacépède's comments, cited above). But Koch could certainly lay claim to having been the late-eighteenth-century concerto's most articulate, eloquent and impassioned proponent. He both defended the concerto against its detractors by engaging in his own 'dialogue' – sometimes direct, sometimes covert – with Sulzer, Schulz, and Kirnberger, and offered a fervent account of the hitherto unacknowledged vital quality of solo/orchestra relations.

Following his commentary on the expressive qualities of the late-eighteenth-century concerto in the *Versuch* and the *Musikalisches Lexikon*, Koch explicitly cites C. P. E. Bach's and Mozart's piano concertos respectively as exemplary models of an orchestra actively engaged in dramatic dialogue with the soloist.[63] While his acknowledgement of C. P. E. Bach's concertos strikes a chord with Triest's remark in 1801 that the composer 'opened a path to greater and more *reliable* skillfulness, which consists not in high-wire acrobatics but in the power to represent every playable series of tones the way their creator conceived them',[64] his recognition of the importance of dramatic dialogue in Mozart's concertos is especially revealing in regard to contemporary writings. Two critics in early issues of the *Allgemeine Musikalische Zeitung*, for example, draw attention to the increased prominence of the orchestra – a decisive component in Koch's argument for dramatic dialogue as we have seen – in Mozart's concertos. The first critic, in a brief article on No. 15, K. 450, refers in passing to the elevated role of the oboe in the third movement: there are some short passages, he explains, 'which . . . if executed properly, require perhaps as much practice and assurance as any passages in the piano'.[65] The second critic, however, writing on *Breitkopf und Härtel*'s 'Œuvres Complettes de Wolfgang Amadeus Mozart', gives a detailed account of the centrality of Mozart's concertos in the development of the genre in the eighteenth century.[66] Arguing that the orchestra's role in concertos prior to Mozart's is utterly subservient – in

[62] Karl Ludwig Junker, *Betrachtungen über Mahlerey, Ton-, und Bildhauerkunst* (Basel, 1778), pp. 84–5. Quoted in Hosler, *Changing Aesthetic Views*, p. 176.

[63] See *Introductory Essay*, pp. 211–12, and *Musikalisches Lexikon*, col. 854.

[64] Triest, 'Remarks', p. 350.

[65] See *Allgemeine Musikalische Zeitung* 2 (October 1799), col. 14.

[66] *Allgemeine Musikalische Zeitung* 3 (October 1800), cols. 25–35, 51–4. No author is given for this article. The editor of *AMZ* at this time was Johann Friedrich Rochlitz.

both ideas and execution – to that of the soloist, he explains that the orchestra, which 'only accompanies', must 'lay aside anything of consequence [*Erhebliche*]' in order to serve the soloist. In complete contrast, he continues, Mozart thoroughly works all instruments, allowing the soloist to be only the 'most striking [*hervorstechendsten*] *among* these [all performers]'. Now the ritornello sections, as well as the solo sections, 'arouse expectations' and 'excite the spirit'.[67]

Just as Koch's commentary is framed as a response to other writings on the concerto (especially those of Sulzer, Kirnberger and Schulz in the *Allgemeine Theorie*), so the *AMZ* critic's remarks are closely tied to contemporary criticism. A few months after the *AMZ* article in October 1800, Triest, also writing in volume 3 of *AMZ*, touched on a number of the same issues, although without citing Mozart's concertos. While some artists in the 'third period' of the eighteenth century (which he defines as 'From Mozart to the end of the century') 'took advantage of the more developed internal and external tonal mechanism to transform voices that had been mere accompaniments into more obbligato parts', many failed to do so, on account of '[composing] only as *virtuosos*, i.e. . . . [working] for *artists*, not for *art*'. Triest excuses the concerto as 'the special proving ground of virtuosity', where in any case, 'hardly one in a hundred can claim to possess any inner artistic value', but states that such an emphasis on virtuosity to detrimental effect is also found 'in pieces that, supposedly, are intended to elevate all the participating instruments to an equal or near equal rank, for example in quartets (literally: musical conversations for four voices)'.[68] The earlier *AMZ* critic, however, had already adduced that Mozart's concertos more than meet the kind of demand raised by Triest for upgrading accompanimental voices; in addition, his positive comment on Mozart's ritornello sections pre-empts Triest's criticism that concerto ritornellos in general are 'nothing but rests for the lungs or the fingers'.[69]

Koch, and the *AMZ* critic of 1800, then, both locate full orchestral participation – with the corollary of lively solo/orchestra relations – as a defining feature of the concerto genre, and both identify Mozart's works as paradigms. Their attention to the prominent role of the accompanying orchestra, moreover, cannot be interpreted simply as evidence of an increasingly symphonic conception on Mozart's part. The *AMZ* critic, for example, distinguishes the symphonic and concerto genres, explaining that for Mozart 'the concerto is the greatest *from the point of view of intimacy* [*im Zarten*], in contrast to the symphony which is the greatest *where grandeur is concerned* [*im Grossen*]'.[70] Instead, both writers reveal that *relations* between the soloist and the orchestra in Mozart's concertos – previously lopsided in favour of the soloist – have moved in the direction of greater orchestral participation. Mozart's concertos

[67] *Allgemeine Musikalische Zeitung* 3 (October 1800), col. 28.
[68] Triest, 'Remarks', p. 370.
[69] Ibid., p. 370.
[70] *Allgemeine Musikalische Zeitung* 3 (October 1800), col. 28.

have made the orchestra's active interaction with the concerto soloist not merely desirable but rather compulsory in order to 'excite the spirit' or engage in 'passionate dialogue'.

Ultimately, Koch's explanation of the expressive qualities of the concerto, together with the remarks of the *AMZ* critic, suggest that historically-informed analyses of dramatic dialogue and solo/orchestra relations in the late-eighteenth-century concerto will be particularly relevant for Mozart's works. Although Koch's invocation of dialogue does not appear at first glance to be very different from vague twentieth-century invocations of dialogue in Mozart's concertos (to which I drew attention in my Introduction), there is at least one indication that Koch had a precise understanding in mind. For in the middle of his description of first-movement concerto form in the *Versuch* (which comes immediately after the passage I have been discussing), he explains that the '[orchestral] voices do not always wait for the conclusion of the incise or phrase in the principal part, but throughout its performance may be heard alternately in brief imitations'.[71] Koch's 'brief imitations' strongly resemble the 'little imitations' (*petites imitations*) to which Antoine Reicha draws attention in his detailed and technically specific codification of dialogue in 1814.[72] It is to the emergence of dialogue as a theoretical concept in the eighteenth century and to Reicha's understanding in particular, as well as to the historical definitions of dialogue most applicable to Mozart's piano concertos, that we shall turn our attention in Chapter Two.

[71] Koch, *Introductory Essay*, p. 211.

[72] Antoine Reicha, *Traité de mélodie* (Paris: Richault, 1814), p. 89.

2

Antoine Reicha's *Dialogue*

The Emergence of a Theoretical Concept in the Eighteenth and Early Nineteenth Centuries and its Applicability to Mozart's Piano Concertos

In spite of dialogue's popularity as a general metaphor for instrumental interaction in the eighteenth century, and its importance to aesthetic discourse on the late-eighteenth-century concerto in particular, its constituent musical elements remained unsystematically delimited. Just as an historical study of dramatic dialogue and piano/orchestra relations in Mozart's concertos must situate these works in the context of contemporary aesthetics, so it must establish a way of probing dialogue that is grounded in theoretical writings from the classical period, even if these writings date from slightly after Mozart's time. To this end, we turn our attention in the present chapter to the first orderly codification of dialogue, undertaken in 1814 by a cosmopolitan Czech theorist, composer and teacher of high repute, Antoine Reicha (1770–1836). After establishing the properties of melodic syntax in the first half of his *Traité de mélodie*, Reicha devoted the eighth of nine 'suggestions' ('propositions') of how to treat a melody to the technique of dialogue.[1] He begins this section with a succinct definition:

> To *dialogue the melody* is to distribute the phrases and the members, the ideas, and the periods between two or more voices or instruments, or even between an instrument and a voice . . .
>
> There are only the following four ways of dialoguing a melody: first by executing the full periods alternately; second by distributing the phrases (or members of the periods) among the different voices that are to execute the melody; third by motives [*dessins*], that is to say, by little imitations; fourth by starting a phrase with one voice and finishing it with another.[2]

[1] Antoine Reicha, 'Huitième Proposition, Qui a pour but de dialoguer la Mélodie', in *Traité de mélodie*, pp. 89–92. ('Eighth Suggestion, the aim of which is to dialogue the melody'). The 'Huitième Proposition' and accompanying musical examples are reprinted unchanged in the revised 1832 edition of *Traité de mélodie*. All citations of this work refer to the 1814 edition, unless otherwise indicated.

[2] Ibid., p. 89. '*Dialoguer la Mélodie* veut dire en distribuer les phrases et les membres, les idées, les périodes entre deux ou plusieurs voix ou instrumens, ou bien entre un instrument et une voix. Il n'y a que les quatre manières suivantes de dialoguer une Mélodie: 1°. les périodes entières s'exécutent alternativement; 2°. en distribuant les phrases (ou membres de périodes) entre les

Without doubt, Reicha's intensely systematic consideration of melody in general (of which his definition and explanation of dialogue forms only one part) is a theoretical landmark of the early nineteenth century. Whereas his grand proclamation regarding the originality of the *Traité de mélodie* ('For several centuries, a quantity of treatises on harmony have been published, and not a single one on melody') seems over zealous, as his contemporaries François-Joseph Fétis and Alexandre-Étienne Choron pointed out, it is difficult to establish which eighteenth-century writings influenced the formulation of his melodic system.[3] An explanation and historical contextualization of his discussion of dialogue, however, shows that he was deeply ingrained both in eighteenth-century accounts of instrumental dialogue and the operatic 'dialogued duet' alike, and highly original in his comprehensiveness, precision and imaginative recourse to non-musical writings. As we shall see, moreover, references to instrumental and operatic dialogue in Reicha's later theoretical tracts, the *Traité de haute composition musicale* (1824–6) and the *Art du Compositeur dramatique, ou Cours complet de composition vocale* (1833), as well as the *Traité de mélodie*, finally reveal a firm theoretical foundation for this hitherto elusive musical concept. Thus, Reicha's writings provide important theoretical material for probing dialogue – including its dramatic dimension – in Mozart's piano concertos. After investigating the musical characteristics ascribed to instrumental dialogue by diverse eighteenth- and early-nineteenth-century writers and exploring both Reicha's debt to earlier understandings of dialogue (instrumental and vocal) and his decisive move beyond them, we explain precisely how Reicha's theories are applicable to dialogue in Mozart's works.

Understandings of Musical Dialogue in the Eighteenth Century

A brief definition of musical dialogue appeared in every important music dictionary of the eighteenth and early nineteenth centuries; together these

différentes voix qui doivent exécuter la Mélodie; 3°. on dialogue par dessins, c'est-à-dire par de petites imitations; 4°. on commence une phrase par une voix, et on achève par une autre'. For lucid summaries of Reicha's understanding of terms such as 'rhythme', 'période', 'membre' and 'dessin', see Nancy Kovaleff Baker, 'An *Ars Poetica* for Music: Reicha's System of Syntax and Structure', in *Musical Humanism and its Legacy: Essays in Honor of Claude Palisca*, eds. Baker and Barbara Russano Hanning (Stuyvesant, New York: Pendragon, 1992), pp. 426–9; and Ian Bent with William Drabkin, *Analysis* (London: Macmillan, 1987), pp. 16–17. Reicha's historically important explanations of *la grande Coupe binaire* (large binary form) are discussed in Roger Graybill, 'Sonata Form and Reicha's *Grande Coupe Binaire* of 1814', *Theoria* 4 (1989), pp. 89–105; Baker, 'Reicha's System of Syntax and Structure', pp. 442–5; Peter A. Hoyt, 'The Concept of *développement* in the Early Nineteenth Century', in *Music Theory in the Age of Romanticism*, ed. Ian Bent (Cambridge: Cambridge University Press, 1996), pp. 141–62.

[3] See Baker, 'Reicha's System of Syntax and Structure', pp. 422–5. (Reicha's statement is quoted in the above translation on p. 422.)

entries provide a useful gauge of understandings of 'dialogue' in the century before Reicha's *Traité de mélodie.*[4] The definitions below, given by the principal dictionary writers of the period, are strikingly similar: all of them explain that two or more voices or instruments can interact in dialogue, thus demonstrating that musical dialogue is not necessarily a text-generated concept; all emphasise responses or alternation; and almost all point to a unification of the interlocutors at some stage (or stages) of the dialogued piece.

> Composition with at least two voices, or two instruments which answer one another and which often come together at the end, making a trio with the B–C [basso continuo] (Sebastien de Brossard, 1705).[5]
>
> Composition with at least two voices, or as many instruments, heard alternately (Johann Gottfried Walther, 1732).[6]
>
> [Dialogue] signifies a piece of music for at least two voices, or two instruments, which answer one another; and which frequently uniting, make a trio with the thorough bass (James Grassineau, 1740).[7]
>
> Composition for two voices or two instruments which answer one another, and which often unite. . . . [T]his word applies more precisely to the organ [than to operatic scenes]; it is on this instrument that an organist plays dialogues, answering himself with different [organ] stops, or on different keyboards (Jean-Jacques Rousseau, 1768).[8]
>
> A composition for two or more voices or instruments, which answer one another, and which frequently uniting at the close make a trio with the thorough bass. It is much used by the Italians in their operas, oratorios, serenades, &c. (John Hoyle, 1770).[9]

[4] For a succinct account of sacred and secular textual dialogues from the late Middle Ages onwards, see David Nutter and John Whenham, 'Dialogue', in *New Grove Dictionary of Music and Musicians,* ed. Stanley Sadie (London, 1980), vol. 5, pp. 415–21.

[5] Sebastien de Brossard, *Dictionnaire de Musique* (Paris, 1705; reprint, The Hague: Hilversum, 1965), 'Dialogue', p. 18: 'Composition au moins à deux voix, ou deux Instrumens, qui se répondent l'un à l'autre et qui souvent se réunissant sur la fin, font un trio avec la B–C [Basso Continuo]'.

[6] Johann Gottfried Walther, *Musicalisches Lexikon* (Leipzig: Wolfgang Deer, 1732), 'Gespräch', quoted in Würtz, *Dialogué,* p. 15. 'eine Composition wenigstens von zwo Stimmen, oder so viel Instrumenten, so wechselsweise sich hören lassen'.

[7] James Grassineau, *A Musical Dictionary* (London, 1740; reprint, New York: Broude Brothers, 1966), 'Dialogue', p. 55.

[8] Jean-Jacques Rousseau, *Dictionnaire de Musique* (Paris: Duchesne, 1768; reprint, Hildesheim: Georg Olms, 1969), 'Dialogue', p. 145. 'Composition à deux voix ou deux Instrumens qui se répondent l'un à l'autre, et qui souvent se réunissent. . . . [C]e mot s'applique plus précisément à l'orgue; c'est sur cet instrument qu'un organiste joue des *dialogues,* en se répondant avec différens jeux, ou sur différens claviers'.

[9] John Hoyle, *Dictionarium Musica, being a complete Dictionary or Treasury of Music* (London, 1770), 'Dialogue', p. 25. Hoyle's reference to dialogue in Italian opera is almost certainly to the well-established 'dialogued duet' (discussed in the section 'Reicha's Understanding of Dialogue' below).

> Composition for two voices or for two instruments which answer one another by turns. It is the word organists use for elements of imitation from one keyboard to another, one hand to the other (J. J. O. de Meude-Monpas, 1787).[10]

> A vocal or instrumental composition of two parts, in which the performers, for the most part, sing or play alternately, but occasionally unite. The instrumental *dialogue* not only affords considerable scope for the display of the composer's ingenuity and science, but from the attention and exactitude which it demands in performance, is particularly calculated for the improvement of young practitioners (H. W. Pilkington, 1812).[11]

The precise musical nature of the instrumental responses, alternations, and unifications suggested by the dictionary writers, however, remains unclear. Meude-Monpas, at least, specifies imitation (in the technical not the mimetic sense) as an important attribute of instrumental dialogue. In this respect, his account reflects other late-eighteenth-century understandings that recognise instrumental imitation as a component of dialogue, most notably the so-called *dialogué* style. Popular among composers of Parisian quartets during the period c.1770–1800, the *style dialogué* consisted, paradigmatically, of short motifs imitated freely among instrumental voices, assuring adequate distribution of motivic material.[12]

This type of imitation, characteristic of *dialogué* quartets, encouraged theoretical parallels to be drawn between imitation and dialogue. Descriptions of relaxed and spontaneous imitation, for example, resonated with descriptions of the fine art of salon conversation.[13] Rousseau, for example, pointed out that in music 'we treat imitation as we like; we abandon it, we take it up again, we begin another [imitation] at will', and Laborde remarked in a very similar fashion that 'we leave the first [imitation], we take it up, we abandon it at will'.[14]

[10] J. J. O. de Meude-Monpas, *Dictionnaire de Musique* (Paris, 1787; reprint, Geneva: Minkoff, 1981), 'Dialogue', p. 47: 'Composition à deux voix ou à deux instruments, qui se répondent tour-à-tour. Les Organistes appellent ainsi des traits d'imitation d'un clavier et d'une main à l'autre'. The notion that imitative traits on the organ constituted dialogue is corroborated by Jérome Joseph de Momigny, who identifies 'a lively [imitative] dialogue between the top part and the tenor' in one of his own fugues. See *La seule vraie théorie de la musique: ou le moyen le plus court pour devenir Mélodiste, Harmoniste, Contrepointiste et Compositeur* (Paris, 1821; reprint, Geneva: Minkoff, 1980), pp. 165, 167.

[11] H. W. Pilkington, *A Musical Dictionary, Comprising the Etymology and Different Meanings of all the Terms that most frequently occur in Modern Composition* (Boston: Watson & Bangs, 1812), 'Dialogue', pp. 23–4.

[12] The second chapter of Würtz's *Dialogué: Vorrevolutionäre Kammermusik*, 'Analysen', extrapolates the principal characteristics of the *dialogué* style from an examination of late-eighteenth-century French chamber music. Würtz describes the imitation of short motifs in the outer voices of a Cambini quartet as a 'model example' ('Musterbeispiel') of dialogue (p. 84).

[13] General parallels between the art of conversation and the *style dialogué* are explored in Hanning, 'Conversation and Musical Style'.

[14] See Rousseau, *Dictionnaire de Musique*, p. 251 ('On traite l'Imitation comme en veut; on l'abandonne, on la reprend, on en commence une autre à volonté') and Jean-Benjamin de Laborde, *Essai sur la musique ancienne et moderne* (Paris: E. Orfroy, 1780), vol. 2, pp. 49–50 ('On ne demande point à l'imitation, la sévérité qu'on exige pour la fugue. On quite [*sic*] la

In comparison, Mme de Staël, one of the principal writers on conversation, defined that art as 'a certain manner of acting upon one another, of giving mutual and instantaneous delight, of speaking the moment one thinks'.[15] In a similar vein, Jean d'Alembert identified conversation as a 'relaxation'.[16]

Just as musical material freely imitated among voices was a defining component of dialogue, so fugal imitation was identified as a dialogic type, albeit a formal kind removed from the spontaneity of salon conversation. To be sure, the term fugal 'answer', in currency by the middle of the eighteenth century, would have immediately suggested a dialogic context to contemporary theorists, but invocations of dialogue extended beyond this specific term.[17] In the first volume of his *Allgemeine Geschichte* (1788), for example, Forkel characterised the fugue as a number of statements and responses among members of a group:

> Let us imagine a people made emotional by the account of a great event, envisaging initially a single member of this group, perhaps through the intensity of his feelings, being driven to make a short powerful statement as the expression of his feelings. Will not this emotional outpouring gradually grip the collective members of this people and will he not be followed by first one, then several, then the majority, each singing the same song with him, modifying it according to his own way of feeling to be sure, but on the whole concording with him as to the basic feeling?[18]

première, on la prend, on l'abandonne à volonté'). As Susan Snook-Luther points out, the discussion of imitation evolves considerably during the eighteenth century. In 1722 Rameau 'scarcely distinguishes between imitation and repetition', while Marpurg, in 1753, 'explicitly distinguishes between repetition, transposition, and imitation'. In the second half of the eighteenth century, Daube, Sulzer and Kirnberger all distinguish between free and strict imitation. See Johann Friedrich Daube, *The Musical Dilettante: A Treatise on Composition*, trans. and ed. Susan P. Snook-Luther (Cambridge: Cambridge University Press, 1992), pp. 144–5, n. 95.

[15] See Anne Louise Germain Staël-Holstein, *Germany*, trans. from the French (New York: Eastburn, 1814), p. 61.

[16] See Franz Swediaur, ed., *The Philosophical Dictionary or, the Opinions of Modern Philosophers on Metaphysical, Moral and Political Subjects* (London: Elliot, 1786), vol. 1, pp. 150–1.

[17] The notion that fugal entries constitute 'guiding' and 'following' parts originates in the mid sixteenth-century work of Vicentino and Zarlino. The more precise concepts of 'subject' and 'answer', however, develop no earlier than the seventeenth century. See Roger Bullivant, 'Fugue', in *New Grove*, ed. Sadie, vol. 7, p. 18. In any case, the 'answer' had become an established term by the eighteenth century. Johann Mattheson (1739), for example, explains that the French and Italians refer to the consequent as a 'réponse' or 'riposta' and he equates the 'answer' with the consequent. See Ernest C. Harriss, *Johann Mattheson's 'Der Vollkommene Capellmeister': A Revised Translation and Critical Commentary* (Ann Arbor: UMI Research Press, 1983), pp. 694–5. Rameau uses the term 'réponse', as Mattheson points out, in 1722. See Jean-Philippe Rameau, *Treatise on Harmony*, trans. Philip Gossett (New York: Dover, 1971), p. 352.

[18] *Allgemeine Geschichte der Musik* (Leipzig, 1788, 1801), vol. 1, pp. 47–8. Translation adapted from Hosler, *Changing Aesthetic Views of Instrumental Music in 18th-Century Germany*, pp. 185–6. Heinrich Koch quotes Forkel's passage in his article on the fugue in *Musikalisches Lexikon*, cols. 612–13.

Later in the same passage Forkel asserted that the voices 'seem to be going by different routes to one and the same goal . . . first gradually aris[ing], but then pour[ing] themselves out in a universal stream'.[19] He therefore invoked a 'uniting' of interlocutors, in a similar fashion to dictionary writers.

Like Forkel, Georg Joseph Vogler and Johann Abraham Peter Schulz also made general connections between fugal imitation and dialogue. Vogler stated that 'the fugue is a conversation among a multitude of singers . . . a musical artwork where no one accompanies, no one submits, where nobody plays a secondary role, but each a principal part'.[20] Schulz linked fugal imitation to dialogue in his explanation of the trio: in quick succession he remarked that 'The proper trio . . . contains three main parts which . . . maintain a dialogue in tones' and that the successful composer 'must not only understand three-part composition, but . . . have total command of everything that belongs to fugue and double counterpoint'.[21]

The theorist William Jones offered a more complex interpretation of fugal dialogue in *A Treatise on the Art of Music* (1784).[22] Jones understood 'the form of a dialogue' as two different subjects that are interchanged, rather than as one subject imitated from voice to voice. He described an example, a double fugue by Corelli, in the following way:

> The melody of the whole [i.e. both subjects] is extremely simple, being confined chiefly to four notes descending to a half-close in the first subject; and to the same four notes ascending by different intervals. . . . These notes contain the simple matter of the two subjects. When adorned with melody and expression, and set together in harmony, they make a very different figure.[23]

The four-note shapes of the two dialoguing subjects quoted by Jones (see Example 1A below) – the first 'descending to a half-close', the second 'ascending

[19] See Forkel, *Allgemeine Geschichte*, vol. 1, p. 48. Quoted in Hosler, *Changing Aesthetic Views*, pp. 185–6.

[20] *System für den Fugenbau* (Offenbach, 1811), p. 28. Quoted (in translation) in Neal Zaslaw, *Mozart's Symphonies: Context, Performance Practice, Reception* (Oxford: Clarendon Press, 1989), p. 544. It is likely that both Forkel (1788) and Vogler (1811) were directly countering Rousseau (1768), who had a very low opinion of the fugue. Rousseau remarks that the fugue is, 'in general . . . more noisy than agreeable' ('plus bruyante qu'agréable') giving the listener only 'mediocre' pleasure. See *Dictionnaire de Musique*, pp. 221–2. In his article 'L'Unité de Mélodie' from the *Dictionnaire*, Rousseau disparages music which, like the fugue, often presents two or more melodic lines simultaneously: 'all music in which several melodic lines may be determined is bad, producing the same effect as two or more conversations ['discours'] going on at the same time'. See Ibid., pp. 538–9, quoted (in trans.) in le Huray and Day, eds., *Music and Aesthetics*, p. 117. Forkel and Vogler, like Rousseau, notice conversation at work, but, unlike Rousseau, cast their fugal conversations in a positive light.

[21] 'Trio', in *Allgemeine Theorie*, vol. 4, p. 599. (Schulz was responsible for all the articles on music from S onwards.) Schulz contrasts the 'proper trio' ('eigentliche Trio') with 'Trios in name only' ('uneigentliche Trios') which have only two main parts and a purely accompanimental bass (pp. 599–600).

[22] William Jones, *A Treatise on the Art of Music in which the Elements of Harmony and Air are practically considered* (Colchester, 1784).

[23] Ibid., p. 50.

by different intervals' – exist in a kind of antecedent-consequent relationship and are based on closely related motifs. Yet the fully 'adorned' subjects are strikingly dissimilar (see Example 1B below).[24]

Example 1A: From William Jones, *A Treatise on the Art of Music* (Colchester, 1784), p. 28.

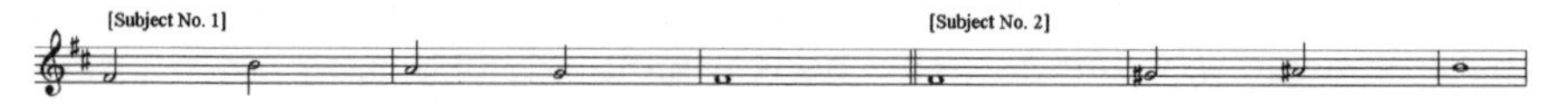

Example 1B: From William Jones, *A Treatise on the Art of Music* (Colchester, 1784), p. 28.

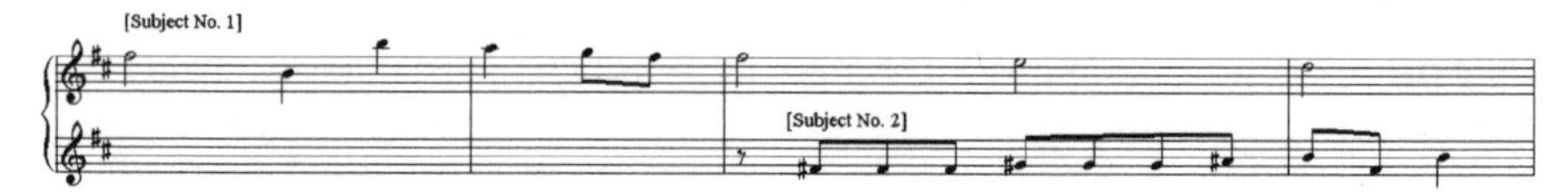

We can determine from the above quotation and from Jones's comment that this double fugue '[diversifies] the original air [subject] without departing from the sense of it',[25] that dialogue brings together contrasting *and* similar material. Although Jones thus goes further than other eighteenth-century writers in elucidating dialogue's precise musical characteristics and functions, he does not investigate these in a methodical fashion. It falls to Antoine Reicha to standardise dialogic conventions, determining when dialoguing voices present contrasting material and when they present similar material, and to analyze dialogue's musical characteristics and formal functions in a more meticulous and systematic manner.

Reicha's Understanding of Dialogue

Several facets of musical dialogue present in the eighteenth-century sources discussed above resurface in Antoine Reicha's explanation of dialogue in the *Traité de mélodie.* Reicha repeatedly emphasises alternation, in keeping with the definitions of eighteenth-century dictionary writers; draws on the prevalent concept of dialogue as imitation in the third of his four categories of dialogue, 'by motives, that is to say, by little imitations'; and invokes the kind of precise antecedent-consequent distribution advocated by William Jones for 'the melody as a whole' in his second category, 'distributing the phrases (or members of the periods) among the different voices that are to execute the melody' in a systematic fashion whereby each phrase is allotted an identical number of measures.

As well as drawing on eighteenth-century understandings of dialogue in the *Traité de mélodie,* Reicha provides a textbook example of the type of dialogue described by eighteenth-century dictionary writers in the first volume of his

[24] These musical examples are given by William Jones as Ex. CXXIX and Ex. CXXX in Ibid., p. 28.
[25] Ibid., p. 50.

Traité de haute composition musicale (1824). In the 'Chorus dialogued by the wind instruments' ('Choeur dialogué par les instruments à vent') written by Reicha himself,[26] alternation between the winds and the voices is strictly preserved until the end of the piece; here, the two interlocutors 'unite', mostly doubling each other.[27] Reicha's dialogued chorus also contains illustrations of specific dialogue types categorised in the *Traité de mélodie*, for example melodies split between the interlocutors and 'little imitations'. In short, Reicha's musical illustration both follows the standard pattern of dialogue described by eighteenth-century dictionary writers, and, in keeping with his attempt to systematise the treatment of melody, also reinforces a more exact definition by providing examples of his new subcategories.

Reicha's concern with the formal function of dialogue in his dialogued chorus – it leads to a uniting of the vocal and wind forces at the end – intersects with his theoretical discussion of the operatic 'dialogued duet' in the *Art du compositeur dramatique* (1833). In dealing with this genre, Reicha was on familiar eighteenth-century ground. As Elisabeth Cook has shown, the Italian 'dialogued duet', comprising a pattern of alternating, imitating, overlapping and uniting voices, had firmly established itself in the operatic repertory by the 1730s.[28] Jean-Jacques Rousseau first introduced dialogue into theoretical writings on the duet in the early 1750s, considering it essential to the supremacy of melody.[29] Rousseau's emphasis on dialogue acquired seminal importance in the second half of the eighteenth century, providing the starting point for subsequent theoretical discussion of the duet. While Marc-Antoine Laugier (1754) and Jean-Louis Aubert (1754) found Rousseau's assessment of the pre-eminence of dialogue unnecessarily limiting, others, including Jean d'Alembert (1750s), Jacques Lacombe (1758) and Baron Grimm (1765), assimilated Rousseau's views unquestioningly. Later writers such as V. de la Jonchère (1772) and Laurent Garcin (1772) expanded upon them, advocating more complex types of duets, in which dramatic function and musical effectiveness were prioritised over slavish adherence to dialogue.[30] Critics recognised the pivotal significance of Rousseau's position even at the end of the eighteenth century; Pierre-Louis Ginguené, for example, reproduced Rousseau's article 'Duo' from the *Dictionnaire de musique* in the *Encyclopédie méthodique* (1791), revising those aspects of Rousseau's theory that he considered redundant (such as the prohibition of strongly articulated contrast between the characters).[31]

[26] Peter Eliot Stone includes the 'Choeur dialogué par les instruments à vent' in his list of Reicha's compositions. See 'Reicha, Antoine', in *New Grove*, ed. Sadie, vol. 15, p. 699. The composition, with a brief description, is given in *Traité de haute composition musicale*, vol. 1 (Paris, 1824), pp. 74–9.

[27] Reicha mentions the composer 'uniting the two sections' ('réunissant les deux masses'). See *Traité de haute composition musicale*, p. 74.

[28] See Elisabeth Cook, *Duet and Ensemble in the Early Opéra-Comique* (London: Garland, 1995), p. 29.

[29] Ibid., p. 228.

[30] Ibid., pp. 228–45.

[31] See the article 'Duo' in Framery and Ginguené, eds., *Encyclopédie méthodique*, pp. 465–72.

Reicha, surely aware of eighteenth-century theoretical discussion of the 'dialogued duet', gives a characteristically systematic analysis of dialogue's formal function in this genre. He points out that although it usually allows the composer only rare opportunities to unite the voices, 'in all the cases the means of uniting them from time to time – above all near the end of the piece – must be found'.[32] Reicha then outlines *several* ways in which a composer might write a 'dialogued duet', elaborating on dialogue's formal function in the process:

> I. The duet is dialogued up to the coda, without repeating the words, or repeating them according to the circumstances. The two voices are united in the coda.
> II. The two voices are alternately dialogued and united from the beginning to the end of the duet.
> III. Adopting the *coupe binaire* which divides the duet into two sections, one unites the two voices towards the end of each section and the rest is dialogued.
> IV. Using a *coupe ternaire* which divides the duet into three parts, one can dialogue the first two sections and devote the third to the uniting process. Or one can even dialogue just the second section and unite the voices in the two others. These two others, furthermore, could be similar, apart from the coda added to end the piece.[33]

Just as his explanation of the dialogued chorus brings a specific identification of instrumental dialogue's musical attributes to bear on more general eighteenth-century understandings, so his systematic discussion of the formal functions of dialogue in the 'dialogued duet' provides more detailed and precise technical instructions to the operatic composer than eighteenth-century writings.

Reicha's orderly consideration of dialogue (instrumental and vocal) extends not only to its constituent elements and its formal function but also to distinctions between dialogue as repeated material and dialogue as contrasting material first raised in an instrumental context by William Jones. In the *Traité de mélodie*, Reicha develops the second of his categories, 'distributing the phrases (or members of the periods) among the different voices that are to execute the melody' more fully, providing musical examples that include both types of dialogued material. In certain illustrations, 'the *responding* phrases are of the same character as their *opening* phrases' or they are only 'varied

[32] *Art du compositeur dramatique, ou Cours complet de composition vocale* (Paris, 1833), p. 40: 'il faut trouver dans tous les cas le moyen de les réunir de temps en temps, surtout vers la fin du morceau'.

[33] Ibid., p. 41. 'I. On dialogue le Duo jusqu'à la coda, sans répéter les paroles, ou en les répétant selon les circonstances. Dans la coda, on réunit les deux voix. II. On dialogue et l'on réunit alternativement les deux voix du commencement jusqu'à la fin du Duo. III. En adoptant la coupe binaire qui devise le Duo en deux parties, on réunit les deux voix vers la fin de chaque partie, en dialoguant le reste. IV. Prenant une coupe ternaire qui partage le duo en trois parties, on peut dialoguer les deux premières parties en consacrant la troisième à la réunion. Ou bien on peut dialoguer seulement la seconde partie et réunir les voix dans les deux autres, qui du reste pourraient être semblables, sauf la coda que l'on y ajoutera pour terminer le morceau'.

repetitions'.[34] In other cases, however, 'all the *responding* phrases are of an opposed character to that of the *opening* phrases: it is a continual contrast'.[35]

Reicha continues his discussion of contrasting dialogue by clarifying when it should be written:

> two people of different character or with different feelings can perfectly well question one another and reply to one another in this way, and create a strong opposition between the parts they have to sing. A melody dialogued in this fashion can become very cutting, can seem quite natural and can produce a great deal of effect, if it is done well, and above all if it is well placed. An effective use could be made of it in dramatic music in particular; and I am surprised not to know of a duet dialogued entirely in that manner.[36]

Whereas these remarks are aimed at opera 'in particular' and are part of a long-running debate about the suitability of strongly conflicting emotions in duets,[37] further remarks on oppositional effects in both the *Traité de mélodie* and the *Art du compositeur dramatique* apply equally well to interaction in instrumental music. In the *Traité de mélodie* Reicha points to changes in tempo, and 'continual change from major to minor and from minor to major (of the same key)' as indicators of confrontation.[38] He goes into more detail in the *Art du compositeur dramatique*, specifying numerous purely 'musical means for finding opposed effects'. These reside 'in the difference between instruments and the difference in their timbres; in the difference in the value of notes; in the different chords; in the *forte* and the *piano*; in the choice of keys; in high and low notes; in the succession of unison and harmony; in the different sections of which the orchestra is composed, etc. etc.'[39]

Reicha's techniques for producing dialogic opposition and his association of contrasting dialogue with dramatic dialogue, moreover, do not resonate *exclusively* with operatic practice. Changes in tonality and tempo in C. P. E. Bach's trio sonata in C, H. 579 (W. 161/1), a programmatic 'Conversation

[34] *Traité de mélodie*, pp. 90–1.

[35] Ibid., p. 91: 'toutes les phrases *répondantes* sont dans un caractère opposé à celui des phrases *commençantes*: c'est un contraste continuel'.

[36] Ibid., p. 91: 'deux personnes de différent caractère ou de différent sentiment, peuvent parfaitement bien se questionner et se répondre de la sorte, et mettre une forte opposition entre ce qu'elles ont à chanter. Une mélodie dialoguée de la sorte peut devenir très-piquante, paraître fort naturelle et produire beaucoup d'effet, si elle est bien faite, et surtout bien placée. C'est particulièrement dans la musique dramatique qu'on en pourrait faire un usage heureux; et je suis étonné de n'y point connaître un *duo* dialogué entièrement de la sorte'.

[37] Cook, *Duet and Ensemble*, pp. 221–45. See also Framery and Ginguené eds., *Encyclopédie méthodique*, vol. 1, pp. 465–72.

[38] Ibid., p. 91: 'changement continuel de majeur en mineur et de mineur en majeur (du même ton)'.

[39] *Art du compositeur dramatique*, p. 43: 'les moyens musicaux pour trouver des effets opposés ne manquent pas: il les trouvera dans la différence des instruments et de leur timbre; dans celle des valeurs de notes; dans les différents accords; dans le *forté* et le *piano*; dans le choix de tons; dans les notes élevées et les notes graves; dans la succession de l'unisson et de l'harmonie, dans les différentes masses dont se compose l'orchestre, etc. etc.'

between a Cheerful Man [*Sanguineus*] and a Melancholy Man [*Melancholicus*]', set two 'characters' in opposition, and offer a famous precedent in eighteenth-century instrumental music for two of Reicha's forms of dialogic confrontation.[40] Reicha's remarks on dialogic contrast and opposition in the *Traité de mélodie* are also strikingly similar to remarks made by late-eighteenth-century French neo-classical writers on the much-admired style of confrontational dialogue in the theatre. Just as Denis Diderot, Joseph de Laporte, Louis Sébastien Mercier and Jean Marmontel identify confrontational dialogue as the ideal style for the theatre – Marmontel remarking that 'the interlocutors have views, feelings or passions which are in opposition to one another, and this is the form most suitable to the theatre'[41] – so Reicha explains that 'an effective use could be made of [oppositional dialogue] in dramatic music in particular'.[42] Reicha's comments that the two characters in dialogue provide 'a continual contrast', 'put a strong opposition between what they have to sing' and demonstrate opposing sentiments, also relate to specific remarks on theatrical dialogue made by the French dramatists: Diderot states that the characters 'strike blows and ward them off at the same time; it is a struggle'; Mercier points out that they are 'by turns conquering, by turns conquered . . . always in an eternal struggle'; and Laporte identifies a 'battle of feelings between them – feelings which clash, repel one another, or triumph over one another'.[43] Given that Reicha's notion of *développement* – the presentation of ideas 'in different guises' their combination 'in many interesting manners' and the creation of 'unexpected and novel effects with ideas known in advance' – is indebted to neo-classical dramatic theory,[44] it would be no surprise if his formulation for contrasting, dramatic dialogue in music deliberately invoked neo-classical dramatic writings as well.

[40] For a perceptive examination of C. P. E. Bach's *Sanguineus und Melancholicus* in the context of confrontation in classical instrumental music, see Will, 'When God met the Sinner'.

[41] Jean Marmontel, 'Dialogue' in *Encyclopédie, ou Dictionnaire raisonné des sciences, des Arts et des Métiers, par une société de gens de lettres*, ed. Denis Diderot, Jean d'Alembert et al. (Paris, 1751–65), vol. 10, p. 883: 'les interlocuteurs ont des vues, des sentimens ou des passions qui se combattent, et c'est la forme la plus favorable au théâtre'.

[42] *Traité de mélodie*, p. 91: 'C'est particulierement dans la Musique dramatique qu'on en pourrait faire un usage heureux'.

[43] Denis Diderot, *De la poésie dramatique* (1758), in *Diderot's Writings on the Theatre*, ed. F. C. Green (Cambridge: Cambridge University Press, 1936; reprint, New York: AMS Press, 1978), pp. 177–8 ('Ses personnages se pressent sans ménagements; ils parent et portent en même temps; c'est une lutte'). Louis Sébastien Mercier, *Du Théâtre, ou nouvel Essai sur l'Art Dramatique* (Amsterdam, 1773), p. 182 ('tour à tour vainqueurs, tour à tour vaincus, ils sont toujours dans une lutte eternelle'). Joseph de Laporte, *Dictionnaire Dramatique* (Paris, 1776), vol. 1, p. 385 ('un combat de sentimens qui se choquent, qui se repoussent, ou qui triomphent les uns des autres').

[44] See Hoyt, 'The Concept of *développement* in the Early Nineteenth Century'. Reicha's definition of 'développement' is given in the above translation on p. 144.

Definitions of Musical Dialogue in the Context of Mozart's Piano Concertos

Characteristics of Dialogue in Mozart's Piano Concertos

Antoine Reicha's extended discussion of dialogue in the *Traité de mélodie* and subsequent elaborations in the *Traité de haute composition musicale* and *Art du Compositeur dramatique* firmly establish dialogue as a theoretical concept applicable to instrumental music from the classical period. His precise categorisation and establishment of definite formal functions for instrumental dialogue transcend the vagaries of eighteenth-century writings on the subject and therefore provide an analytical tool for probing such interaction in an historically informed fashion.

In the sphere of instrumental music, Reicha's definitions and explanations of dialogue are especially relevant to Mozart's piano concertos. Reicha analyses the first movement of the String Quartet in B♭, K. 458 (1784) and the *Figaro* overture (1786) in the *Traité de haute composition musicale*, for example, to illustrate his concept of 'development', thus giving no reason to doubt the applicability of his theoretical ideas in general to Mozart's concerto repertory. Moreover, several components of dialogue, as he explains it, resonate specifically with discussions of the expressive dimensions of the late-eighteenth-century concerto (see Chapter One). The association of the classical concerto with dramatic rather than conversational dialogue, for example, lends historical justification to grounding an understanding of Mozart's concerto dialogue in Reicha's formal definition rather than in the *style dialogué* more appropriate to the conversational exchange of classical chamber music. Furthermore, Reicha's clear differentiation of dialogue as repeated material and dialogue as contrasting material suggests that motivations for instrumental 'characters' can be determined through the dialogue in which they engage. This topic has particular relevance to Mozart's concertos, since (as we shall see in Chapter Three) much of the critical discourse on solo/orchestra relations from the late eighteenth century onwards is framed in terms of the co-operation and competition of the solo and orchestral forces.

The fact that Reicha requires basic timbral contrast among participants in an instrumental dialogue, whatever the motivations of the participants, suggests a practical way of establishing the make-up of interlocutors in Mozart's piano concertos. In his discussion of the 'Choeur dialogué par les instruments à vent', Reicha clarifies: 'We must represent the choir No. 1 sufficiently removed from the wind instruments. The former must not be accompanied by the organ, which has too much resemblance to the wind instruments'.[45] Reicha also links dialogue with timbral variety on other occasions, explaining that if one

[45] Reicha, *Traité de haute composition musicale*, p. 74: 'Il faut se representer le choeur No. 1 suffisamment éloigné des instruments à vent. Le premier ne doit pas être accompagné par l'orgue, qui a trop de rapport avec les instruments à vent'.

particular canon 'had been destined for the orchestra, we could have dialogued it, introducing each reprise with string instruments, while the repetition will have been done by the wind instruments',[46] and commenting that another 'can first be executed as we see below, putting it in a duo, trio, quartet, quintet or even in a symphony; but we can also dialogue it, that is to say to change the instruments repeating each reprise'.[47] Since there are, of course, two fundamental groups in a Mozart concerto – the solo piano and the accompanying orchestra – and since the orchestra itself divides into two timbrally distinct units of winds and strings, I represent the piano, the winds and the strings as the three principal interlocutors, with the winds and strings conceived (for the purposes of tracing piano/orchestra relations) as the subspecies of a larger orchestral interlocutor. Dialogue among instruments of the same group must also be held to account, of course, although it demands a different status from piano/strings/winds dialogue given the relative absence of timbral contrast (particularly among the string instruments and between the right and left hand of the piano). I refer to this type, therefore, as 'internal dialogue'. In any case, identifying the piano, winds and strings as the three interlocutors in Mozart's concertos offers a reasonable compromise between interpreting the orchestra exclusively as a single speaker (Koch's Greek Chorus) and interpreting every orchestral instrument as an autonomous speaker in its own right.

Although Reicha's categorisation of musical dialogue provides a firm foundation for an analytical investigation of dialogue in Mozart's piano concertos, it cannot be applied slavishly to these works. For example, Reicha's prescriptiveness in regard to the symmetrical organization of melody (including dialogue) – whereby the 'rhythm' (*rhythme*) 'helps preserve the symmetry within the melody by equalizing the members [melodic patterns] in terms of their number of measures' and 'places cadences symmetrically'[48] – does not do justice to the flexibility of melody and phrasing encountered in Mozart's concertos. Equally, the analysis of these works will profit from broadening the notion of dialogue to include closely related melodic concepts explained by Reicha and others, albeit not necessarily in the context of dialogue. Several facets of melodic treatment in Koch's formulation, when placed in the context of alternation between interlocutors, will be identified as dialogue. His 'appendices' and phrase extensions, for example, are particularly relevant in this respect. Koch's explanations of these techniques, which involve (among other things) 'a section of the phrase itself, whose repetition makes the meaning of the phrase more emphatic'; 'an incomplete segment which is not yet present in the phrase but which is able to define its substance more closely'; an

[46] Reicha, *Traité de haute composition musicale*, p. 212: 'Si le No. 3 était destiné à l'orchestre, on pourrait le dialoguer en exposant chaque reprise avec les instruments à cordes, tandis que la repetition se ferait par les instruments à vent'.

[47] Ibid., p. 211: 'Ce canon peut d'abord s'exécuter tel qu'on le voit ci-dessus, en le placant dans un duo, trio, quatuor, quintette, ou même dans une symphonie; mais on peut aussi le dialoguer, c'est à dire changer d'instruments en répétant chaque réprise'.

[48] Baker, 'Reicha's System of Syntax and Structure', p. 428.

'immediate continuation of an idea in a phrase'; an '[extension] through the repetition of only a single measure'; and a 'parenthesis, or . . . interpolation of incidental melodic sections . . . placed either between the segments of a phrase or between a complete melodic section and its repetition, in order to portray still more accurately the feeling which is to be expressed'[49] are supported by musical examples that demonstrate motivic links ('little' or 'brief' imitations' in dialogic terms) between the original and the appended material. Also, Koch's description of the smooth joining of two phrases is partially similar to Reicha's explanation of phrase joining through 'supposition', and applicable to an investigation of concerto dialogue. Although Reicha's 'supposition' involves direct overlapping of phrases, whereby 'a member [is] composed so that the last measure of the first member is also the first measure of the second'[50] and is designed in part to validate the symmetrical design of phrases, it also ensures a smooth transition from one musical phrase to the next.[51] Similarly, Koch's demonstration of how 'the space from a caesura note struck in the strong part of the measure or delayed by an appoggiatura is filled with notes until the tone with which the following phrase begins' in such a way that 'the following phrase is connected more closely with the preceding one'[52] marks a fluid phrase-to-phrase segue. In the spirit of these descriptions, I identify smooth transitions between phrases, in which the piano or the orchestra is at pains to relate its material closely to the surrounding thematic material presented by the other party, as dialogic segues.[53]

The fact that Mozart's piano/orchestra dialogue in practice goes well beyond Reicha's theoretical descriptions in its subtlety and sophistication and in its intricate manipulation of solo and orchestral interlocutors, results in occasional analytical haziness in regard to whether or not dialogue is taking place. (I justify questionable assignations of dialogue in my analyses on a case-by-case basis.) Although a construction of dialogue based on late-eighteenth and early-nineteenth-century historical sources cannot constitute a ready-made analytical system, its status (for some, perhaps, a limitation) in this respect is intrinsic to

[49] Koch, *Introductory Essay*, pp. 45, 52, 41, 160.

[50] Baker, 'Reicha's System of Syntax and Structure', p. 432.

[51] Reicha mentions that 'supposition' is applicable to voices in dialogue. See *Traité de mélodie*, p. 90. 'Supposition' originates in Rameau's harmonic theory and designates a note placed below the sounding notes of a chord. See Joel Lester, *Compositional Theory in the Eighteenth Century* (Cambridge, Mass.: Harvard University Press, 1992), pp. 100, 108–14.

[52] Koch, *Introductory Essay*, p. 34.

[53] Other common musical characteristics of dialogue in Mozart's piano concertos (as identified in Chapters Three, Four, Five and Six) that follow the spirit if not the letter of Reicha's explanation include: the answering voice presenting a continuation to the lead-off voice simultaneously with a different continuation in the original voice (see, for example, bars 470–86 of K. 459/iii); the answering voice engaging in dialogic repetition of a theme while the lead-off voice (invariably the piano) introduces flourishes, embellishments and/or accompanimental figurations (e.g. K. 537/i, bars 164ff. illustrated at bars 174–5, and K. 459/i, bars 72–87). When a lead-off voice doubles an answering voice, dialogue is only deemed to have taken place if the latter presents a substantial portion of the answer *by itself* (e.g. K. 595/i, bars 143–53, illustrated by the piano at bars 149–53).

the very nature of dialogue, non-musical and musical alike. In late-eighteenth-century plays and operas it is not always clear that dialogue – in the meaningful sense of one interlocutor reacting to the words of another as opposed to making a statement oblivious to whatever else is said – is, in fact, happening.[54] Inevitably, given the lack of a text, the presence or absence of dialogue in Mozart's piano concertos can be even more of a grey area. It is sufficient to point out here, however, that dialogue does not occur at *every* alternation of material in the piano, strings and winds; that the absence of piano/orchestra dialogue in sections and at junctures at which it is usually present – for example, in the solo expositions of first movements in general and at the secondary theme and the piano's initial solo entry in particular – itself provides cause for comment; and that the nature of the dialogue in which piano and orchestral interlocutors engage correlates directly with the relations established between them. Just as one influential writer has recently suggested that music 'is not narrative, but . . . possesses moments of narration' and is all the more forceful as a result,[55] so I propose that Mozart's piano concertos are not dialogues but contain instances of dialogue, these instances carrying a powerful ability – in light of late-eighteenth-century aesthetic commentary – to define relations between the soloist and the orchestra.

Dialogue and Form in Mozart's Piano Concertos

The basic structural alternation of solo and orchestral forces in Mozart's piano concertos and the emphasis upon alternation as a central component of dialogue (with general and specific connotations for eighteenth-century dictionary writers and Reicha respectively), requires clarification of the theoretical connection between dialogue and musical form in these concertos. Does dialogue, as understood in this chapter, necessitate a new understanding of the form of individual movements? Or is dialogue not, in fact, formally defining?

Dialogue's status in regard to the formal structure of Mozart's piano concerto movements can be determined by considering its place in the compositional process. In his *Versuch*, Koch explains in detail the 'Order of Composing', but does not mention dialogue specifically, in spite of his richly imaginative reference to it in the concerto. To be sure, dialogue would have constituted part of Koch's second or third stage, either the 'Ausführung' (Realization), in which the composer decides 'the distinguishing content of the subsidiary voices' and the presentation of 'the main phrases of the movement', or the 'Aus-

[54] For one famous example, see the 'dialogue' between Orestes and Pylades in Act 2 of Goethe's *Iphigenie auf Tauris* in which Orestes wallows in self-pity, paying little heed to Pylades' remarks. See Johann Wolfgang von Goethe, '*Iphigenia in Tauris*: a Play in Five Acts', trans. David Luke in *Verse Plays and Epic*, ed. Cyrus Hamlin and Frank Ryder (New York: Suhrkamp, 1987), pp. 15–20.

[55] See Carolyn Abbate, *Unsung Voices: Opera and Musical Narration in the Nineteenth Century* (Princeton: Princeton University Press, 1991), p. 29.

arbeitung' (Elaboration), in which the composer completes both 'those voices whose content has been determined in part' and 'the remaining voices meant to accompany the main part'.[56] Nevertheless, dialogue's *exact* position in the compositional process, as outlined by Koch, remains uncertain. In contrast, Reicha's 'General Remark on the Use of Counterpoint' ('Remarque générale sur l'emploi du contrepoint') in the *Traité de haute composition musicale* clarifies precisely when dialogue should be conceived. Extolling the virtues of two- and three-part counterpoint and suggesting it be worked into the finale of a quartet or symphony, Reicha then explains:

> [the composer] will begin by creating the model of his counterpoint, the main subject of which will be taken from the motif of his piece, in order to integrate the counterpoint with the other ideas; once that is done, he will look for places suitable for the reverberation of his counterpoint; he will dialogue these reverberations with other ideas in order to give adequate variety to his piece; if the whole produces a good effect, his goal will be attained.[57]

The sequential nature of Reicha's compositional method, in which dialogue is written only after a skeletal structure has been established (in this case a 'model of counterpoint'), invites further comparison with dramatic theory. Just as his oppositional dialogue is similar to neo-classical writings on confrontational dialogue, so his positioning of dialogue after the determination of basic structure in the compositional process strikes a chord with the subservient position assigned by eighteenth-century dramatists to individual dialogues in the overall plan of a play. In the seventh section of his treatise *De la poésie dramatique* (1758), Diderot emphasises the skills required for coming up with plans ('having an excellent imagination; thinking about the order of things and the way in which one thing leads to the next; . . . getting to the heart of your subject; seeing clearly at what moment the action should begin').[58] Only once a plan is established, Diderot explains, can dialogues be written.[59] The influential Austrian critic Joseph von Sonnenfels remarks in 1768 that 'dialogue proceeds only according to a plan'.[60] Furthermore, in 1796, Goethe's protaganist Wilhelm

[56] See Koch, *Versuch*, vol. 2, pp. 124–5. Translation by Baker in *Aesthetics and the Art of Musical Composition in the German Enlightenment*, p. 200. For a cogent summary of the three different stages in Koch's process, see Ian Bent, 'The "Compositional Process" in Music Theory, 1713–1850', *Music Analysis* 3 (1984), pp. 29–36.

[57] *Traité de haute composition musicale*, vol. 1, p. 157: 'il commencera par créer le modèle de son contrepoint, dont le principal sujet sera pris dans le motif de son morceau pour assimiler le contrepoint aux autres idées; cela étant fait, il cherchera les endroits favorables à la répercussion de son contrepoint; il dialoguera ces répercussions avec d'autres idées pour donner une variété suffisante à son morceau; si le tout ensemble produit de l'effet, son but sera atteint'.

[58] Diderot, 'De la Poésie dramatique', p. 132: 'Avoir une belle imagination; consulter l'ordre et l'enchaînement des choses; . . . entrer par le centre de son sujet; bien discerner le moment ou l'action doit commencer'.

[59] Ibid., p. 132.

[60] Joseph von Sonnenfels, *Briefe über die Wienerische Schaubühne* (1768), ed. Hilde Haider-Pregler (Graz: Akademische Druck- und Verlagsanstalt, 1988), p. 265: 'und das Gespräch folgt nur dem Plane'.

Meister gives a practical example of a plan being formulated before dialogue. Once 'the structure . . . [of a play he was writing] became clear to him . . . he spent most of the night and the next morning carefully composing dialogue and songs'.[61] For Reicha, as for eighteenth-century neo-classical dramatists, dialogue functions within a pre-existent formal structure rather than dictating the organization of that structure.

Even though dialogue was not considered formally defining in the classical period – and will not be treated as such in my analyses – its development over the course of a piece is intrinsically linked to the formal 'shape' of the piece. As we have seen, eighteenth-century dictionary writers talk of interlocutors 'uniting' in dialogues; Forkel of them 'pour[ing] themselves out in a universal stream'; and Reicha of characters in a dialogued duet 'uniting from time to time – above all near the end of the piece'. Equally, late-eighteenth-century dramatic critics recognise correspondingly close connections between dialogue in a play and the play's overall form: Sonnenfels remarks that dramatic dialogue is vital in order 'to introduce subjects spontaneously' ('die Gegenstände ungezwungen herbeizuführen'), a procedure 'especially important in the first act during the exposition, where above all the spectator must be made aware [of things] so that he does not find the ensuing parts confusing';[62] and Lessing recognises the tight bond between the two, stating 'I do not understand how it is possible to shorten a scene without changing the whole sequence of a dialogue.'[63]

We imply the kind of progression towards resolution or agreement acknowledged by writers on musical dialogue in our categorisation of the first movements of Mozart's piano concertos in terms of sonata form. The 'double exposition' ('orchestral' and 'solo') receives only one recapitulation, suggesting a general kind of 'unification' of the piano and the orchestra in this final section. In practice too – as we shall see in Chapters 3 and 4 – piano/orchestra dialogue often effects relational reconciliation or reaffirms collaboration in the recapitulation in a remarkably concise and powerful way. The formal labels of orchestral exposition, solo exposition, development and recapitulation for concerto form might represent something of an anachronism,[64] but they remain in the spirit of the incipient sonata structure recognised by Koch and are therefore used in my analyses. Although the divisions do not account for the alternation of ritornello and solo sections outlined by Koch and others in the

[61] *Wilhelm Meisters Lehrjahre*, trans. Eric A. Blackall as *Wilhelm Meister's Apprenticeship* (New York: Suhrkamp, 1989), p. 99.

[62] Sonnenfels, *Wienerische Schaubühne*, p. 264: 'Die ungezwungene Herbeiführung der Gegenstände, ist hauptsächlich in den ersten Auftritt wesentlich, wo die Exposition geschehen, und der Zuschauer von allen unterrichtet werden muss, ohne welches er die folgenden Theile dunkel finden könnte'.

[63] Lessing, *Hamburg Dramaturgy*, p. 38.

[64] In all likelihood the English theorist Ebenezer Prout was responsible for coining the term 'double exposition' in his *Applied Forms* of 1895. See Stevens, 'An 18th-Century Description of Concerto First-Movement Form', p. 85.

late eighteenth century, they recognise the four-fold 'punctuation' of Mozart's first movements, thus staying close to Koch's theory.[65]

Reicha's concept of dialogue – which forms the basis for my investigation of solo/orchestra relations in Mozart's piano concertos – bears witness to a rich and constructive 'dialogue' with other writings on the subject, instrumental, vocal and non-musical descriptions alike. Just as our understanding of Reicha's concept has been informed by descriptions of musical and dramatic (that is, operatic *and* theatrical) dialogue from the late eighteenth century, so our analysis of dialogue in Mozart's piano concertos will draw on a similarly broad contextual framework. Equipped with an aesthetic and historical-theoretical foundation, we are now in a position to investigate how Mozart's piano and orchestra behave towards each other in dialogue and to determine precisely how the piano concertos take their place alongside dramatic criticism, music criticism, spoken plays, and Mozart's own operas, as a medium of Enlightenment.

[65] Karol Berger's studies of punctuation form in Mozart's piano concertos, generated from Koch's theories, divide Mozart's first movements into four 'periods'. The ends of the first, second and third periods correlate with the ends of the orchestral exposition, solo exposition and development sections respectively. See Berger, 'Toward a History of Hearing' and 'The First-Movement Punctuation Form'.

PART II
STYLE

3

Mozart's Piano Concertos and Late-Eighteenth-Century Dramatic Dialogue

A Study of Competition and Co-operation in Three First Movements

How exactly can we interpret the ways in which the soloist and the orchestra relate to each other in a Mozart piano concerto, in light of our theoretical investigations in Chapters 1 and 2? Many writers on solo/orchestra relations in this repertory have taken the easy way out, calling attention to striking, 'dramatic' moments of piano/orchestra interaction without placing those moments in historical or structural contexts. To be sure, the analyst is faced with intrinsic limitations in assessing the process of behavioural change among 'characters' over the course of a Mozart concerto. Not the least of these difficulties is the near impossibility of distinguishing on musical and historical grounds between finely refined behavioural types, such as co-operation and collaboration, and competition, confrontation, conflict and struggle.[1] As we shall see, however, the systematic identification of alterations in general types of behaviour is an important and a realistic goal, especially when dramatic dialogue is the focal point of our investigation.[2] By comparing ideas on dialogic behaviour introduced in late-eighteenth-century dramatic theory and music theory and by adding these points of comparison to our understanding of dialogue established in Chapter 2, we will clarify the dramatic development of

[1] In light of the difficulty of differentiating among closely related motivations, I shall consider 'collaboration' synonymous with 'co-operation', and shall regard conflict, confrontation and struggle as manifestations of a general category of competitive interaction.

[2] Similarly, alterations in general types of *feelings* in instrumental music would be more discernible along historical lines than alterations in specific types. As Heinrich Koch explains: 'if music alone [i.e. untexted] is to awaken feelings, then the composer must adhere to more general feelings. . . . He may only try to awaken a specific kind of pleasant or unpleasant feeling in his listeners in so far as he is capable of making the expressions of this feeling distinctive enough. For example, in the class of pleasant feelings, the composer can most clearly differentiate for the hearts of his listeners joy from tenderness, the sublime [*Erhabne*] from the playful; he will therefore also be able to awaken in them these different kinds of pleasant feelings. But never will he be able to bring forth a precise enough distinction between fear and pity through his music alone, without running the risk of being misunderstood by all his listeners. Thus, if it is to awaken feelings, more narrow limits are set for music by itself than when it is united with poetry'. See Koch, 'Introductory Essay, Vol. 2, Part 1', in *Aesthetics and the Art of Musical Composition*, eds. Baker and Christensen, p. 152.

interaction between the soloist and the orchestra in Mozart's concertos, using the first movements of K. 449, 450 and 482 as case studies.

The confusing etymology of the word 'concerto' has often encouraged critics to identify co-operative and competitive behaviour in these works. The term may have derived from any one of three sources: the Latin 'concertare' ('to compete, contend'), the Italian 'concertare' ('to agree, act together') or the Latin 'conserere' ('to consort').[3] Eighteenth-century writers on the concerto collectively reflect this etymological uncertainty, identifying a mixture of co-operative and competitive attitudes in the interaction between soloist(s) and orchestra. Mattheson and Walther, in the first half of the eighteenth century, recognised the baroque concerto's co-operative and competitive qualities.[4] Koch, A. F. C. Kollmann and François Jean de Chastellux, in the second half of the eighteenth century, emphasised one or the other motivation, all three situating interaction in a dialogic context. Koch's remark that the orchestra 'signals [the soloist] through short interspersed phrases sometimes approval, sometimes acceptance of his expression, as it were'[5] emphasises co-operative dialogue. In contrast, Kollmann's suggestion that a concerto might 'express a Conversation between a Melancholicus and Sanguineus' insinuates the kind of confrontation and argument worked into C. P. E. Bach's famous programmatic sonata, 'a Conversation between a Cheerful Man and a Melancholy Man'.[6] Chastellux – in the context of his discussion of German symphonists – associates the concerto with the articulation and resolution of confrontational dialogue: 'Their symphonies are a type of *Concerto*, in which the instruments shine in turn, in which they provoke each other and respond; they dispute and reconcile among themselves. It is a lively and sustained conversation'.[7]

References to co-operation and competition also surface in influential nineteenth- and twentieth-century writings on Mozart's piano concertos, the two motivations often being combined within a single interpretation. Otto Jahn, for example, identifies in these works a 'combination of the orchestra and the solo instrument into a whole, by means of the co-operation of all their separate and

[3] One of the most detailed accounts of the changing meanings of 'concerto', including a discussion of the word's confusing etymology, is Erich Reimer's 'Concerto/Konzert', in *Handwörterbuch der Musikalischen Terminologie*, ed. Hans Heinrich Eggebrecht (Stuttgart: Fritz Steiner Verlag, 1972–), vol. 1, pp. 1–17. See also Arthur Hutchings, 'Concerto', in *New Grove*, ed. Sadie, vol. 2, p. 627; Siegfried Kross, 'Concerto – Concertare und Conserere', in *Bericht über den internationalen musikwissenschaftlichen Kongress Leipzig 1966*, ed. Carl Dahlhaus (Kassel: Bärenreiter, 1970), pp. 216–20; and Michael Marissen, *The Social and Religious Designs of J. S. Bach's Brandenburg Concertos* (Princeton: Princeton University Press, 1995), pp. 99–100.

[4] See Reimer, 'Concerto/Konzert', pp. 9, 11; and Marissen, *Bach's Brandenburg Concertos*, pp. 99–100.

[5] See Koch, *Introductory Essay*, p. 209.

[6] Augustus Frederick Christopher Kollmann, *An Essay on Practical Musical Composition* (London, 1799; reprint, New York: Da Capo, 1973), p. 20.

[7] Chastellux, *Essai sur l'union de la poësie et de la musique* (Paris, 1765), pp. 49–50. Translation from Mark Evan Bonds, 'The Symphony as Pindaric Ode', in *Haydn and His World*, ed. Elaine Sisman, p. 143.

independent elements'.[8] Co-operation, however, is not universal, as conflicts sometimes emerge. Mozart keeps the attention of the audience, for example, 'by the competition of the rival forces'.[9] Cuthbert Girdlestone, while considering the 'essence' of the concerto to be the 'struggle' between the solo and the orchestra, nonetheless points out that '[the] struggle is broken by truces during which the orchestra and solo collaborate on friendly terms'.[10] And Charles Rosen, concerned above all with 'contrast and struggle', offers analyses that stress the collaborative nature of Mozart's concertos.[11]

Not surprisingly, piano/orchestra competition – with its related notions of confrontation, conflict and struggle – has often been recognised (particularly in the works of Mozart) as a central dramatic component of the late-eighteenth-century concerto. Donald Tovey, for example, describes the classical concerto as 'a highly dramatic and poetic art-form'[12] characterised by a 'thrilling . . . antithesis of the individual and the crowd'.[13] Charles Rosen, clearly informed by Tovey, sees 'the contrast and struggle of one individual voice against many' as 'the latent pathetic nature of the form'.[14] The classical concerto, he argues, was dramatised 'in the most literally scenic way – the soloist was seen to be different'.[15] Leonard G. Ratner also identifies a 'dramatic confrontation' between the soloist and the orchestra.[16] And most recently Susan McClary interprets the late-eighteenth-century concerto as 'a soloist and a large, communal group, the orchestra . . . [enacting] as a spectacle the dramatic tensions between individual and society'.[17]

There is, therefore, a long and venerable tradition both of drawing attention to co-operation and competition in Mozart's piano concertos and to associating solo/orchestra competition with the dramatic nature of these works. As Janet Levy among others has perceptively observed, the pre-eminence of dramatic metaphors to describe solo/orchestra interaction may be to some extent 'rooted in primordial aspects of human experience', namely antithesis, opposition and reconciliation.[18] Anthropomorphic accounts of the dramatic nature of piano/orchestra interaction have yielded, in fact, many intuitively

[8] *Life of Mozart*, trans. Pauline D. Townsend (New York: Cooper Square Publishers, 1970), 3 vols., vol. 2, p. 470. (Original publication, 1891; first German edition, 1859.)

[9] Ibid., vol. 2, p. 471.

[10] Girdlestone, *Mozart and His Piano Concertos*, p. 15.

[11] See in particular Rosen's analysis of the first movement of K. 271 in *The Classical Style*, pp. 198–211.

[12] Tovey, *Concertos and Choral Works*, p. 6.

[13] Ibid., p. 6.

[14] Rosen, *The Classical Style*, p. 233.

[15] Ibid., p. 196.

[16] Leonard G. Ratner, *Classic Music: Expression, Form and Style* (New York: Schirmer, 1980), p. 283.

[17] Susan McClary, 'A Musical Dialectic from the Enlightenment: Mozart's *Piano Concerto in G Major, K. 453*, Movement 2', *Cultural Critique* 5 (1986), p. 138. For an article that is, in part, a reply to McClary's analysis of K. 453/ii, see Harold Powers, 'Reading Mozart's Music: Text and Topic, Syntax and Sense', *Current Musicology* 57 (1995), pp. 5–43.

[18] Janet Muriel Levy, 'Contexts and Experience: Problems and Issues', in *Mozart's Piano Concertos*, ed. Zaslaw, p. 143.

satisfying interpretations of individual moments of interaction in Mozart's piano concertos. Nevertheless, a more methodical examination of co-operation and competition over extended sections and movements will greatly enhance our understanding of interaction in these works. While we could undertake a rigorously theoretical approach – categorizing every type of interaction in Mozart's concertos and assigning motivations to specific instruments at specific moments on the basis of pre-determined theoretical/analytical criteria – there would be innumerable practical difficulties in establishing such a comprehensive system. Instead, by situating interaction in Mozart's piano concertos within the historical context of dramatic dialogue – the most revered type of interaction in late-eighteenth-century dramatic theory – we can uncover the ways in which co-operation and competition manifest drama in these works.

Co-operation and Competition in Late-Eighteenth-Century Dramatic Dialogue and Concerto Dialogue

Koch's explicit statement that 'passionate dialogue' between the concerto's soloist and orchestra takes place in a dramatic context – 'by a concerto, I imagine something similar to the tragedy of the ancients, where the actor [the soloist] expressed his feelings not towards the pit, but to the chorus [the orchestra]'[19] – belies deeper connections between his conception of solo/orchestra dialogue in the concerto and dramatic theorists' understanding of dialogue in spoken plays. For Koch, like his contemporaries in the theatrical community, explains dialogue both as an extended process and as immediate exchange. In addition to participating actively across the concerto as a whole ('Now in the allegro it tries to stimulate [the soloist's] noble feelings still more; now it commiserates, now it comforts him in the adagio'), the orchestra engages in 'brief imitations':

> In well-composed concertos, every single part of the accompanying orchestra makes its contribution to the main part [the three main periods, or solo sections], according to the ideal [of passionate dialogue] described before. As a segment of the whole, it is involved in the passionate dialogue and has the right to show its feeling concerning the main part through short phrases. To this end, these voices do not always wait for the conclusion of the incise or phrase in the principal part, but throughout its performance may be heard in brief imitations; yet they must be placed and arranged so that they do not obscure the performance of the main part.[20]

Thus, 'brief imitations' and the process whereby solo/orchestra relations develop – the orchestra 'stimulat[ing] noble feelings', 'commiserating', 'comforting', etc. – together constitute 'passionate dialogue'.

The components attributed to concerto dialogue by Koch – immediate

[19] Koch, *Introductory Essay*, p. 209.
[20] Ibid., p. 211.

exchange and extended process – are broadly comparable to those assigned to dramatic dialogue by late-eighteenth-century dramatists. Joseph von Sonnenfels comments that as a whole the dialogue of a Brandes play is good (that is, the division of the dialogue and the progression of material therein), but that at the 'technical' level (immediate exchange), the dialogue is deficient.[21] Denis Diderot points out that the most effective dramatic dialogue in the form of immediate give-and-take will probe issues and ideas central to a play: 'The reply [in dialogue] does not attach to the last words of the speaker; it relates to the content, the heart of the matter.'[22] And Jean Marmontel, like Diderot, explains that individual instances of dramatic dialogue must function in a wider context as well, contributing directly and effectively to the advancement of the plot. Thus, 'each reply [in dialogue] would be to the scene what the scene is to the act' – in other words, functioning in a long-range context (advancing the plot) in addition to an immediate one.[23]

In light of the general theoretical similarity between components of dramatic dialogue and concerto dialogue, clues to the dialogic behaviour between concerto characters can be located in late-eighteenth-century dramatic theory. For example, dramatists are especially explicit in their admiration for carefully executed confrontation. Whereas for Diderot the direct, outright opposition of characters can lead only to an unproductive 'string of little ideas and antitheses' ('Un tissu de petites idées, d'antithèses'),[24] the ebb and flow of effective dialogue relies on characters simultaneously confronting and holding off each other. Of Corneille's dramatic dialogue, Diderot writes:

> This infinitely difficult art of dramatic dialogue has perhaps not been mastered by anyone to the same extent as by Corneille. His characters press one another without concessions; they strike blows and ward them off at the same time; it is a struggle.[25]

Joseph de Laporte strikes a very similar note in his article on dramatic dialogue in the *Dictionnaire Dramatique* of 1776:

> It is not natural that, in the midst of violent conflicts of interest which arouse all the characters, they should give themselves, as it were, the luxury of haranguing one another. It should be a battle of feelings between them – feelings which clash,

[21] Sonnenfels, *Briefe über die Wienerische Schaubühne*, p. 293.

[22] Diderot, 'De la Poésie dramatique', in *Diderot's Writings on the Theatre*, ed. F. C. Green (Cambridge: Cambridge University Press, 1936; reprint, New York: AMS Press, 1978), p. 178. 'La réponse ne s'accroche pas au dernier mot de l'interlocuteur; elle touche à la chose et au fond'.

[23] Denis Diderot, Jean d'Alembert, eds., *Encyclopédie, ou Dictionnaire raisonné des sciences, des Arts et des Métiers, par une société de gens de lettres* (Paris, 1751–72), vol. 10, p. 383: '[C]haque réplique serroit à la scene ce que la scene est à l'acte, c'est-à-dire, un nouveau moyen de nouer ou de dénouer'.

[24] Diderot, 'Poésie dramatique', p. 164.

[25] Ibid., pp. 177–8: 'Cet art du dialogue dramatique, si difficile, personne peut-être ne l'a possédé au même degré que Corneille. Ses personnages se pressent sans ménagements; ils parent et portent en même temps; c'est une lutte'.

> repel one another, or triumph over one another. It is above all in this game that Corneille is superior.[26]

Louis Sébastien Mercier, in *Du Théâtre* of 1773, and Jean Marmontel, writing in the *Encyclopédie* (1751–72), also consider confrontation essential to dramatic dialogue. Mercier states that characters should be 'by turns conquering, by turns conquered . . . always in an eternal struggle'.[27] Similarly, Marmontel, identifying four pre-eminent types of dialogue, declares that 'In the fourth, the interlocutors have views, sentiments or passions which combat one another, and this is the form most favourable to the theatre.'[28]

Although critics such as Diderot, Laporte, Mercier and Marmontel admired confrontation, it is highly unlikely that they would have recommended sustaining it through every moment of a play. After all, dramatic dialogues in eighteenth-century plays come in all varieties, ranging from the blatantly confrontational to the completely amicable and collaborative, a fact reflected in Marmontel's four-fold definition.[29] In any case, Laporte's example of effective dramatic dialogue – one of Oedipus's pivotal encounters with Jocasta in Voltaire's *Oedipe* – illustrates that dialogic confrontation is especially suited to projecting moments of great relational intensity:

> Oedipus: I killed your husband.
> Jocasta: But you are mine.
> Oedipus: I am yours by virtue of a crime.
> Jocasta: It was involuntary.
> Oedipus: Nevertheless, it was committed.
> Jocasta: Oh, woe of woes!
> Oedipus: Oh, wedlock all-too-fatal! Oh love that once burned so fiercely!
> Jocasta: It is not extinguished; you are my husband.
> Oedipus: No, I am no longer your husband &C.[30]

[26] Laporte, *Dictionnaire Dramatique*, vol. 1, p. 385: 'Il n'est pas naturel qu'au milieu d'intérêts violens qui agitent tous les personnages, ils se donnent, pour ainsi dire, le loisir de se haranguer réciproquement. Ce doit être entr'eux un combat de sentiments qui se choquent, qui se repoussent, ou qui triomphent les uns des autres; c'est sur-tout dans cette partie que Corneille est supérieur'.

[27] Mercier, *Du Théâtre*, p. 182: 'tour à tour vainqueurs, tour à tour vaincus, ils sont toujours dans une lutte eternelle'.

[28] See Marmontel, 'Dialogue', in *Encyclopédie*, eds. Diderot and d'Alembert, vol. 10, p. 883: 'Dans la quartrième, les interlocuteurs ont des vues, des sentiments ou des passions qui se combattent, et c'est la forme la plus favorable au théâtre.'

[29] Although Marmontel's fourth type quoted above is 'most favourable to the theatre', his second and third types – collaborative in intent – are not explicitly discouraged in dramatic usage. In the second: 'the interlocutors have a common plan that they devise together, or interesting secrets that they communicate to one another'. In the third: 'one of the interlocutors has a project or sentiments that he wants to inspire in the other'. See 'Dialogue' in *Encyclopédie*, eds. Diderot and d'Alembert, vol. 10, p. 882.

[30] Laporte, *Dictionnaire Dramatique*, pp. 390–1.

> 'Oedipe: J'ai tué votre époux.
> Jocaste: Mais vous êtes le mien.
> Oedipe: Je le suis par le crime.

Laporte explains that these lines are especially effective because they are 'like fencing thrusts, given and warded off at the same time'.[31]

The dialogic technique used by Voltaire in Laporte's example is *stichomythia*, a confrontational style originating with the Greek tragedians. It has been defined in the *Shorter Oxford Dictionary* as 'dialogue in alternate lines, employed in sharp disputation, and characterised by antithesis and rhetorical repetition or taking up of opponent's words'.[32] Goethe also used this dialogic technique at moments of great intensity in his early classical plays *Iphigenie* (1787) and *Torquato Tasso* (1790). In *Tasso*, for example, *stichomythia* appears immediately before Antonio's and Tasso's crucial altercation (the end of Act 2, scene 3, lines 1393–1406),[33] and at the moment at which the Princess and Leonora disagree on whether Tasso should be sent away to Florence as a punishment for his violent behaviour (Act 3, scene 2, lines 1728–40); and in *Iphigenie*, it surfaces when Pylades and Iphigenie argue over their escape from Tauris (Act 4, lines 1643–53). In every case, 'disputation', 'repetition' and the 'taking up of an opponent's words' are evident.

Although interactive behaviour between characters in musical dialogue is explained by music theorists less clearly than that between characters in dramatic dialogue is explained by dramatists, musical dialogue is at least considered capable, like its dramatic counterpart, of embodying competitive as well as co-operative motivation. In addition to Kollmann's insinuation that competition could be worked into dialogue in the concerto, J. J. de Momigny compares the fugue to 'a very animated debate between two lawyers who, through their logic and eloquence try to conquer each other, and who

Jocaste: Il est involontaire.
Oedipe: N'importe il est commis.
Jocaste: O comble de misere!
Oedipe: O trop fatal hymen! Ô feux jadis si doux!
Jocaste: Ils ne font point éteints; vous êtes mon époux.
Oedipe: Non, je ne le suis plus &C'.

[31] Ibid., p. 390: 'ressemblent à des coups d'escrime poussés et parés en même temps'.

[32] Quoted in Andrew K. Kennedy, *Dramatic Dialogue: The Duologue of Personal Encounter* (Cambridge: Cambridge University Press, 1983), p. 39.

[33] See '*Torquato Tasso:* A Drama', trans. Michael Hamburger, in *Johann Wolfgang von Goethe: Verse Plays and Epic*, eds. Cyrus Hamlin and Frank Ryder (New York: Suhrkamp, 1987), p. 89:

ANTONIO: What lofty spirit in a narrow chest!
TASSO: There's space enough to vent its fullness here!
ANTONIO: The rabble, too, vents passion in mere words.
TASSO: If you're a gentleman, as I am, show it!
ANTONIO: I am, but I am conscious where I am.
TASSO: Come down with me, where weapons can decide.
ANTONIO: As you've no right to challenge, I won't follow.
TASSO: A welcome subterfuge for cowardice.
ANTONIO: A coward threatens only where he's safe.
TASSO: Gladly I can dispense with that protection.
ANTONIO: Forgive yourself! This place will not forgive you.
TASSO: May this place forgive my long forbearance.

sometimes interrupt each other'.[34] Momigny's further comparison of fugal entries and 'thrusts' ('bottes') in fencing – the two participants 'come close to each other, pursue each other and follow each other'[35] – as well as Antoine Reicha's explanation of confrontational dialogue in music – 'the *responding* phrases are of an opposed character to that of their *opening* phrases: it is a continual contrast'[36] – may be indebted to Diderot's, Mercier's and Laporte's descriptions of confrontational dramatic dialogue; in any case, Momigny characterises fugal entries in an identical manner to how Laporte characterises Voltaire's dramatic dialogue (that is, as fencing 'thrusts'). Also, likening the duet genre to a conversation, Momigny suggests that the 'true' ('vrai') duet can display either co-operation or competition: 'the two parties are like two friends who are conversing or two adversaries who are fighting'.[37]

However, not all critics recognised confrontation in musical dialogue just as theoretical notions of confrontational dramatic dialogue did not always inform practice. The music dictionary writers Sebastien de Brossard, James Grassineau, Jean-Jacques Rousseau, J. J. O. de Meude-Monpas and H. W. Pilkington, for example, give no indication that dialogic 'responses', 'answers', and 'alternations' are anything but co-operative;[38] Nikolaus Forkel's account in the *Allgemeine Geschichte* of a fugal dialogue involves voices 'concording' with one another;[39] Charles Avison, likening his own sonatas to 'a Conversation among friends', states that the interlocutors 'are of one Mind and Propose their mutual Sentiments';[40] and Koch's 'passionate dialogue between the concerto player and the accompanying orchestra' incorporates only co-operative concepts such as 'approval', 'acceptance', 'commiseration' and 'comfort'.[41] A study of dialogic interaction in Mozart's concertos, therefore, must account for both competitive and co-operative behavioural types.

[34] Momigny, *La Seule Vraie Théorie de la Musique*, p. 146: 'On peut considérer la fugue comme un débat très animé de deux avocats, qui, par leur logique et leur éloquence, cherchent à se vaincre mutuellement, et qui se coupent quelquefois la parole'.

[35] Ibid., p. 146: 'se serrent, se poursuivent et se mettent en suite'.

[36] Reicha, *Traité de mélodie*, p. 91: 'toutes les phrases *répondantes* sont dans un caractère opposé à celui des phrases *commençantes*: c'est un contraste continuel'.

[37] Momigny, *La Seule Vraie Théorie de la Musique*, p. 175: 'Dans le vrai Duo, les deux Parties sont comme deux amis qui conversent ou comme deux adversaires qui combattent'.

[38] See Brossard, *Dictionnaire de Musique*, p. 18; Grassineau, *A Musical Dictionary*, p. 55; Rousseau, *Dictionnaire de Musique*, p. 145; Meude-Monpas, *Dictionnaire de Musique*, p. 47; Pilkington, *A Musical Dictionary*, pp. 23–4.

[39] *Allgemeine Geschichte*, vol. 1, pp. 47–8.

[40] See Avison's 'Advertisement' for his Opus 7, *Six Sonatas for the Harpsichord, with Accompaniments for 2 violins, and a violoncello* (London, 1760). Quoted in Katalin Komlós, *Fortepianos and their Music: Germany, Austria and England, 1760–1800* (Oxford: Clarendon Press, 1995), p. 85.

[41] Koch, *Introductory Essay*, p. 209.

Dramatic Dialogue and Piano/Orchestra Relations in the First Movements of K. 449, 450 and 482[42]

The important analytical question that must now be addressed is whether in practice piano/orchestra dialogue in Mozart's concertos is attuned to the theoretical understandings of musical and dramatic dialogue described above. As we established earlier, there is a long tradition of considering piano/orchestra competition (with related notions of confrontation, conflict and struggle) as a fundamentally dramatic characteristic of Mozart's concertos. But the dramatic credentials of these concertos can be strengthened and refined both by linking late-eighteenth-century theoretical discussions of dialogic interaction to examples of dialogue in Mozart's concertos, and by connecting dialogic processes in Mozart's concertos to dialogic processes in contemporary spoken plays.

Because of the large volume of dialogue in which members of the orchestra engage independently of the piano and in which the piano engages with separate instruments of the orchestra, we shall regard the strings and woodwinds in Mozart's concertos as separate interlocutors (see Chapter Two).[43] It is important to note, however, that there are very few indications in Mozart's concertos that the strings and woodwinds partake in anything but completely co-operative exchange with each other. As we shall see, relational tensions, when they do arise, are a product of the piano's behaviour towards the *entire* accompanying orchestra (rather than simply isolated segments thereof). For the purposes of detecting co-operation and competition, therefore, we shall regard Mozart's piano and orchestra as separate, indivisible entities.

Let us begin our analysis with one of the most succinct and powerful piano/orchestra dialogues in all of Mozart's piano concertos: the dialogue at the beginning of the development section from the first movement of No. 22 in E♭, K. 482 (Example 2, bars 214–22). The piano begins with 'little imitations', the third of Antoine Reicha's four types of dialogue, of the violin's closing gesture from bars 214–15 (in bars 216–18). The three-note stepwise ascent is then passed between the piano and the woodwinds and the piano and the full orchestra (bars 218–22), each three-note segment cadencing in a new key (B♭ minor, F minor, A♭ and C minor respectively). The full orchestra, with its emphatic final segment (marked *forte*), usurps the piano by putting an authoritative – and to all intents and purposes unanswerable – stamp on the dialogue.

[42] Although many of the analytical observations in Chapters Three, Four, Five and Six are illustrated with musical examples, some are not. It is expected that the reader wishing to follow the analytical argument in its entirety will have scores of Mozart's piano concertos K. 271–595 to hand (and, for Chapter 5, scores of *Idomeneo, Entführung, Figaro* and *Don Giovanni*).

[43] For a discussion of the prominent role played by the woodwinds in Mozart's concertos after K. 450, see Irving R. Eisley, 'Mozart's Concertato Orchestra', *Mozart-Jahrbuch 1976/77*, pp. 9–20.

Example 2: Mozart, Piano Concerto K. 482, 1st movement, bars 214-22.

Bars 214–22 can be considered analogous to *stichomythia*, the confrontational style of dialogue outlined above. The piano initiates dialogue by taking up the orchestra's 'words' (bars 214–17); the piano and the orchestra alternate a short segment; the two parties apparently disagree about where the dialogue should lead (each segment cadences in a different key); and the orchestra is openly confrontational in its decisive and imposing final contribution (the C minor cadence in bars 221–2).

In addition to specific technical parallels with *stichomythia*, Mozart's piano/orchestra dialogue in bars 214–22 of K. 482/i functions in its wider context in a somewhat similar way to a *stichomythia* dialogue. Just as the dialogues in Voltaire's *Oedipe* and in Goethe's *Iphigenie* and *Tasso*, cited above, are pivotal in terms of plot development and relations between characters, so Mozart's dialogue in K. 482/i marks a crucial and decisive moment in the interaction between the piano and the orchestra.

The confrontational style of dialogue at the beginning of the development section of K. 482/i is in large part a product of the unsettled piano/orchestra relations in the solo exposition. The two parties in the solo exposition, it seems, are on different wavelengths. For example, the piano *alone* carries out the crucial, initial phase of the first modulation to the dominant (bars 114–18), the return modulation to the dominant (bars 149–51) following an interlude in B♭ minor, and also the presentation of all new thematic material; the orchestra involves itself neither in the modulatory processes nor in the exposition of significant material. In addition, the piano restates none of the orchestra's themes from the orchestral exposition. Two specific moments, furthermore, seem to reveal competitive rather than co-operative inclinations on the part of the piano and the orchestra. First, the two parties are not synchronised at the piano's entry, the piano sacrificing precise alignment with the orchestra for increased forward momentum. The E$\flat^4$–D^4 (I–V) motion of the piano's first phrase (bars 77–80), for example, demands the resolution D^4–E$\flat^4$ (V–I). The D^4, however, is prolonged through an interrupted cadence (V-vi, bar 84) and then resolved an octave too low (V–I, bar 94). E$\flat^4$ is finally heard six bars later (bar 100). Above all, the D^4–E$\flat^4$ resolution does *not* coincide with the beginning of the tutti (bar 94); the goal lies beyond it. Second, in a pseudo-dialogue with the orchestra marked 'forte' (bars 128–9, Example 3), the piano blatantly contradicts the orchestra's two-bar affirmation of the dominant (bars 126–7) by abruptly moving to the dominant minor. Just as the piano advocates forward momentum at the start of the solo exposition by delaying resolution in the correct register, it does the same in bars 128–9 by abruptly shifting the mode.

Example 3. Mozart, Piano Concerto K. 482, 1st movement, bars 126-29.

While the confrontational dialogue at the opening of the development – especially the orchestra's final emphatic remark – is a *product* of relational tension in the preceding solo exposition, the dialogue itself also begins the process of *resolving* relational tension. The piano, for example, reveals – merely by engaging in its first genuine dialogue with the orchestra in the movement – that it is no longer oblivious to material presented by the orchestra. In addition, the orchestra resolutely discards the passive role it had adopted in the solo exposition, taking part in the thematic and modulatory processes from which it was absent in the previous section. Following the dialogue of bars 214–22, the orchestra assumes an integrated thematic and tonal role in the development section: ascending/descending arpeggios are dialogued between the strings and the woodwinds (bars 224–47); and the piano and the orchestra prepare *together* for the A$\flat$ tonality of the new theme in bar 248 by both presenting a half-step descending bass line (A$\flat$–E$\flat$, bars 236–47).

The remaining relational tensions from the solo exposition are resolved over the course of the recapitulation. The piano, for example, no longer propels itself beyond the onset of the main theme at the beginning of the recapitulation by delaying the 'correct' resolution to E♭. The B♭ minor passage from the solo exposition (bars 128–51) is also omitted: the piano no longer diverts the music into the minor without, as it were, the orchestra's consent. Correspondingly, the three-bar preparation for the secondary theme in the solo exposition (bars 152ff.), one of the piano's assertions of modulatory superiority (B♭m–B♭), is also omitted. Now, the piano and the orchestra *together* reconfirm E♭ (bars 329–30), in preparation for the reappearance of the secondary theme (bar 330). Above all, the piano and the orchestra demonstrate mutual co-operation by finally engaging in three instances of dialogue that avoid the competitive edge of the dialogue from the beginning of the development section. First, the piano and the woodwinds exchange the full theme from bar 13 (Reicha's first type of dialogue) in bars 276–92; second, the piano imitates the orchestra's three-note closing gesture from bars 308–9 (see bars 309–10); third, the piano and the full orchestra alternately present the theme from bar 51 (bars 314–30).

The defining moment in the shift from competitive piano/orchestra relations in the solo exposition to co-operative relations in the recapitulation is the dialogue at the beginning of the development section. This dialogue must be considered dramatic not only by virtue of its analogies with *stichomythia* but also more generally because it injects dynamic relational change into the process of piano/orchestra interaction. At one and the same time, the succinct and potent dialogue embodies existing relational tensions and presents the beginnings of a resolution to these tensions.

The dramatic significance of dialogue in K. 482/i – comprising, above all, its crucial role in bars 214–22 as a pivot between competitive and co-operative relations – encourages us to investigate dialogue's dramatic function in other Mozart concertos. To be sure, decisive dialogue will not always invite specific parallels with dramatic devices such as *stichomythia*. As K. 482/i demonstrates, however, dialogue emphasises both crucial shifts in piano/orchestra relations and also carefully planned processes of exchange.

The development section of the first movement of Mozart's Piano Concerto No. 15 in B♭ begins, like the corresponding section of K. 482/i, with the first genuine piano/orchestra dialogue of the movement (see Example 4). While the dialogue, consisting of the piano's imitation (and elaboration) of a two-bar figure in the orchestra, does not feature an audibly authoritative gesture as in bars 221–2 of K. 482, it does have a competitive edge. By situating this dialogue in the context of piano/orchestra exchanges from the solo exposition, we will see clearly why this is the case.

The piano's entry at the beginning of the solo exposition of K. 450/i immediately suggests uneasy relations between the piano and the orchestra. After an initial rapid, scalar descent, the piano begins an eight-bar build-up to the return of the main theme in bar 71 (see Example 5). This build-up loses steam for three reasons. First and most important, the piano states predominantly tonic harmony in its eight-bar build-up (exclusively tonic in bars 67–70).

Example 4. Mozart, Piano Concerto K. 450, 1st movement, bars 149-56.

This not only lends an harmonically static quality to the music, uncharacteristic of the movement thus far, but also – by virtue of being exclusively tonic rather than, say, dominant – nullifies any sense of harmonic expectation (in the build-up) or harmonic arrival (at the restatement of the main theme beginning in bar 71). Second, the piano gradually ascends, peaking in bar 68. As soon as the high point is reached, however, the piano has to recede (bars 68–70) so as to accommodate the restatement of the main theme. The registral climax, then, leads to nothing. Third, the two pauses in the piano in bar 70 (brief cadenzas are often added by performers here) establish once and for all that the return of the main theme will not be perceived as the focal point of the piano's virtuosic elaborations.[44]

In short, the piano's entry in K. 450 disrupts a musical flow that had certainly not been endangered by the orchestra in the orchestral exposition. To be sure, the piano's tonic pedals and the gradual, stepwise ascents from the piano's entry are also evident in the orchestral exposition;[45] in fact, the piano writing in bars 63–8 might be considered something of a composite of bars 41–5 and sixteenth-note figurations traceable to bars 9–13. But the piano far exceeds anything found in the orchestral exposition, standing aloof from the orchestra both in the

[44] Ellwood Derr argues that 'the scheme of making initial solo entries on foreign material [as in K. 450/i] had apparently been transferred by Mozart into his piano concertos from a practice established for arias . . . namely a fermata for the soloist typically initiated after the completion of the opening ritornello cadence'. See 'Mozart's Transfer of the Vocal "fermata sospesa" to his Piano Concerto First Movements', in *Mozart-Jahrbuch 1991*, p. 155.

[45] See, for example, bars 41–5, which combine an octave melodic ascent (first violin) with a tonic pedal (cello).

Example 5. Mozart, Piano Concerto K. 450, 1st movement, bars 63-74.

type of music it performs and in the harmonic stasis and absence of directional thrust that the writing brings with it. The lack of piano/orchestra dialogue – both in the eight-bar build-up and subsequently in the first period of the restatement of the main theme (bars 71–8, exquisitely split between the woodwinds and strings in bars 1–8 and an example of Reicha's second type of dialogue) – may not, in itself, be a sign that co-operation between the piano and the orchestra is missing. Nevertheless, the fact that the passages in question also expose strong dissimilarities in the piano and orchestral writing reinforces the impression that, at this juncture at least, the piano and the orchestra are not exactly seeing eye-to-eye.[46]

[46] Other critics have noticed uncertainty at the piano's entry in K. 450. Cuthbert Girdlestone, for example, observes that the 'piano entry drives the orchestra into the background', and the orchestra becomes 'neither collaborator nor adversary but just accompanist'. See *Mozart and his*

Following the piano's flamboyant entry and monopolization of the first eight bars of the main theme, the uneasy piano/orchestra relations come to a head. Admittedly, the piano and woodwinds in bars 78–80 follow a pattern established by the strings and woodwinds in the orchestral exposition (bars 8–10) in subjecting an ascending chromatic scale and descending semiquavers to a kind of split-theme dialogue. But the dialogue does not initiate co-operative exchange. Instead of adhering to the orchestra's cadential pattern from bars 13–14 of the orchestral exposition, the piano at the corresponding point in the solo exposition anchors itself on B♭ root position harmony for two full bars (bars 83–4, Example 6). Just as the piano's preparation for the return of the main theme (bars 63–70 in Example 5) gets stuck on B♭ and is accompanied by virtuosic flourishes and an indecisive registral ascent which have nowhere to go, so bars 83–4 stagnate on B♭ and offer scalar flourishes (very similar to bars 67–8) which reach a peak and then descend anti-climactically. The piano's reconfirmation of the tonic (bars 85–6) is greeted with disdain by the strings, which directly confront the piano's behaviour by effecting a loud and abrupt shift to G minor harmony for the beginning of the transition. Whereas the piano seems content, then, to dwell on B♭ harmony, the orchestra is evidently eager to move the harmony along.

Example 6. Mozart, Piano Concerto K. 450, 1st movement, bars 83-87.

It is striking that, in addition to the moments of relational tension described above, none of the principal themes treated in dialogue between the woodwinds and the strings in the orchestral exposition of K. 450 (Examples 7, 8 and 9) return in dialogue between the piano and the orchestra in the solo exposition.[47] (For a diagrammatic representation of the reappearance of these three themes in dialogue, as explained below, see Fig. 1.)

Piano Concertos, p. 199. Denis Forman also points out a kind of indecision on the piano's part. Whereas the 'piano introduction [bars 59–70]' constitutes 'a majestic assertion of the key of B flat and fit to stand at the head of the grandest symphonic First Concerto [that is, the solo exposition]', its return to the main theme (bars 71ff.) is somewhat anticlimactic, marking a moment of 'carefully contrived bathos'. See Forman, *Mozart's Concerto Form: The First Movements of the Piano Concertos* (New York: Praeger, 1971), pp. 177–8.

[47] As we have seen, there is a brief dialogue in bars 78–80, corresponding to bars 8–10, although most of the main theme (bars 1–8) is not dialogued on its reappearance in the solo exposition (bars 71–8).

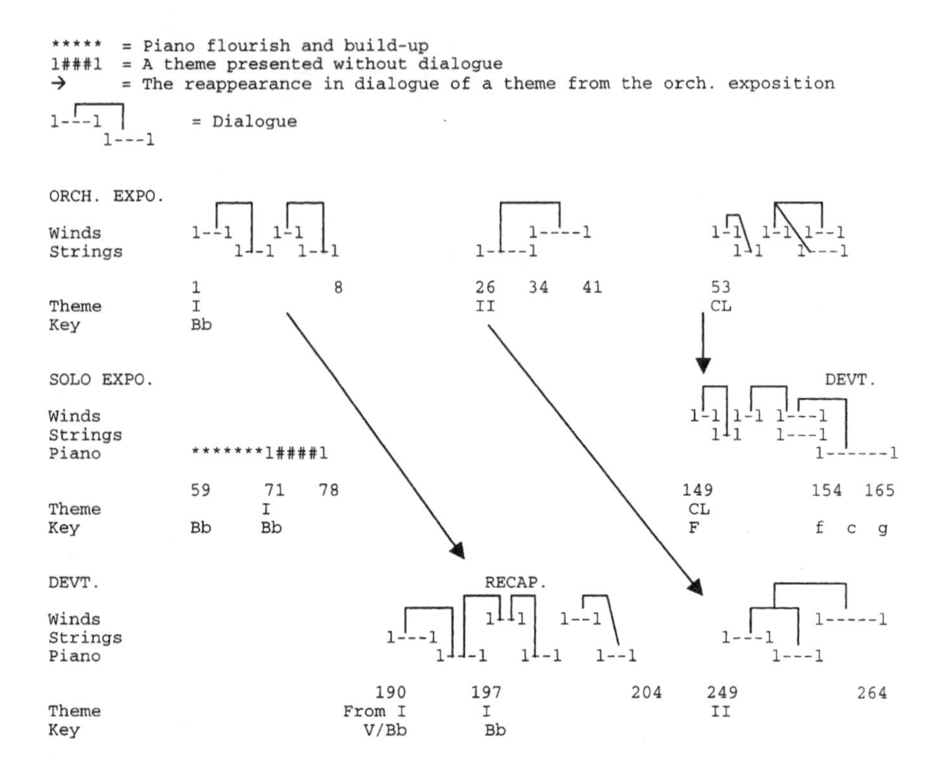

Fig. 1: The reappearance in dialogue of the three themes dialogued in the orchestral exposition of K. 450/1.

The shift in attitude towards dialogue between the orchestral and solo expositions is accentuated by the exquisite way in which the strings and woodwinds interlocutors are balanced in the orchestral exposition. The woodwinds lead the first dialogue (Example 7) and the strings lead the second (Example 8). Appropriately, in the third dialogue (Example 9) which the woodwinds initiate, the strings and woodwinds 'come together' (bars 57–8)

just as eighteenth-century dictionary writers on musical dialogue such as Rousseau, Meude-Monpas, Grassineau, and Pilkington advocate.[48]

Example 7. Mozart, Piano Concerto K. 450, 1st movement, bars 1-4.

Example 8. Mozart, Piano Concerto K. 450, 1st movement, bars 26-41.

Example 9. Mozart, Piano Concerto K. 450, 1st movement, bars 53-59.

The piano/orchestra dialogue at the beginning of the development section of K. 450 (Example 4) therefore occurs in the context of uneasy exchanges between the piano and the orchestra in the solo exposition, in which dialogue is conspicuous by its absence. That the piano is at last willing to engage in dialogue of any kind is a sign that relations with the orchestra are improving. In addition, a specific relational tension inherited from the solo exposition is resolved. The piano uses the material arrived at through dialoguing with the orchestra's consequent (bars 153^2–4^1 dialogued in bars 154^2–6^1) to produce a sequential modulation from F minor to C minor to G minor. Whereas the initial exchange between the orchestra and the piano at the end of the orchestral

[48] See Rousseau, *Dictionnaire de Musique*, p. 145; Meude-Monpas, *Dictionnaire de Musique*, p. 47; Grassineau, *A Musical Dictionary*, p. 55; and Pilkington, *A Musical Dictionary*, pp. 23–4.

exposition going into the beginning of the solo exposition involves no dialogue and leads to an uncomfortable harmonic stasis, the corresponding dialogic exchange at the end of the solo exposition going into the development features the requisite tonal movement. In short, dialogue appears to have 'corrected' an earlier 'flaw' (the piano's harmonic stasis), one that had lent considerable tension to piano/orchestra relations.

We must not overlook, however, a competitive edge to the dialogue at the beginning of the development section. Antoine Reicha proposes sudden changes in dialogue from a major to a parallel minor key as an effective way of accentuating contrast between interlocutors;[49] indeed, the piano's answer moves *immediately* from the orchestra's key of F major to F minor. In addition, the piano disguises the dialogued phrase to some extent through semiquaver elaboration and chromaticisation. Thus, the piano's continuation of the kind of intricate, ornate and individualistic music that helps to create relational tension between the piano and the orchestra at the beginning of the solo exposition, co-exists with an exchange that begins at least to resolve this tension. Just as at the opening of the development section in K. 482/i, dialogue at the corresponding moment in K. 450/i demonstrates at one and the same time relational tension and partial resolution of that tension.

If the opening of the development section initiates dialogue between the piano and the orchestra and combines competition and co-operation, the end of the development moving into the recapitulation (bars 189–200, Example 10) continues the dialogue, but now with fully co-operating parties. Above all, this passage finally unveils a three-way dialogue to match the intricate two-way dialogues between the strings and woodwinds in the orchestral exposition: all three parties play an active role in dialoguing the main theme, the strings and piano smoothly preparing for, and effortlessly leading into, the woodwinds' statement. Another source of relational tension inherited from the solo exposition is also resolved. The dialogue between the strings and the piano (bars 190–6) before the onset of the recapitulation includes a six-bar pedal on F in the piano (bars 189–94). In its earlier incarnation immediately before the return of the main theme in the solo exposition, a piano pedal had contributed to the unsettling harmonic stasis. Here, however, the pedal heightens the sense of harmonic anticipation (by virtue of its placement on F, in the context of an eight-bar dominant build-up). It consequently emphasises, rather than detracts from, the return of the main theme (bars 197).

Three-way dialogue resurfaces in the recapitulation at bars 249–64 (Example 11), reinforcing the air of graceful co-operation established at the end of the development and beginning of the recapitulation. Here we encounter the final strings/woodwinds theme from the orchestral exposition yet to reappear in dialogue. Not only is the theme split between the strings and piano and then passed to the woodwinds, but the piano pedal, now fully

[49] See Reicha, *Traité de mélodie*, p. 91.

Example 10. Mozart, Piano Concerto K. 450, 1st Movement, bars 189-200.

assimilated as a co-operative element, also returns in its anticipatory role (bars 250–2, predicting the piano's contribution to the dialogue).[50]

Piano/orchestra relations alter over the course of K. 450 and 482 in very similar fashions. (This is striking because the sources of piano/orchestra tension in the solo expositions of the two movements are very different: in K. 450, the piano advocates harmonic and tonal stasis and the orchestra forward propulsion; in K. 482, the reverse is true.) Both movements follow a broad trajectory

Example 11. Mozart, Piano Concerto K. 450, 1st Movement, bars 248-60.

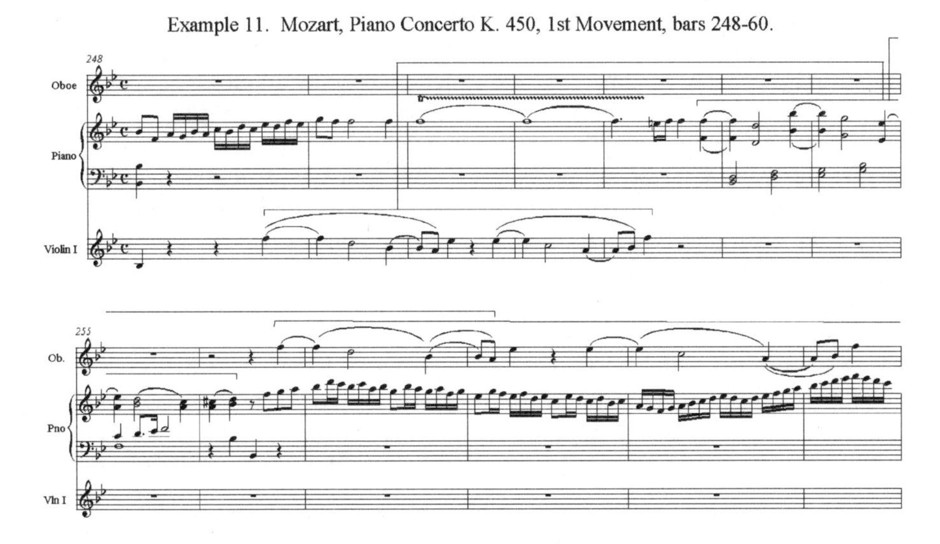

[50] We might also draw attention to the dialogue between the strings/woodwinds and the piano immediately before, and at the beginning of, the cadenza of K. 450/i. As I explain in note 53 below, such dialogue is rare in the cadenzas of the first movements of Mozart's piano concertos.

from competition in the solo exposition to full co-operation in the recapitulation; both combine co-operation and competition in a dramatic dialogue at the beginning of the development; and both utilise this dialogue as a crucial pivot between competitive and co-operative motivations. Above all, dialogue between the piano and the orchestra underscores a carefully crafted process of relational change. As we have seen above, Heinrich Koch and late-eighteenth-century dramatic theorists readily recognised dialogue's ability to function in both an immediate and progressive capacity. There can be no better practical illustrations of this than K. 450 and K. 482.

Not all of Mozart's first movements, however, follow the competition-to-co-operation trajectory exemplified by K. 482/i and 450/i; in fact, the vast majority follow a pattern rooted in piano/orchestra co-operation, as we shall see in Chapter Four. Yet other movements do exhibit the kind of intense relation-defining dramatic dialogue characteristic of K. 450/i and 482/i, and situate it, moreover, in the context of taut and coherent dialogic processes. In order to show how this is the case, let us consider powerful dramatic dialogue in K. 449/i, a movement that does not follow a competition-to-co-operation trajectory, but nonetheless uses dialogue to underscore dynamic relational change.

The beginning of the recapitulation of K. 449/i (see Example 12), like the beginnings of the development sections of K. 450/i and 482/i, marks a decisive moment in the relationship between the piano and the orchestra. The dominant is established (bar 219) in adequate time for K. 449/i's recapitulation (bar 234), and is then coloured by inflections to the minor (see the G♭s and D♭s in bars 223–9). Drawing upon the modal ambiguity of the previous bars, the piano ascends chromatically in all three lines (bars 230–3) leading directly to the return of the main theme in the tonic (bar 234). This effect is jarring: the piano not only leaves the modal ambiguity of bars 223–9 unresolved in bars 230–3, but also, by virtue of its chromatic movement, embodies an indecisive harmonic progression (♭VI–IV6–♭VII–V6) which lends the music neither the clear dominant preparation nor the harmonic propulsion expected at this juncture of the movement.[51] The arrival of the main theme is extremely abrupt, the orchestra asserting tonal stability in a manner that forcefully breaks the piano's chromatic ascent and suggests conflict with the soloist.

A remarkably ingenious dialogue, however, swiftly and succinctly resolves the piano/orchestra conflict. The semitone motion in the piano (bars 230–3, Example 12), forcefully interrupted by the full orchestra (bar 234), immediately reappears in the following bars (242–3). The piano, taking its cue directly from the final bar of its first semitone ascent (bar 233), starts semitone ascents in all three voices on B♭, D and F (bars 242–3^2). The piano's ascent in bars 242–3^2 forms part of a split-theme dialogue with the strings (the first time in the

[51] To be sure, the piano's chromatic writing in bars 230–3 (C♭, C, D♭, D) could be interpreted merely as filling the gap between the dominant harmony (on B♭) of bar 226, and the tonic harmony (on E♭) of bar 234. But this explanation in itself would not do justice to the unusual and peculiar harmonic effect of the four bars immediately preceding the recapitulation.

Example 12. Mozart, Piano Concerto K. 449, 1st Movement, bars 228-45.

movement that the main theme has been treated in this way). The formerly disruptive semitone ascent is, therefore, instantly assimilated as a co-operative element. Moreover, just as this brilliant and uncannily lucid moment of dialogue realises the 'coming together' of interlocutors in relationship terms recognised by eighteenth-century writers on dialogue and expressed with greatest clarity by Reicha in his discussion of the 'dialogued duet', so it effects unification in formal terms. At a basic level, of course, first-movement concerto form requires two expositions to 'come together' in a single recapitulation. In this movement, however, the formal unification through dialogue is especially succinct: the orchestra repeat bars 1–8 from the orchestral exposition in bars 234–41 and the piano repeats bars 97–104 from the solo exposition in bars 242–9.

Although the harmonic rupture at the moment of recapitulation in K. 449 is resolved in an extraordinary fashion a few bars later, the rupture radiates beyond its immediate confines. In bars 319–20, shortly before the cadenza (see Example 13), there is a similarly abrasive harmonic confrontation between the orchestra and the piano: the orchestra violently interrupts the piano's final cadential trill, thrusting the music into C minor. Here, the orchestra's intrusion is not only harmonically confrontational but dynamically and thematically confrontational as well: its sudden, forceful shift into C minor is all the more startling for the fact that its figure in bar 319, originating in bar 3 and (more directly) in bar 16, takes thematic attention away from the piano's final cadential trill. Resolution of this conflict is swift and every bit as ingenious as that of the earlier conflict at the beginning of the recapitulation. First, the orchestra, which was responsible for the harmonic disturbance, resolves the conflict with an emphatic reconfirmation of the tonic, E♭ (IV–II6/5–I6/4 [bars 324–8], Example 14), using a progression that incorporates an ostentatious chromatic ascent in the cellos and basses, A♭ (bars 324–5) – A

Example 13. Mozart, Piano Concerto K. 449, 1st Movement, bars 318-20.

(bars 326–7) – B♭ (bar 328). Although this type of ascent is of course common immediately before a Mozart cadenza, it is imbued here with considerable significance: the chromatic ascent, formerly a catalyst for piano/orchestra confrontation at an important structural juncture (the end of the development going into the recapitulation), now returns in a reconciliatory role at another pivotal structural moment (the preparation for the piano cadenza).[52] Second, the thematic conflict brought about by bars 319–20 is resolved by the dialoguing of the arpeggiated semiquaver figure between the first violin (bars 320–6) and the piano (the very opening of the cadenza, Example 14).[53] Just as at the beginning of the recapitulation, dialogue emphasises in a concise and direct fashion that co-operation between the piano and the orchestra has been re-established.

Bars 319–20 represent a moment of intense conflict, but not the first occasion in the movement that the material from bars 16–17 has been at the centre of relational tension. The beginning of the development section, for example, includes a confrontational piano/orchestra dialogue, featuring the rhythm from bars 16–17 in its very earliest incarnation (that is, in its bar 3 form). Whereas subtle piano/orchestra dialogue is characteristic of the solo exposition (see, for example, bars 95–104, 112–17, 137–46), it disappears at the beginning of the development and is replaced by markedly contrasting material in the piano and the orchestra. The piano begins the section in a straightforward full-theme dialogue with the orchestra (bars 176–85),[54] but the dialogue does not lead to

[52] We might also note parenthetically that the half-step ascent beginning on A♭ 'rescues' the cellos and basses from completing their 'lamento' descent from C–B♭–A♭[–G].

[53] It is difficult to generalize about the way in which Mozart begins his first-movement cadenzas, as no cadenzas survive for six of the Viennese concertos – K. 466, 467, 482, 491, 503 and 537. Of those first movements of Mozart's Viennese piano concertos with extant cadenzas (K. 413, 414, 415, 449, 450, 451, 453, 456, 459, 488, 595), only K. 415, 449 and 450's cadenzas begin with the piano instantly dialoguing an immediately preceding orchestral figure. Both the K. 451 cadenza and one of the three surviving cadenzas for K. 456 begin with scalar flourishes and only then dialogue material from the orchestra's previous passage. For brief considerations of Mozart's extant cadenzas, see Christoph Wolff, 'Cadenzas and Styles of Interpretation in Mozart's Piano Concertos', in *Perspectives on Mozart Performance*, ed. R. Larry Todd and Peter Williams (Cambridge: Cambridge University Press, 1991), pp. 228–38; and Frederick Neumann, 'Instrumental Cadenzas', *Ornamentation and Improvisation in Mozart* (Princeton: Princeton University Press, 1986), Chapter 17.

[54] The piano reverses the position of the orchestra's stepwise descent and trill figure, as do the strings in bars 70–8 of the orchestral exposition.

Example 14. Mozart, Piano Concerto K. 449, 1st Movement, bars 324-28.

further collaborative exchange. Initially (bars 186–7) the piano states arpeggiated semiquavers. In the next seventeen bars (188–204), it simply juxtaposes figuration deriving from the arpeggiations in dialogue with the orchestra's abrasive, *forte* presentations of the figure from bar 3 (see Example 15). No attempt is made by either party to reintroduce collaborative dialogue. In fact, the piano and the orchestra at this juncture exploit several of the musical effects listed by Reicha for contrasting dialogue: the 'opposed character' of the phrases (the full orchestral *forte* against the piano *legato*); 'the succession of unison [orchestra] and harmony [piano]'; the 'change from major to minor . . . (of the same key)' (B♭ major–B♭ minor harmony, bars 188–90); and pronounced timbral fluctuation.[55]

Whereas the close co-operation of the solo exposition is no longer evident in bars 188–203 and is fully recaptured only with the split-theme dialogue at the beginning of the recapitulation, the intervening dialogue (bars 204–18) occupies a middle ground, in relational terms, between these two poles. On the one hand, dialogue occurs only internally (the trill figure in the left and right hands of the piano, and the stepwise quaver figures in the strings, bars 204–12, 214–18, see

[55] Also, the piano and orchestra's alternated phrases are the same length, one of Reicha's prerequisites for the second of his dialogue categories, which includes dialogic opposition. See Reicha, *Traité de mélodie*, p. 90.

Example 15. Mozart, Piano Concerto K. 449, 1st Movement, bars 188-96.

Example 16), with no attempt made to re-engage harmonious piano/orchestra dialogue; on the other hand, the striking oppositional effects from the preceding dialogue disappear.

Overall, piano/orchestra dialogue in K. 449/i – like dialogue in K. 450/i and 482/i – is carefully designed to emphasise changes in the behaviour of the two parties towards each other over the course of the entire movement. There is a shift in K. 450 and 482 from competition in the solo exposition to co-operation in the recapitulation, pivoting around the crucial confrontations (in dramatic dialogue) at the beginning of the development sections. K. 449/i, on the other hand, moves from co-operation in the solo exposition to competition in the early part of the development section and back to co-operation, albeit punctuated by moments of competition (resolved to co-operation through dialogue) in the recapitulation.

Whereas an individual dialogue such as the one in bars 214–22 of K. 482 is dramatic by virtue of its similarity to a specific dramatic technique (*sticho-mythia*), dialogue in all three works serves a dramatic function as it constitutes an extended formal process stretching across an entire movement. As we have seen, each piano/orchestra dialogue is a product of earlier exchanges between the two parties and has a direct bearing on future exchanges. This kind of process is accentuated, moreover, by the extraordinary

Example 16. Mozart, Piano Concerto K. 449, 1st Movement, bars 204-208.

vitality that dialogues such as bars 214–22 of K. 482 (Example 2), bars 150ff. of K. 450 (Example 4) and bars 234ff. of K. 449 (Example 12) lend to piano/orchestra relations.

Mozart's K. 449, 450 and 482 thus offer powerful practical realizations of the late-eighteenth-century theoretical positions outlined above. In accordance with Koch's account, distinct dialogic processes map out broad alterations in the interactive behaviour of the piano and orchestra; as eighteenth-century writers on musical dialogue collectively imply, piano/orchestra dialogue is usually co-operative, but from time to time competitive; and, as dramatic theorists make clear, confrontational dialogue underscores decisive alterations in relations between characters.

It is not surprising – given the connections between theory and practice outlined above – that a further analogy can be drawn between the interactions between dramatic characters in classical plays and the interactions between the piano and the orchestra in Mozart's concertos. Diderot and Lessing protest repeatedly against straightforward character oppositions and unexpected and abrupt transformations in relations between characters ('coups de théâtre' in Diderot's words). Both favour a more carefully crafted process whereby differences among characters are gradually revealed.[56] Mozart, as we have seen, adopts a similar position. He is careful not to oppose directly the piano and the orchestra at the beginning of the solo expositions of K. 450/i and 482/i through a 'momentary effect' (to quote Diderot). Instead, he reveals only gradually during the piano's initial entry that the instrument is on a different wavelength from the orchestra. In addition, sudden and unsubtle changes in relations characteristic of 'coups de théâtre' are shunned in favour of subtly graded processes of change.

Similarities between Piano/Orchestra Relations in Mozart's Concertos and Character Relations in Late-Eighteenth-Century Classical Plays

In light of the practical manifestations in Mozart's piano concertos of theoretical positions espoused by dramatists, we might also identify (albeit somewhat tentatively) parallels between dialogic processes in Mozart's piano concertos and those in late-eighteenth-century classical plays. Four important and influential German classical plays, Goethe's *Clavigo* (1774) and *Iphigenie auf Tauris* (1787) and Lessing's *Minna von Barnhelm* (1767) and *Nathan der Weise* (1779), were either familiar to the Viennese theatre-going public during Mozart's time (*Minna* and *Clavigo*), or were written almost contemporaneously with the main body of Mozart's Viennese piano concertos, including K. 449, 450

[56] See, for example, Diderot, 'De la Poésie dramatique', p. 166, and Lessing, *Hamburg Dramaturgy*, p. 221.

and 482 (*Iphigenie* and *Nathan*),[57] thus rendering all of them good sources for comparative study. *Minna* was staged at the *Burgtheater* in 1781 and 1782,[58] and again on 16 August, 1785, and 18 November, 1786.[59] *Clavigo*, performed on 7 January, 30 March and 7 September 1786,[60] would no doubt have held special interest for Mozart, given that it was based on Beaumarchais' memoirs and that Mozart was himself setting Da Ponte's libretto to Beaumarchais' *Figaro* from October 1785 to May 1786. Although *Iphigenie* and *Nathan* only received their Viennese premieres in 1800 and 1819 respectively, they are also especially well suited to comparison with Mozart's concertos. Most important for the purposes of examining the dramatic significance of dialogue in Mozart concertos, both *Iphigenie* and *Nathan* privilege dialogue over action.[61]

We noticed, in all three of Mozart's movements discussed above, that dialogue directly stimulates changes in relations between the piano and the orchestra. In a similar way, Goethe's *Iphigenie* offers a famous dramatic realization of dialogue that directly stimulates relational change. As Benjamin Bennett has recently explained, Act 2, scene 1 of *Iphigenie* is dominated by Orestes's 'obsessive hypochondriac despair' in which he is unable to communicate. He and Pylades continually talk at cross-purposes. After falling into a trance 'in which he perfects his withdrawal from reality', Orestes is '[pulled] back into the real world' by *dialogue* (albeit 'totally illusory communication') between Iphigenie and Pylades (Act 3, lines 1317–40). Bennett concludes: 'If we even imagine ourselves in contact with others, this is already a step toward openness; toward a social rather than an obstinately individual mode of perceiving and acting'.[62] The same point could be made for the opening of the development sections of Mozart's K. 450/i and 482/i concertos. The simple act of engaging in dialogue begins the process of replacing the piano's and orchestra's self-absorption with a kind of openness; social exchange thus supersedes individualism and isolationism.

Structural rather than topical parallels can also be drawn between piano/orchestra dialogue in Mozart's three first movements (K. 449, 450, 482) and the two-person dialogues that dominate Lessing's *Nathan* and *Minna von Barn-*

[57] Goethe wrote a prose version of *Iphigenie* during February and March of 1779, while living in Weimar. See Cyrus Hamlin and Frank Ryder, 'Postcript: *Iphigenia in Tauris*', in *Johann Wolfgang von Goethe: Verse Plays and Epic*, eds. Hamlin and Ryder (New York: Suhrkamp, 1987), p. 309.

[58] See Maria von Alth and Gertrude Obzyna, eds., *Burgtheater 1776–1976: Aufführungen und Besetzungen von zweihundert Jahren* (Vienna: Salzer-Überreuter, 1979), p. 2.

[59] Link, *The National Court Theatre in Mozart's Vienna*, pp. 66, 94.

[60] Ibid., pp. 75, 81, 90. Mozart could have attended any of these three performances of *Clavigo*, as he was in Vienna without interruption in 1786. See Peter Dimond, compiler, *A Mozart Diary: A Chronological Reconstruction of the Composer's Life, 1761–1791* (Westport, Connecticut: Greenwood Press, 1997), pp. 171–6.

[61] Benjamin Bennett makes this somewhat obvious but very important point in *Modern Drama and German Classicism: Renaissance from Lessing to Brecht* (Ithaca, New York: Cornell University Press, 1979), p. 97.

[62] Ibid., pp. 114–15.

helm. For example, differences in the way in which interaction develops in *Nathan*'s Act 2, scene 5 (Nathan and the Templar) and *Minna*'s Act 3, scene 2 on the one hand, and *Nathan*'s Act 3, scenes 5–7 (Nathan and the Sultan Saladin) on the other,[63] are analogous to differences in the way in which interaction develops in Mozart's K. 450, 482 and 449. Just as K. 450/i and 482/i progress from uneasy competition to full co-operation, so Nathan and the Templar in Act 2, scene 5 of *Nathan* and Franziska and Just in Act 3, scene 2 of *Minna* move from distrust, cynicism and a reluctance to engage in productive dialogue, to solid agreement and amicable mutual respect.[64] In contrast, the Nathan/Saladin dialogue, like K. 449/i, does not contain a striking development in the relations between the two characters; there is, for example, no obvious disagreement between the characters at the beginning. Just as the piano and the orchestra in the solo exposition of K. 449/i assume a co-operative relationship but test this co-operation at the beginning and end of the recapitulation, so Saladin believes in Nathan's wisdom at the beginning of their exchange (Act 3, scene 5) but subsequently asks him to prove his wisdom on the question of which of the three religions (Judaism, Christianity and Islam) is 'true'. In K. 449/i, the piano and orchestra meet the self-imposed challenge to their co-operation in an emphatic and convincing fashion, thereby strengthening their bond; similarly, in Act 3, scene 7 of Lessing's play, Nathan famously recounts the fable of the rings (a metaphor for the absence of one single religious truth) in such a way as to reinforce Saladin's belief in his wisdom.

Similar parallels in relational trajectories can be found between Mozart's

[63] See Gotthold Ephraim Lessing, *Nathan the Wise*, trans. Bayard Quincy Morgan (New York: Frederick Ungar, 1989 [First edition 1955]), pp. 48–53 and 71–82; and Lessing, *Minna von Barnhelm*, trans. Kenneth J. Northcott (Chicago: University of Chicago Press, 1972), pp. 42–6.

[64] At the beginning of the dialogue, Nathan remarks 'I am a wealthy Jew' to which the Templar replies nastily 'I never thought the richer Jew the better.' Also the Templar interrupts Nathan forcefully when Nathan tries to explain his purpose:

> 'NATHAN: My name is Nathan; I'm the maiden's father
> Whom your great heart delivered from the flames;
> I come . . .
> TEMPLAR: Why, if to thank me: – stop! I have
> Endured already for this trifling thing
> Too many thanks' (pp. 48–9).

By the end of the dialogue, however, the Templar agrees enthusiastically with Nathan's belief in religious tolerance and exclaims 'Yes, Nathan, yes; we must, we must become good friends' (p. 52). Similarly, Franziska's dialogue with Just (Tellheim's servant) begins with distain on the part of Franziska, culminating in her exclamation:

> 'FRANZISKA: Well I declare! Letting so many good people go and keeping the worst one of all [i.e. Just]. I'd like to know what your master sees in you.
> JUST: Perhaps he thinks I'm an honest man.
> FRANZISKA: People who are just honest don't amount to much' (p. 44).

But by the end of the dialogue, after Just has proved the importance of honesty by giving examples of servants who were dishonest, Franziska is much more respectful: 'I deserved that. Thank you, Just. I set too low a price on honesty. I won't forget the lesson you've taught me' (p. 46).

three concerto movements and Goethe's two-person dialogues in *Clavigo*.[65] The exchange between Clavigo and Beaumarchais in Act 2 of Goethe's play, for example, follows an analogous pattern of exchange between the piano and the orchestra in the first movements of K. 450 and 482. Just as relational tension is evident when Beaumarchais narrates the story of Marie's lover's desertion and leads to a climactic confrontation when he identifies Clavigo as that lover, so the piano and orchestra initially demonstrate relational unease at the beginning of the solo expositions of K. 450/i and 482/i and only later come to blows more directly. Equally, the tension in the *Clavigo* exchange begins to diffuse when the two characters make concessions – Clavigo to sign the *mea culpa* declaration and Beaumarchais to put in a good word for Clavigo to Marie – just as relational tensions in Mozart's concerto movements begin to disappear when the piano and the orchestra change their behaviour in regard to harmonic stasis and forward propulsion. In contrast to the Clavigo/Beaumarchais exchange, the exchange between Clavigo and Carlos in the first part of Act 4 develops in a manner akin to piano/orchestra exchange in K. 449. Just as Clavigo mostly co-operates with Carlos's attempt to persuade him to reject Marie, sometimes voices strong disagreement – for example when Carlos criticises his prospective marriage to Marie and when he hears that Beaumarchais will be mistreated – but always comes around to Carlos's point of view, so the piano and the orchestra in K. 449/i engage mostly in co-operative exchange (the solo exposition and recapitulation), sometimes punctuated by confrontations that always resolve to co-operation.

The similarities I have located between Mozart's concerto dialogue in K. 449, 450 and 482 and dramatic dialogue in Goethe's *Clavigo* and *Iphigenie*, and Lessing's *Minna* and *Nathan*, are by no means exhaustive; nor should these specific parallels suggest that equally convincing ones cannot be found in other contemporary plays. At the very least, however, correlations such as these provide practical evidence of the dramatic credentials of piano/orchestra interaction in Mozart's concertos.

The connections between dialogue in Mozart's concerto movements and theoretical discussions and examples of dramatic dialogue from late-eighteenth-century plays suggest that Mozart's concertos might have conveyed meaning to their audiences in a somewhat analogous way to contemporary dramatic works. Although this can be best understood in the context of Mozart's complete three-movement cycles (and is therefore discussed at greater length in Chapter 6), it is also evident at the level of individual movements. In both theory and practice Lessing emphasised that audiences must engage closely with the process of development in a play, in order to grasp the full significance of the message (or messages) contained therein. In the *Hamburgische Drama-*

[65] See Johann Wolfgang von Goethe, 'Clavigo: a Tragedy', trans. Robert M. Browning, in *Johann Wolfgang von Goethe: Early Verse Drama and Prose Plays*, ed. Cyrus Hamlin and Frank Ryder (New York: Suhrkamp, 1988), pp. 153–88.

turgie, for example, he stresses that Euripides (in his view one of the greatest of all tragedians) 'deliberately let his spectators know as much of the coming action as any god might know, . . . [promising] to awaken their emotions, not so much by that which should occur, as by the mode in which it should occur'.[66] And from *Nathan* we can certainly deduce, as many critics have, that the *pursuit* of truth is just as important as truth itself.[67] Similarly, in Mozart's piano concertos it would not have been enough for audiences simply to observe that the piano and the orchestra co-operate or even that they move from competitive to co-operative relations over the course of a movement. It would have been essential for audiences to grasp the full significance of *how* a state of co-operation is attained (K. 450, 482) or reinforced (K. 449). They would have to understand, for example, the complex means by which dialogue functions as a pivot between competitive and co-operative relations. Only in this way would an audience have comprehended the full dramatic impact of movements such as K. 449/i, 450/i and 482/i.

When we adopt a late-eighteenth-century dramatic perspective on competition and co-operation in Mozart's piano concertos, we realise that these works challenged their classical audiences far more stringently than has hitherto been acknowledged. Joseph Kerman and Susan McClary have recently proposed that piano/orchestra relations in Mozart's piano concertos represent, respectively, 'a composite metaphor for Mozart and his audience and *their* relationship' and a 'dramatization' of the tension between an individual and society.[68] We can conclude from our investigation of dialogue, however, that works such as K. 449/i, 450/i and 482/i carried intellectual as well as metaphorical significance for their late-eighteenth-century listener. Following every stage in the process of relational change in each movement would have been a highly demanding exercise for a contemporary listener; Mozart's concertos would certainly have provided a prime example of the kind of instrumental music which, according to Adam Smith, can 'occupy, and as it were fill up completely the whole capacity of the mind, so as to leave no part of its attention vacant for thinking of anything else'.[69] By engaging his listener in a challenging intellectual pursuit, Mozart offered him or her an excellent vehicle for learning about co-operation (or, more precisely, the quest for co-operation), a value deeply

[66] Lessing, *Hamburg Dramaturgy*, p. 151. There are, Lessing points out, 'hundreds of instances when we cannot do better than to tell [the spectator] straight out what is going to occur' (p. 149). Also, in a letter to Nicolai, Lessing emphasises the processive nature of evoking pity in a spectator; that is, through terror and admiration, lower 'rungs' on the 'ladder'. See the letter to Nicolai of November 13, 1756, translated in Henry Hitch Adams and Baxter Hathaway, eds., *Dramatic Essays of the Neoclassic Age* (New York: Columbia University Press, 1950), p. 330.

[67] See, for example, John A. McCarthy, '"Verständigung" and "Dialectik": On Consensus Theory and the Dialectic of Enlightenment', in *Impure Reason: Dialectic of Enlightenment in Germany*, eds. W. Daniel Wilson and Robert C. Holub (Detroit: Wayne State University Press, 1993), p. 26.

[68] See Kerman, 'Mozart's Piano Concertos and their Audience', p. 153; McClary, 'A Musical Dialectic', p. 138.

[69] Smith, *Essays on Philosophical Subjects*, p. 205.

cherished in the Age of Enlightenment. Mozart's concertos thus fulfilled the single most important requirement for all late-eighteenth-century music and drama: the general instruction of the listener/spectator. In this respect, concertos such as K. 449, 450 and 482 provided their classical audiences with a splendid complement to the very best that late-eighteenth-century spoken theatre had to offer.

4

Towards a Dialogic Apotheosis

The First Movements of Mozart's Piano Concertos K. 271–491 and Beyond

Now that we have established the dramatic credentials of co-operative and competitive interaction in general and dialogue in particular in Mozart's concertos, we must explain patterns of interaction in a more systematic and methodical fashion. Since all of the first movements follow the same formal schemata – concerto form – they provide a particularly cogent body of movements for stylistic investigation, and enable us to demonstrate the evolution of piano/orchestra interaction across Mozart's *œuvre.* Whereas the comparative study of concerto and operatic dialogue in Chapter 5 explains the inter-generic and dramatic significance of this evolution, the current investigation, focussing more narrowly on the first movements of the piano concertos K. 271–595, demonstrates precisely how the prevalent pattern of relational development in these movements culminates in the extraordinary sophistication and intensity of the Piano Concerto No. 24 in C minor, K. 491, and how it is adapted in the first movements of the three remaining concertos, K. 503, 537 and 595.

As we will see in the analyses below, the vast majority of the first movements of Mozart's piano concertos from 1777–86 (K. 271–491) – including K. 449 discussed in Chapter 3 – follow a similar pattern of relational development, in terms of the dialogue (or lack thereof) in which the solo and orchestral forces participate. In the solo exposition, the piano and the orchestra engage in intimate dialogue that bonds rather than separates the two forces; in the development, they either partake in dialogue among themselves (internal dialogue), move away from dialogue all together, or engage in confrontational dialogue, along the lines described by Reicha; and in the recapitulation, they re-establish the intimate dialogue of the solo exposition, often adding dialogic subtleties not included in the earlier section.[1] The only exceptions are the first movements of K. 415, 450, 467 and 482. We observed in Chapter 3 that K. 450/i and 482/i follow a competition-to-co-operation trajectory from the solo exposition to the recapitulation; K. 467/i also resolves relational unease from the solo exposition later in the movement, although

[1] The recapitulation of K. 449/i is the exception rather than the rule in terms of its integration of confrontational interaction into the reinforcement of co-operation.

competition in the solo exposition as a whole is less pronounced than in K. 450/i and 482/i.[2] K. 415/i, in contrast, is a bit of an anomaly. While there is virtually no dialogue between the piano and the orchestra in the solo exposition,[3] there are none of the signs of relational unease that characterise K. 450, 467 and 482 either.[4] In keeping with this trend, neither the development nor the recapitulation incorporates significant piano/orchestra dialogue. To be sure, the piano and the strings engage in internal dialogue in the development (see, for example, bars 160–3, 167–72, 176–9, 181–6 [strings] and 190–4 [piano]), as the strings had done in the orchestral exposition (bars 1–6, 25–31, 36–43), but neither party makes an attempt to engage in substantive dialogue with the other. Although Girdlestone's description of K. 415 as 'an unequal and heterogeneous work where great beauties remain unknown because they lie side by side with weaknesses and banalities' is overly harsh,[5] there is no doubt that K. 415 lacks the subtlety and intricacy of exchange characteristic of Mozart's other Viennese concertos.[6]

In order to clarify the workings of Mozart's paradigm of relational development – intimate dialogue in the solo exposition and recapitulation sections contrasting with less tightly-knit exchange in the development sections – and to explain why he broke with it in his final three works, I shall look at the first movements of K. 271, 413, 414, 449, 451, 453, 456, 459, 466, 488, 503, 537, 595 in the context of an extended analysis of the first movement of K. 491. Two basic dialogic similarities among these movements distinguish them from the first movements of Mozart's remaining four piano concertos (K. 415, 450, 467, 482) and justify comparative analysis of them as a group. With the exception of K. 491, for example, all of the works immediately introduce the solo piano in some form of dialogue with the orchestra (see Table 1 below), integrating the soloist smoothly into the musical fabric and establishing co-operative relations from the outset, whereas

[2] See the discussion of K. 467/i in Chapter Six, pp. 154–6.

[3] An exception is the one small fragment of dialogue in the secondary theme (bars 93ff.). The piano joins its antecedent and consequent phrases with a descending chromatic figure (D–C♯–C–B) very similar – in pitch, rhythm and register – to the figure used by the first violin to introduce the theme (D–C♯–C–A–B, bars 92–3).

[4] The piano's initial entry does not generate a forward momentum that projects the new theme beyond the restatement of the main theme (as in K. 482/i); nor does the new theme itself usurp the restatement (as in K. 450/i). Equally, the piano and the orchestra do not incorporate dialogue at the entry of the soloist, although this is true of every concerto movement up to K. 491 considered in this chapter (K. 271, 413, 414, 449, 451, 453, 456, 459, 466, 488). Ellwood Derr, in his article on musical connections among K. 413, 414 and 415, suggests that the piano's initial theme is 'a minimally altered setting of the pianist's first solo entry from [J. C.] Bach's then widely circulated Concerto in C, Op. 1/5/i'. See Derr, 'Some Thoughts on the Design of Mozart's Opus 4, the "Subscription Concertos"', in *Mozart's Piano Concertos*, ed. Zaslaw, p. 202.

[5] See Girdlestone, *Mozart and His Piano Concertos*, p. 147.

[6] Denis Forman makes a similar point in regard to K. 415: 'The perfect synthesis of the two voices is not yet there, but instead there is an equally satisfactory but entirely different balance of contrast, the piano speaking in one voice and the orchestra in another.' See Forman, *Mozart's Concerto Form*, pp. 167–8.

three of the remaining four movements do not.[7] In addition, all movements in the group feature dialogue in the presentation of the secondary theme in the solo exposition[8] – reiterating piano/orchestra co-operation at this important formal juncture – again in contrast to three of the four remaining movements (see Table 2).[9]

Table 1: Types of Piano/Orchestra Dialogue at the Initial Entry of the Soloist (K. 271–595)

Alternating full theme	: K. 459 (bars 72–87)
Split theme (for example, antecedent/consequent)	: K. 413 (bars 68–81)*, K. 271 (bars 1–7)*
Imitation	: K. 413 (bars 53–60)*, K. 414 (bars 80–4)*, K. 449 (bars 95–6, 101–104), K. 451 (bars 75–6), K. 456 (bars 68, 79)*, K. 467 (bars 68–75)**, K. 503 (bars 91–6)*, K. 595 (bars 81–9)*
Echo	: K. 453 (bars 75–83)*, K. 537 (bar 88)
Smooth phrase joining	: K. 456 (bars 77–80)* K. 488 (bars 74–5)*
Reshaping of a dialogue from the orchestral exposition	: K. 466 (bars 75–8)*
No dialogue	: K. 415, K. 450, K. 482, K. 491

* Explained in this chapter
** Explained in Chapter 6

There is no shortage of historical and musical reasons for assigning K. 491 a privileged status among Mozart's concertos. Widely considered Mozart's crowning achievement in the medium – 'the glorious culmination of Mozart's work as a concerto writer' in Girdlestone's words[10] – K. 491 was the last of fourteen works completed during Mozart's most productive period of concerto composition (1782–March 1786). One of just two works in the minor mode, it is scored for a richer complement of woodwind instruments

[7] For present purposes the 'introduction' of the piano designates its initial solo entry up until the point at which the orchestra and/or piano begins the re-statement of the main theme, or the orchestra has its first *tutti* interjection.

[8] The 'secondary theme' denotes the theme heard immediately after the confirmation of the secondary key area.

[9] The exception in this category and also in terms of dialogue at the entry of the piano is the first movement of K. 467. As I explain in my discussion of K. 467/i in Chapter 6 pp. 154–6, the solo exposition combines co-operative and confrontational behaviour, occupying a middle ground between the group of movements considered in this chapter, and the more competitively orientated first movements of K. 450 and 482.

[10] See Girdlestone, *Mozart and His Piano Concertos*, p. 389.

Table 2: Types of Piano/Orchestra Dialogue at the Presentation of the Secondary Theme (K. 271–595)

Full theme (antecedent *and* consequent)	: K. 459 (bar 131ff.), K. 466 (bar 127ff.), K. 491 (bar 147ff.), K. 503 (bar 170ff.)
Full theme (piano-orchestra-piano)	: K. 467 (bar 128ff.), K. 537 (bar 164ff.), K. 271 (bar 96ff.)
Dialogued phrases (repeated, elaborated, slightly modified)	: K. 414 (bar 115ff.), K. 451 (bar 128ff.)
Antecedent-Consequent	: K. 456 (bar 128ff.), K. 488 (bar 99ff.), K. 595 (bar 143ff.)
Split phrase	: K. 413 (bar 120ff.), K. 453 (bar 110ff.), K. 459 (bars 131–8)
Imitation	: K. 449 (bar 137ff.)
No substantive dialogue	: K. 415 (bar 93ff.), K. 450 (bar 104ff.)*, K. 482 (bar 152ff.)

* Although the conjunct thirds in the violins (bar 107–108) might be considered a fleeting imitation of the thirds in the piano (bar 107), and the repeated quaver Cs in the piano (bar 103) an obscure imitation of outlined C quavers in the strings (bar 102), this dialogue is far less pronounced than that in the corresponding secondary theme sections of K. 271, 413, 414, 449, 451, 453, 456, 459, 466, 467, 488, 491, 503, 537, 595.

(flute, 2 oboes, 2 clarinets, 2 bassoons) than any other concerto, and features a first movement that is the longest, most intensely expressive and most formally complex of any that Mozart wrote in this genre. The slow movement, uniquely cast in rondo form, and the third movement, one of just two variation form finales (and a more striking affective match for the first movement than any other concerto finale), also demonstrate the striking individuality of this concerto.[11]

While critics have commented eagerly on what is perhaps K. 491's most immediately striking stylistic feature, its affective and expressive intensity, their remarks have failed to clarify the work's special status, namely its position as a climactic and culminating work in Mozart's piano concerto *oeuvre*, firmly linked to its predecessors, yet decisively transcending them at the same time. Interpretations of K. 491's tragic and dramatic qualities, for example, stress either differences from or connections to earlier works, but do not convincingly do both. Some critics emphasise the uniquely grim and dark mood of the work, identifying 'an explosion of the . . . tragic, passionate emotions',[12] a

[11] For a tabulated summary of the formal types of the second and third movements of Mozart's Viennese piano concertos, see James Webster, 'Are Mozart's Concertos "Dramatic"? Concerto Ritornellos versus Aria Introductions in the 1780s', in *Mozart's Piano Concertos: Text, Context, Interpretation*, ed. Neal Zaslaw (Ann Arbor: University of Michigan Press, 1996), p. 113.

[12] Alfred Einstein, *Mozart: His Character, His Work*, trans. Nathan Broder and Arthur Mendel (London: Cassell, 1945), p. 206.

'truly tragic quality',[13] and 'an unrelenting, tragic character'[14] that is new to Mozart's concerto writing. Others discern a profound expressivity more typical of Mozart's earlier concertos. Donald Tovey understands 'the transformation of . . . [Mozart's] originally happy second subject into the tonic minor' in the first movement as 'pathetic but not tragic';[15] Wolfgang Hildesheimer hears in the same movement 'a gloomy agitation, but . . . a major mood, violent and energetic, to be sure, but not "tragic" ';[16] and Volkmar Braunbehrens associates the 'powerful and declarative' elements of the music with a 'tense mood' which has 'nothing to do with 'tragic elements'.[17] In addition, critics who find an absence of drama in K. 491 separate the work from the 'dramatic' type of concerto usually associated with Mozart, particularly K. 466 in D minor. Eric Blom considers K. 491 'less dramatic than the D minor, . . . [and] more declamatory';[18] Cuthbert Girdlestone points out that the 'prominent mood is elegiac rather than dramatic';[19] and Charles Rosen, for whom drama is synonymous with Mozart's concerto style, states that K. 491 'evades the theatricality of the earlier work [K. 466]' and is 'less operatic'.[20] In an attempt, then, to paint a more precise picture of the pivotal role played by K. 491 in Mozart's repertory, particularly in regard to the intensity of piano/orchestra relations, I shall proceed chronologically through the first movement of K. 491, comparing dialogic interaction in the solo exposition, development and recapitulation sections to dialogic interaction in the corresponding sections of Mozart's earlier piano concertos. I shall then go on to trace the stylistic impact that this extraordinary movement had on Mozart's final three piano concertos.[21]

[13] Philip Radcliffe, *Mozart Piano Concertos* (Seattle: University of Washington Press, 1978), p. 62.

[14] Mario M. Mercado, *The Evolution of Mozart's Pianistic Style* (Carbondale, Illinois: Southern Illinois University Press, 1992), p. 93.

[15] Tovey, *Concertos and Choral Works*, p. 177.

[16] Wolfgang Hildesheimer, *Mozart*, trans. Marion Faber (New York: Vintage, 1983), p. 163.

[17] Volkmar Braunbehrens, *Mozart in Vienna 1781–1791*, trans. Timothy Bell (New York: Grove, 1989), pp. 276–7.

[18] Blom, *Mozart* (New York: Collier, 1966 [first published 1935]), p. 206.

[19] Girdlestone, *Mozart and His Piano Concertos*, p. 390.

[20] Rosen, *The Classical Style*, p. 245.

[21] A number of studies have been devoted to critical and analytical consideration of K. 491/i exclusively, although none has addressed the stylistic position of the first movement among Mozart's concertos in a systematic fashion. Recent probing studies include: John A. Meyer, 'Mozart's "Pathétique" Concerto', in *Music Review* 39 (1978), pp. 196–210; Eric Wen, 'Enharmonic Transformation in the First Movement of Mozart's Piano Concerto in C Minor, K. 491', in *Schenker Studies*, ed. Hedi Siegel (Cambridge: Cambridge University Press, 1990), pp. 107–24; and William Kinderman, 'Dramatic Development and Narrative Design in the First Movement of Mozart's Concerto in C Minor, K. 491', in *Mozart's Piano Concertos*, ed. Zaslaw, pp. 285–301. Charles Rosen also analyzes K. 491/i in *The Classical Style*, pp. 245–50.

The First Movement of K. 491 in Comparison to Mozart's Earlier Piano Concertos

Solo Exposition

As a means of establishing close relations in the solo expositions of many of the first movements of Mozart's concertos (including K. 491), the piano and orchestra elaborate upon dialogue introduced in the orchestral exposition. K. 453, 456 and 414 offer good illustrations of this process in works preceding K. 491. In the orchestral exposition of K. 453, for example, the main theme contains echo answers (a sort of 'little imitation' in Reicha's terminology) in the winds (bars 4, 8). Not only are the echoes repeated in the main theme's antecedent and consequent phrases at the beginning of the solo exposition (see Example 17), but the piano adds the echo's distinctive semiquaver embellishments to the main theme (bars 80 and 81), drawing the solo exposition's consequent melodically and rhythmically closer to its echo answer than the orchestral exposition's consequent had been. Similarly, the piano's echo in octaves of part of the winds' secondary theme played in octaves (bars 147, 149)

Example 17. Mozart, Piano Concerto K. 453, 1st Movement, bars 74-83.

creates a stronger link between statement and echo than was present at the corresponding moment of the orchestral exposition (bars 43 and 45, winds and first violin), where the first violins played the echo at a single pitch level. The beginning of the solo exposition in K. 456 (see Example 18) includes two instances of dialogic elaboration. The subtle division of a four-bar antecedent between the winds and the violins in the orchestral exposition (bars 9–12) is retained in the solo exposition (bars 78–81), while flourishes in the piano's antecedent and consequent (bars 79, 81 and 85) add semiquaver elaborations (bars 79^2, 81^2 and 85) reminiscent of the trill-like figurations of the orchestral exposition's penultimate bar (winds and violins, bar 68). In the same thematic statement, the piano and the winds also engage in dialogue with previously undialogued material. In bars 10–13 the violins' chromatic ascents grow out of their own preceding F–B♭ chromatic ascent (bars 8–9), while at the corresponding point in the solo exposition (bars 79–82) the winds take their lead directly from the piano (bars 77–8). In the solo exposition of K. 414 (see Example 19), the piano's presentation of the main theme's consequent elaborates the internal dialogue from the corresponding segment of the orchestral exposition (bars 13–16). The piano's semiquaver figures (bars 76–8) are first transformed into the ascending semiquaver figures from the end of the orchestral exposition (bars 58, 60) and then dialogued between the piano (bar 80) and the first violin (bar 82).

Dialogic elaboration in the solo expositions of K. 271 and 466 takes the form of a more complex manipulation of material than corresponding processes in the solo expositions of K. 453, 456 and 414. In K. 271, the piano famously enters in bar 2 of the orchestral exposition, engaging in a split-theme dialogue with the orchestra (bars 1–7) and then sitting out for the remainder of the section. Immediately after the initial piano/orchestra dialogue, the violin subtly fuses elements from it in the melodic line: the stepwise ascending lines of bars 8–9 and 10–11 and the descending B♭–A♭–G–F line of bar 9 derive from the piano's answer; and the repeated B♭s (bar 7) follow bars 1–2 and 4–5.[22] At the beginning of the solo exposition, the initial dialogue from bars 1–7 is repeated, with semiquavers added to the piano's answer (bars 65, 68). The piano then combines its semiquaver rhythm and the oscillation of its trill in ensuing accompanying figurations (left hand, bars 69–74), bringing the new accompanimental figuration together in turn with a figure deriving from the orchestra's arpeggio in the main theme. In short, the piano elaborates the process of combined dialogue and thematic fusion from the beginning of the orchestral exposition, modifying its answer and using its modification in the subsequent thematic fusion.[23]

In K. 466, the piano and the orchestra engage in an equally sophisticated manipulation of dialogued material. Immediately preceding the entry of the piano, the woodwinds (bars 75–7) derive their minim movement, stepwise motion of voices and sonority (2 oboes, 2 bassoons) from their ascending sequences in bars 33–4, 35–6 and 37–8; the piano, in turn, presents a figure in the right hand originating in the flute in bars 34, 36 and 38, and also recalls the violins' accompanimental thirds from the same bars in the left hand.[24] Although a phrase is not split between the woodwinds and the piano (as in bars 33–8), the

[22] See Rosen's very similar identification of thematic correspondence at this moment in *The Classical Style*, p. 199.

[23] Rosen notices the connection between the piano and orchestral arpeggios, but misses the relationship between the thematic fusions of bars 69 and 7–11. See *The Classical Style*, p. 203.

[24] Rosen also recognises a thematic link between the piano's initial melodic line and the bar 33 material in the form in which it recurs in the solo exposition (bar 115ff.). See Rosen, *The Classical Style*, pp. 233–5.

Example 18. Mozart, Piano Concerto K. 456, 1st Movement, bars 67-82.

earlier dialogue is cleverly reshaped in order to integrate the solo piano smoothly into the movement.

In the solo exposition of K. 491 dialogic elaboration resides in the way types of dialogue are organised across the entire section, a process initiated in the orchestral exposition. In bars 1–3, the strings outline an ascending sixth (C–A♭), complemented by a sequential stepwise descent from A♭ beginning in bar 5 (A♭–G–F–E [bars 5–6], G♭–F–E♭–D [bars 7–8], see Example 20). The implied continuation and resolution of this sequence, which is discontinued after bar 8, occurs at the correct register in the clarinets (F′–E♭′–D′–C) in bars 12–13, resulting in dialogue between the strings and the winds. On a number of occasions later in the section Mozart sidesteps or offsets the resolution of

Example 19. Mozart, Piano Concerto K. 414, 1st Movement, bars 76-84.

the sequential descent (F–E♭–D–C),[25] finally including it again only in the last five bars of the orchestral exposition (first violins, bars 95–9). The first violins in bars 95–9 do not present immediately preceding material in dialogue; they engage rather in a kind of long-range 'dialogue' with bars 1–13 by presenting a resolution to the sequential pattern of bars 3–8 in the original voice (the strings) for the first time, thus bringing the orchestral exposition full circle. Whereas 'dialogue' between the strings and winds occurs at the outer extremes of the orchestral exposition, internal dialogues are concentrated in the middle of the section: for the fifteen bars prior to the midpoint (bar 50) and the twelve bars thereafter, the winds dialogue three different figures among themselves (bars 35–44, 44–51, 52–62).[26] A pattern of dialogic interaction is further marked by the accentuation of the second of these three dialogues by internal dialogue in the strings (1st and 2nd violins, bars 48–52) at the exact midpoint of the orchestral exposition. Thus, the balance exemplified by the main theme – the A♭–D descent in the strings (bars 3–8) resolved by the A♭–C descent in the winds (bars 8–13)[27] – is reinforced by a rudimentary dialogic symmetry across the section as a whole. (Figure 2 graphs dialogue in all four sections of K. 491/i.)

[25] The restatement of the main theme gets stuck on D (bars 20–6) and does not resolve to C; the oboes and clarinets sidestep the resolution of their F–E♭–D figures (bars 62–3); and the F–E♭–D–C movement of bars 72–3 is undercut by an interrupted cadence.

[26] There is also an internal dialogue in the winds in bars 81–7.

[27] See Kinderman, 'Dramatic Development and Narrative Design', pp. 286–7. Kinderman descibes the 'entire theme' (albeit a little simplistically) as 'an example of the remarkable symmetry so characteristic of Mozart, a symmetry that allows for a gradual, and seemingly inevitable, intensification of the music from within'.

Example 20. Mozart, Piano Concerto K. 491, 1st Movement, bars 1-13.

In the solo exposition of K. 491/i, the piano and the orchestra expand the dialogic symmetry from the orchestral exposition by including three-way as well as two-way and internal dialogue. Three-way dialogue appears at both the beginning and end of the solo exposition: the main theme is split among the strings (bars 118–21), winds (121–3) and piano (124ff.) shortly after the soloist enters; repeated quarter- and quaver B♭s are passed from the piano (left hand, bars 241–5) to the strings (245–6), and among the winds, strings and piano (249–55) shortly before the end of the section. These dialogues frame two two-way dialogues in the middle of the section: first the winds dialogue the piano's presentation of the secondary theme (bars 147–64); second, the piano and strings as a single unit dialogue the winds in bars 200–19. Here the symmetry is reinforced by the similar length of the two-way dialogues (sixteen and nineteen bars) and by the reversal of the positions of the interlocutors (piano-winds in the first, winds-piano/strings in the second). The two-way dialogues, in turn, frame internal dialogues in the winds (bars 170–4) and the strings (bars 178–88).

The elaborate dialogic symmetry of the solo exposition of K. 491 constitutes a more developed and intricate dialogic process than is present in any of Mozart's earlier first movements. To be sure, dialogue is systematically organised in the solo expositions of his preceding concertos, but patterns are established most often by highlighting specific dialogic techniques. In No. 23 in A, K. 488, for example, the piano's two presentations of the main theme at the beginning of the solo exposition (Example 21) are joined by a smooth dialogic segue in the first violins that refines the segue from the corresponding moment in the

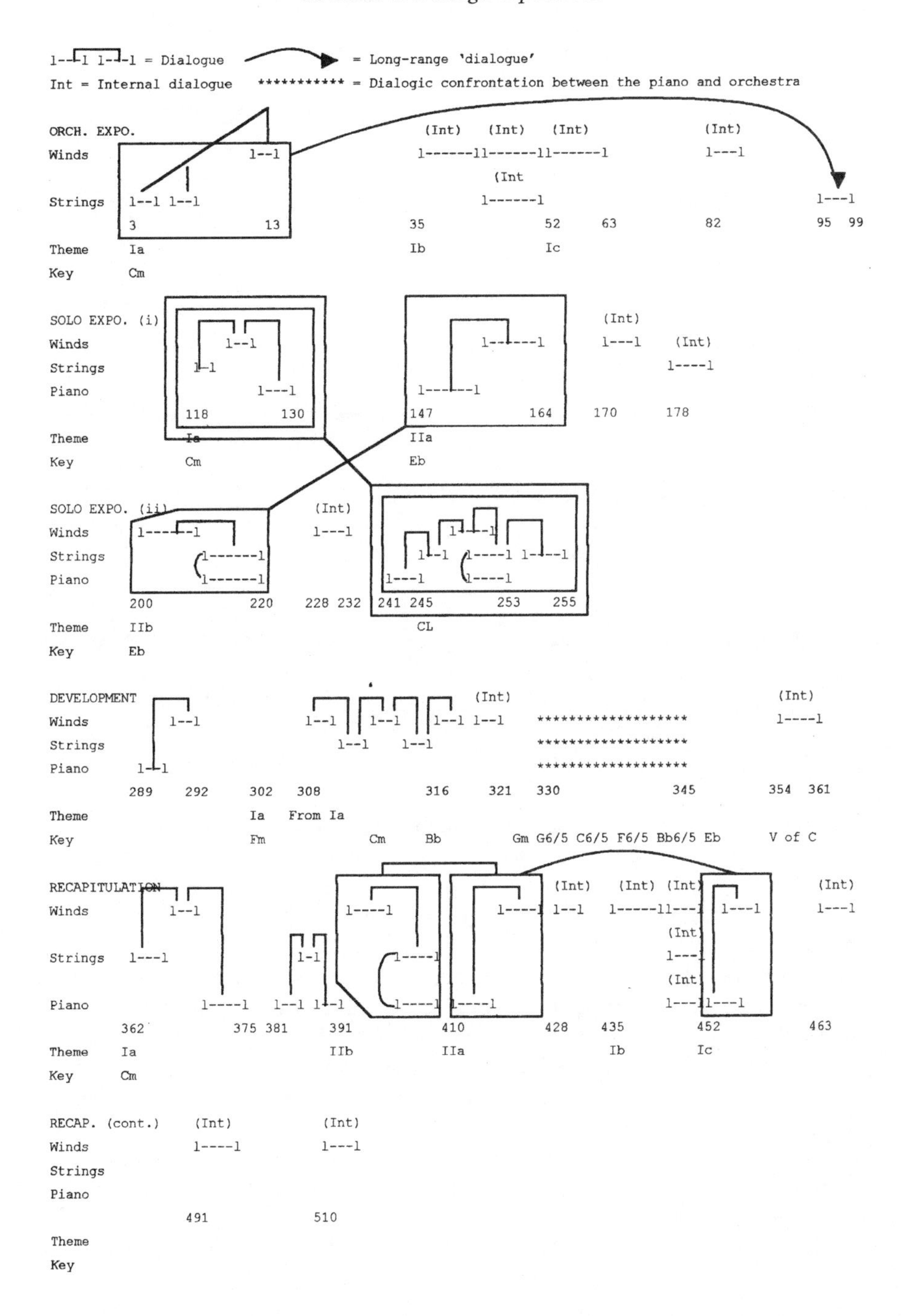

Fig. 2: Dialogue in the First Movement of K. 491

K. 491, 1st Movement: Principal Themes

orchestral exposition (bar 8).[28] This dialogic technique reappears later in the solo exposition: the piano begins the transition in bar 86 (Example 22) by reiterating the repeated quaver Ds (bassoon and cellos) that conclude the first theme section; the piano then leads into a dialogue between strings and piano in the secondary key area (bars 120–2, Example 23) with a figure (bars 119–20) that foreshadows subsequent responses. In No. 11 in F, K. 413, the piano first enters at the beginning of the solo exposition in imitative dialogue, and then splits the main theme with the orchestra. Mozart ingeniously brings together these dialogic procedures when the soloist is reintroduced after its only significant absence from the solo exposition (bars 120–9): the piano engages in a split-theme dialogue with the violins that is also imitative (Example 24). It is only in K. 491, however, that Mozart creates an over-arching dialogic organization that extends to *every* dialogue that appears in the solo exposition.

The symmetrical arrangement of types of dialogue in the solo exposition of

[28] Bars 74–5 from the solo exposition of K. 488/i represent a smoother segue between the two presentations of the main theme than the corresponding segue in the orchestral exposition (bars 8–9), because the violins directly join the piano's B′ (from the end of the first presentation) to the E″ (at the beginning of the second) while also mirroring the piano's half-step descent.

Example 21. Mozart, Piano Concerto K. 488, 1st Movement, bars 67-75.

K. 491 also helps to explain a formal anomaly of the movement: Mozart's 'extension' of the section beyond its first obvious stopping point, the cadential trill in E♭, the secondary key area (bar 199). Whereas in every other Viennese piano concerto Mozart uses a cadential trill to complete the soloist's participation in the solo exposition, the trill in bar 199 of K. 491 leads to a segment that prolongs the section for another eighty-two bars (almost half the solo exposition's total length). It is noteworthy that the two primary dialogues within the 'extension' (bars 200–19 and 241–55) are essential components of the

Example 22. Mozart, Piano Concerto K. 488, 1st Movement, bars 85-88.

Example 23. Mozart, Piano Concerto K. 488, 1st Movement, bars 119-23.

Example 24. Mozart, Piano Concerto K. 413, 1st Movement, bars 120-33.

solo exposition's symmetrical design. It is not unreasonable to suggest, therefore, that Mozart may have taken the very unusual step of extending his solo exposition well beyond the cadential trill, precisely in order to bring about dialogic symmetry.[29]

Development Section

Relational procedures in the development section of K. 491/i, like those in the solo exposition, can best be examined within the context of procedures in earlier movements. In K. 491, as in K. 449, 451, 453, 456, 459, 466 and 488, dialogue among the piano, winds, and strings in the solo exposition gives way to apparent opposition between piano and orchestral forces in the development. Mozart's concertos preceding K. 491 create an oppositional effect in a number of different ways. In K. 453 and 456, for example, piano/orchestra dialogue from the solo exposition is replaced by internal dialogue; Mozart therefore prioritises the independence rather than the mutual dependence of his interlocutors in these development sections. In K. 449, 451 and 488 the kind of intimate piano/orchestra dialogue heard in the solo exposition either breaks down over the course of the section or is replaced by oppositional dialogue that invokes Reicha's paradigm of sharply contrasting phrases alternating between interlocutors (see Chapter 2). In K. 488 strings-to-piano dialogue at the beginning of the development (bars 143–56) and a brief three-way dialogue in the middle of that section (bars 164–9) leads to a separation

[29] Charles Rosen offers another interpretation of the formal 'extension': 'The "double" solo exposition (making a triple exposition with the first ritornello) is a natural consequence of . . . the fragmentation of the larger form corresponding to the inner divisions of the opening statement'. See *The Classical Style*, p. 248.

rather than further integration of piano and orchestral material: first, the winds dialogue internally (bars 170–6); then the strings and winds engage in dialogue (bars 178–85) without the piano. The opposition of the two forces in K. 449 and 451 is more noticeable than in K. 488. Although both development sections begin with the piano dialoguing orchestral material from the end of the solo exposition (bars 176–87 in K. 449 and bars 187–98 in K. 451) in a manner not atypical of the earlier section, the piano adds arpeggiated flourishes not previously introduced into dialogue (bars 186–7 in K. 449 and bars 191–2 in K. 451) that subsequently divide the two forces. In K. 449, *forte* presentations of a trill figure in the full orchestra directly oppose virtuosic arpeggios in the piano in an alternating confrontational dialogue (bars 188–203, see Example 15 in Chapter 3, p. 68); and in K. 451, the piano's arpeggiated figurations, contrasting sharply with the dialogued material in the opening bars, dominate the remainder of the section (bars 199–218), effectively prohibiting intimate dialogue with the orchestra. The piano, in both K. 449 and 451, uses a fragment of its own material, rather than one shared with the orchestra, as a stimulus for development. As a result, co-dependence in the solo expositions gives way to a greater independence of the two forces in the development sections.

K. 491's development section draws on processes of piano/orchestra interaction apparent in corresponding sections of earlier movements. Similar to K. 449, 451 and 488, the development of K. 491 begins with piano/orchestra dialogue (bars 289–92) not unlike dialogue from the solo exposition. The ensuing dialogue between strings and winds (bars 308–17) from which the piano is excluded, and the concurrent internal dialogue in the winds (oboes and clarinets, bars 311–20), invoke procedures similar to those used in the development sections of K. 453, 456 and 488. It is the forceful confrontational dialogue in bars 330–45 of K. 491 (Example 25), however, that contains most allusions to earlier interactive procedures. The stark dialogic opposition of two bars of semiquaver arpeggios in the piano and two bars of *forte* trill-like figurations in the full orchestra strongly resemble K. 449 (bars 188–203); the chain of chromatic oscillations and dominant 7th harmonies in a circle-of-5ths progression, together with arpeggiated writings in the piano, recall a part of the development section of K. 459 (bars 217–28) that contrasts sharply (like the confrontational dialogue from K. 491) with the intimate dialogue of the solo exposition; and the *forte* outbursts in the orchestra, with dominant 7th harmonies signalling forceful harmonic change, invoke similar *forte* orchestral outbursts in alternation with the soloist in K. 466 (bars 204, 218).[30]

[30] Of course, the allusions in this passage to moments from Mozart's earlier development sections should not obscure motivic connections between this passage and other material from K. 491. For a detailed discussion of Neapolitan associations and chromatic processes across the entire concerto – including the orchestra's half-step figure in the development – see John A. Meyer, 'Mozart's "Pathétique" Concerto'. Kinderman also sees a connection between the confrontation and the main theme of the movement 'in the isolation and intensification of the crucial semitone relationship'; see 'Dramatic Development and Narrative Design', p. 291. Leonard

Example 25. Mozart, Piano Concerto K. 491, 1st Movement, bars 329-46.

Although they draw on earlier oppositional effects, the piano and the orchestra in bars 330–45 of K. 491 surpass them in their heightened level of interactional intensity. The colourful array of critical descriptions of the passage reflects its uniqueness in this respect. Tovey writes of the orchestra's 'majestic anger', Girdlestone of the piano's and orchestra's 'duel' in which Mozart makes 'an attempt to move us by the sheer force of the attack' and Arthur Hutchings of the 'daring clashes' between the two forces.[31] Eva and Paul Badura-Skoda call it the 'stormiest outburst' in Mozart's piano concertos, and Joseph Kerman 'a rare example of a real struggle' between an 'aggressive' orchestra and a 'horrified' soloist.[32] In fact, there is no more compelling illustration in Mozart's entire concerto repertory of the style of confrontational dialogue described by Reicha, whereby alternating phrases of equal length, in which the first 'are in a character opposed to those of the [second]', inject 'opposition' into the music.

Thus, interaction in the development section of K. 491 closely follows established interactive procedures, intensifying them considerably through pointed piano/orchestra confrontation (bars 330–45). Just as many of Mozart's earlier development sections turn away from dialogic processes evident in the solo exposition and towards an opposition of the two forces, so K. 491's development abandons the solo exposition's intricate dialogic symmetry in favour of opposition and confrontation.

Recapitulation

The recapitulation of K. 491 builds on relational procedures from the corresponding sections of earlier concerto movements in an even more striking fashion than the solo exposition and development. Many of Mozart's first-movement recapitulations preceding K. 491 elaborate the piano/orchestra interaction from the solo exposition by incorporating new dialogue.[33] The full-theme dialogue initiating the recapitulation of K. 459 (corresponding to the full-theme dialogue at the opening of the solo exposition) is now prefaced by a dialoguing of the head motif in the winds and strings (bars 241–6). In addition, a theme heard only in the orchestral exposition (bars 43–6), returns as an antecedent-consequent (piano-orchestra) dialogue in the recapitulation (bars

B. Meyer points out that if the circle-of-5ths progression initiated in bar 330 had continued beyond the V6/5 of E♭ in bar 342, it would have reached C minor at bar 362, the exact point at which Mozart confirms the tonic at the onset of the recapitulation; see 'Process and Morphology in the Music of Mozart', *Journal of Musicology* 1 (1982), pp. 77–9.

[31] Tovey, *Concertos and Choral Works*, p. 176; Girdlestone, *Mozart and His Piano Concertos*, p. 396; Hutchings, *A Companion to Mozart's Piano Concertos* (Oxford: Oxford University Press, 1989 [7th edition]), p. 170.

[32] Eva and Paul Badura-Skoda, *Interpreting Mozart on the Keyboard*, trans. Leo Black (London: Barrie and Rockliff, 1962), p. 273. Kerman, 'Mozart's Piano Concertos and their Audience', p. 163.

[33] For an extended discussion of Mozart's recapitulatory procedures, see Jane R. Stevens, 'Patterns of Recapitulation in the First Movements of Mozart's Piano Concertos', in *Musical Humanism and its Legacy*, ed. Baker and Hanning (Stuyvesant, New York: Pendragon, 1992), pp. 397–418.

340ff.) with subtle embellishment: the octaves in the piano's final presentation of the antecedent (bars 344^4-5) are answered by octaves in the winds (bars 348–52). In K. 449's recapitulation, as we have seen in Chapter 3, new instances of piano/orchestra dialogue immediately follow moments of relational tension (which in turn echo the opposition of the two forces in the development). In bars 283–96 of K. 451, new dialogue co-exists with an intricate synthesis of earlier dialogues. Here, an antecedent-consequent dialogue originally presented by the winds and strings (bars 60–8) and later adapted in the strings, winds and piano (bars 181–99) is heard for the final time. First, the antecedent-consequent patterns from bars 60–4^1 and 181–5^1 are repeated in bars 283–7^1 (with the piano presenting the consequent); then the antecedent dialogue between the winds and piano from bars 185–9^1 reappears in bars 287–91. On this occasion, however, the latter leads to additional dialogue between the piano and the oboes, who engage in a kind of split-theme dialogue in bars 293–4. (The oboe's figure, in turn, grows into a D–F♯–A ascent in bars 297–8 that alludes rhythmically and melodically to the head motif of the theme from bar 35.) The final presentation of this material thus 'resolves' the opening of the development section by revealing that the antecedent figure dialogued between the piano and the winds, together with the appearance of contrasting triplets in the piano (see bars 185–99), need not create opposition between the interlocutors, but can in fact generate co-operation.

K. 491's recapitulation not only includes new piano/orchestra dialogue (for example bars 381–90 and 452–6) but also organises *all* the dialogue from this section into patterns that invoke the symmetrical arrangements of *both* the orchestral and the solo expositions. The thematic dialogue that initiated the second half of the solo exposition (bars 200ff.) and the presentation of the secondary theme in dialogue (bars 148ff.) in bars 391–409 and bars 410–27 respectively invokes the inner symmetry of the solo exposition (see Fig. 2, p. 85). In addition, these two dialogues are preceded (as in the solo exposition) by a three-way dialoguing of the main theme (bars 362–75).[34] The dialogue in bars 410–27 marks the end of one symmetrical grouping and also initiates another. With the two-way dialogue in bars 452–6, the dialogue in bars 410–27 frames three consecutive internal dialogues in the winds (bars 428–31, 435–44, 444–51);[35] in a similar fashion, the three successive internal wind dialogues in the orchestral exposition are framed by strings/winds dialogue that stretches across the section. Moreover, the final three dialogues of the recapitulation, all in the winds (bars 463–8, 491–7, 510–20), balance the three previous internal wind dialogues (bars 428–51) around the piano/winds dialogue of bars 452–6.[36]

[34] The final three-way dialogue from the solo exposition does not reappear in this segment of the recapitulation. I would argue, however, that enough of the solo exposition's symmetrical design reappears in the recapitulation to invoke the earlier procedure.

[35] Internal dialogue in the strings (bars 444–51) and the piano (448–51) can be heard concurrently with the internal dialogue in the winds in bars 444–51.

[36] According to two recent writers, the piano has experienced a kind of 'defeat' by the end of the recapitulation. William Kinderman points out that the piano's C minor passages in the

Several of Mozart's Viennese concertos before K. 491 also use dialogue to combine processes specific to the orchestral and solo expositions in the recapitulation. This occurs most frequently near the beginning of recapitulation sections. In K. 459, for example, the head motif of the main theme is dialogued between the winds and the strings (bars 241–6) immediately before the recapitulation. When followed by the piano's statement of the main theme, it re-establishes the three-way dialogue characteristic of the solo exposition. At the same time, the collective presentation of the entire period of the main theme by the strings and the winds (bars 255–62) – in turn dialoguing with the piano – invokes bars 1–16 from the orchestral exposition. The beginning of the recapitulation of K. 414 creates dialogue between the orchestra and the piano by repeating bars 1–8 from the orchestral exposition (bars 196–203) and bars 72ff. from the solo exposition (bars 204ff.). In a similar fashion, the split-theme dialogue initiating the recapitulation of K. 449 (see Chapter 3, pp. 64–5) comprises a repeat of bars 1–8 from the orchestral exposition (in bars 234–41) and bars 97–104 from the solo exposition (in bars 242–9). In K. 456, the opening bars of the recapitulation (bars 232–49) combine dialogue from the beginnings of the orchestral and solo expositions: the entire main theme dialogued from strings to winds invokes the orchestral exposition (bars 1–12); the half-step phrase joinings (winds, bars 233–4, 235–6; strings, bars 241–2, 243–4) refer both to the orchestral exposition (bars 10–12) and to the solo exposition (bars 79–81); and the flute's embellishments (bars 241–2, 243–4) are taken from the solo exposition (bars 79–80 and 81–2).[37]

No movement, however, brings orchestral and solo expositions together in the recapitulation as decisively as K. 491/i. Not only are bars 362–456 a dialogic *tour de force*, almost every bar featuring some kind of dialogue, but the dialogic combinations are also organised so as to invoke (and develop) the symmetrical arrangements of the orchestral and solo expositions. In short, dialogue in the recapitulation of K. 491 effects a more forceful union of orchestral and solo

recapitulation 'carry an air . . . of depression'. He locates 'tragic expression' in the 'overarching narrative pattern in which the apparent autonomy of the soloist in much of the solo exposition is subsequently relinquished as a result of the confrontation and combination of solo and tutti materials in the development and recapitulation'. See 'Dramatic Development and Narrative Design', pp. 299–300. Joseph Kerman states: 'After this humbling episode [the piano/orchestra confrontation in the development], the solo loses its form-defining impulse. From now on, in the section of reengagement [the recapitulation], the solo is distinctly subdued'. See Kerman, 'Mozart's Piano Concertos and their Audience', p. 165. I would argue that the piano's minimal contribution to dialogue in the second half of the recapitulation (which might account for a sense of 'resignation') is connected to Mozart's re-invocation of the dialogic symmetry from the orchestral exposition, with its emphasis upon internal dialogues in the winds.

37 There are also subtle additions to the dialogue from the orchestral and solo expositions at this juncture of K. 456/i. A trill in the piano (bars 240–3) engages in dialogue with the flute's trill-like figurations (bars 241^2, 243^2); the winds and the piano carry out a split-theme dialogue (bars 240–9); and the bassoons' half-step ascent (bars 229–32) dialogues with a shorter version of the same half-step ascent in the first violins (bars 239^2–40^1) and leads smoothly (like bars 239–40) to a presentation of the main theme.

exposition sections than occurs in the recapitulation of any other Mozart concerto.[38]

The recapitulation of K. 491 marks a fitting conclusion to a movement that had already – in the solo exposition and development sections – taken intricate dialogue and intense piano/orchestra relations to new heights. The symmetrical organization of dialogue in the solo exposition moves far beyond processes of organization in the corresponding section of earlier movements; the dialogic confrontation between the piano and the orchestra in the development takes piano/orchestra interaction to a higher level of intensity than ever before; and finally, interaction in the recapitulation represents a glorious peroration of dialogic activity.

K. 491 and Beyond

If the intricacy and intensity of piano/orchestra dialogue in the first movements of Mozart's Viennese piano concertos reaches a climax in K. 491, what happens to piano/orchestra dialogue in the first movements of the remaining piano concertos: No. 25 in C (K. 503), No. 26 in D (K. 537) and No. 27 in B♭ (K. 595)? The most striking feature about these movements is that Mozart moves away from his well-established pattern of dialogue and relational development common to the movements discussed above. As we have seen, all but four of Mozart's piano concerto first movements from K. 271 to 491 follow a similar course: in the solo exposition, the piano and orchestra actively engage in intimate dialogue; in the development, the two forces show signs of opposition (with or without dialogue); in the recapitulation, they return to the dialogue from the solo exposition, often reinforcing intimate relations with new dialogic subtleties. Mozart's final three first movements each modify this pattern, particularly in regard to the role of the development section.

The opening bars of the development section of K. 503/i (bars 228–53) exhibit striking dialogic ingenuity, almost rivalling the recapitulation of K. 491. (See Figure 3 for a graph of this process.) In just twenty-five bars Mozart presents each of the six dialogic combinations possible from three pairs of interlocutors (piano/winds, winds/piano, piano/strings, strings/piano, winds/strings, strings/winds). The four dialogic combinations from the solo exposition reappear: the winds answer the piano's theme of bars 228–38 in bars 238–48; the piano takes up the winds' rhythm of bars 248–52 in bars 252^{3}-3^{1}; the piano answers the strings' minim stepwise descents of bars 229–30 and 235–7 in bars

[38] Donald Tovey notices the striking way in which the orchestral and solo expositions are brought together in the recapitulation (although he does not discuss dialogue's role in this process). Tovey considers K. 491 an 'extreme case' among the first movements of Mozart's piano concertos, since 'the first solo [solo exposition] (and hence everything that has to do with the second subject) . . . [is] entirely new'. He claims that in the recapitulation 'we are struck with the full force of the fact that . . . the orchestral and solo materials are for the first time thoroughly combined'. See Tovey, *Concertos and Choral Works*, p. 177.

239–40; and the winds also answer the strings' half-note stepwise descents of bars 245–7 in bars 251–2.[39] Moreover, the two dialogic permutations that did not materialise in the solo exposition – the strings answering the piano (bars 233–4) and the strings answering the winds (bars 243–4) – are also present. Thus, in contrast to the majority of development sections of earlier Viennese concerto first movements, the appearance of the two previously unheard dialogue combinations, and the occurrence of all six combinations in quick succession, add to the intimacy of piano/orchestra dialogue from the solo exposition: all three parties dialogue at the beginning of the development on an apparently equal footing. In bars 260–76 of the development section of K. 503/i dialogue continues to be equally divided among the three interlocutors. The piano, winds and strings pass the head motif of the theme from bar 51 freely back and forth, until it is eventually dialogued internally in the strings (bars 276–81).

1---1 = Dialogue

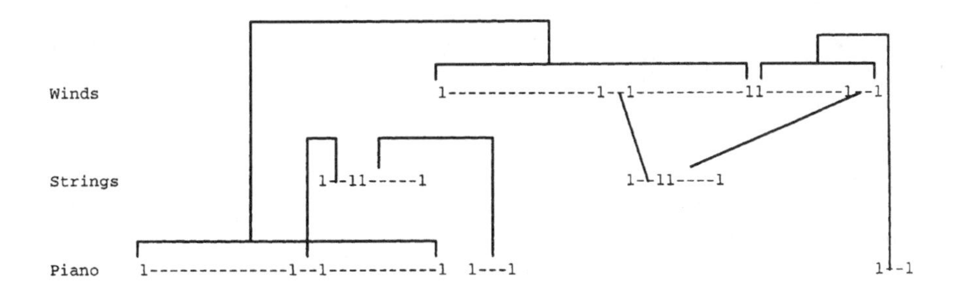

228 29 30 31 32 33 34 35 36 37 38 39 240 41 42 43 44 45 46 47 48 49 250 51 52 53

Fig. 3: Dialogic *tour de force* at the beginning of the development section of K. 503/i

Like K. 503/i, the development section of K. 595/i begins with dialogue among the three interlocutors; unlike K. 503/i and earlier developments, however, dialogue in the section as a whole both contrasts to *and* reinforces the fluid dialogue of the solo exposition. In contrast to the solo exposition, the dialogue at the beginning of the development of K. 595 goes awry (Example 26).[40] Between the two statements of the main theme in B minor and C major in

[39] In the solo exposition of K. 503/i the piano answers the strings at the point of entry (bars 91–6), imitating its outline of the tonic triad and the oscillation of its trill. Also, the piano answers the winds (bars 120–3) and the winds/strings (bars 143–6), while the winds answer the piano (bars 170–87) and both the piano and the strings (bars 194–6, 201–3).

[40] In the solo exposition of K. 595/i, the piano and the orchestra engage in a number of instances of co-operative dialogue. The strings answer the piano's initial statements of the main theme with one-bar imitations of the outlined B♭ arpeggio (see bars 81–9); the piano foreshadows

the piano (bars 191–4 and 197–200 respectively), the strings state the motif from bars 5–6. In the process they outline a diminished harmony – C, D♯, F♯, A – which is subsequently taken up by the winds (bar 196). But this harmony neither confirms B minor nor moves toward C. As Reicha points out, abrupt tonal shifts such as these are characteristic of alternating oppositional dialogue.[41] Tonal contradiction continues in the ensuing three-way dialogue (bars 200–4), each statement of the motif from bars 5–6 outlining a different key (C, c, E♭). Dialogue *without* abrupt tonal contradiction among all three interlocutors is re-established, however, in the second half of the development section moving into the recapitulation (violins, bars 225–9; piano, bars 231–5; winds, bars 235–42; strings bars 242ff.), thus marking a return to the type of fluid and intimate dialogue more characteristic of a solo exposition.[42]

The development section of K. 537 contrasts with the solo exposition in terms of piano/orchestra interaction, but in a very different way from Mozart's normal procedure. Instead of the piano and the orchestra engaging in dialogue in the solo exposition and turning away from it in the development, the reverse is true: piano/orchestra dialogue in the solo exposition is limited to the statement of the second theme (bars 164–77) and two end-of-phrase echoes in the strings (piano/strings, bars 88 and 131); while dialogue is heard in substantial portions of the development section (piano/strings, bars 233–53 and 269–77).

In the first movements of his final three piano concertos, therefore, Mozart experiments with new patterns of piano/orchestra interaction. No longer does dialogue in the development provide a straightforward contrast to dialogue in the solo exposition by setting the two forces in opposition. Instead, new designs emerge. The development of K. 503 adds to the dialogic intricacies of the solo exposition; the development of K. 595 initially contrasts with and later reinforces three-way dialogue from the solo exposition; and the development of K. 537 contrasts with the solo exposition by including substantial passages of piano/orchestra dialogue the like of which did not appear earlier.

The Significance of K. 491 among Mozart's Piano Concertos

In light of the fact that the first movement of K. 491 builds on patterns of relational development and types of relational exchange common to Mozart's earlier piano concertos, and the fact that the three later concertos turn away from these established patterns, we can both re-evaluate K. 491's position

descending semiquavers in the violins and then partakes in imitation (bars 91–6); the piano elaborates orchestral *tutti* interjection (bars 120–4, 139–42); the winds split phrases with the piano (bars 129–36); and the piano and strings share the secondary theme (bars 143–53).

[41] Reicha, *Traité de mélodie*, p. 91.

[42] The dialogue from bars 225–42ff. effects a smooth progression from E♭ back to the tonic B♭ (bar 242). The oscillation of D major and D minor harmony in the piano (bars 231–4), subtly echoed in the winds (bars 235–8), also illustrates the absence of dialogic tonal contradiction at this stage of the movement.

Example 26. Mozart, Piano Concerto K. 595, 1st Movement, bars 189-204.

among Mozart's concertos and assess its impact on Mozart's subsequent concerto writing. Joseph Kerman has also situated piano/orchestra relations in K. 491 at a pivotal juncture in Mozart's concerto repertory. Interpreting 'the solo part and the orchestral part and their relationship [in his concertos] . . . as a composite metaphor for Mozart and his audience and *their* relationship' Kerman suggests that Mozart 'put his tacit contract with them at risk' in K. 491.[43] Although the soloist generally 'traces a broad trajectory from discourse to display' in the solo exposition and recapitulation sections of Mozart's first movements,[44] and the orchestra asserts its authority in the opening orchestral exposition and the final ritornello after the cadenza, 'power relations are in doubt' in K. 491 as the 'issue of discourse versus display remains undecided'.[45] Thus K. 491, 'a deeply subversive work' in which Mozart alienates himself from his audience, leads to the 'strangely cold' K. 503.[46]

It is interesting that neither stylistic nor historical perspectives support Kerman's claim that Mozart was experiencing alienation from his audience in K. 491. It is clear from our study that Mozart closely followed his much-used intimate dialogue – conflict – intimate dialogue paradigm in K. 491/i, furnishing the solo exposition and recapitulation sections with a more elaborate dialogic process, and the development with a more intense conflict, than in any of his other first movements. The fact that Mozart entered K. 491 into his thematic catalogue, the *Verzeichnüss*, on 24 March 1786, only three weeks after K. 488 (another of his most dialogically elaborate concertos), is also noteworthy. If he had not felt alienated from his audience writing K. 488, surely he would not have felt alienated writing K. 491.

But why then did Mozart alter his compositional paradigm in K. 503, 537 and 595? Is it possible that he had in fact 'tired of the Viennese audience', as Kerman suggests?[47] I propose that Mozart's experimentation with piano/orchestra relations in his last three concertos is less a product of disillusionment with his audience than an attempt, after the remarkable sophistication of K. 491, at dialogic renewal. The first movement of K. 491 must have seemed very difficult to follow: the dialogic symmetry and relational complexity it exhibits, contained within Mozart's standard pattern, is extremely sophisticated. Perhaps Mozart felt that the dialogic intricacies and increased interactional intensity of K. 491 had finally exhausted the pattern of relational development that had served him so well in the majority of his Viennese concertos. If K. 491 was, indeed, a watershed for Mozart, it was not because it transformed a pre-existent model of piano/orchestra relations, but rather because it constituted the model's *ne plus ultra.*

Mozart's experimentation with piano/orchestra relations in K. 503, as well as

[43] Kerman, 'Mozart's Piano Concertos and their Audience', pp. 153, 167.
[44] Ibid., p. 155.
[45] Ibid., p. 165.
[46] Ibid., pp. 167–8, p. 166.
[47] Ibid., p. 167.

his broadening of dialogic procedures in that concerto, may have been part of a more general inter-generic trend at the end of 1786 during which he experimented with dialogue and instrumental relations. His 'Prague' Symphony (No. 38, K. 504) and Piano Trio in B♭ (K. 502), completed within days of K. 503, are particularly revealing in this respect.[48] Similarly to K. 503, the first movement of K. 504 comes closest to realizing dialogic equality between the strings and the winds in the development section (see in particular bars 143–70).[49] The fact that K. 504/i 'is not clarified by reference to the traditional concept of sonata form, but must be related to the ritornello structure characteristic of the concerto',[50] also hints that relational issues were weighing on Mozart's mind as he composed the first movement of this symphony. The exposition, development and recapitulation of the first movement of the Piano Trio K. 502 each proceed – unusually for first movements in Mozart's mature chamber music before 1786 – from two-voice dialogue at the beginning of each section to multi-voice dialogue at the end.[51] The opening of the exposition, for example, contains extended passages for the piano and violin (bars 4–9, 17–24, 30–5); the cello becomes a fully active interlocutor only after the secondary theme (bars 41–65 and 79–82). Much of the presentation of thematic material in the development, including the fully dialogued theme initiating the section (bars 83–98) and the repeated quavers in bars 98–108, involves the cello doubling the piano. By the retransition, however, the cello is an independent participant in the dialogue (bars 110–18). The recapitulation follows the pattern established in the exposition.

Thus, even allowing for the different ways in which dialogue operates in concertos and in other instrumental genres, it is at least possible that the

[48] Mozart entered K. 502 into his *Verzeichnüss* on 18 November, K. 503 on 4 December, and K. 504 on 6 December.

[49] The same can be said for dialogic interaction between the piano, violin and cello in the Trio in G, K. 496. The cello partakes in very little dialogue in the exposition, but is an active interlocutor at the beginning of the development section (bars 79–97).

[50] Jens Peter Larsen, 'The Symphonies', in *The Mozart Companion*, eds. H. C. Robbins Landon and Donald Mitchell (New York: Norton, 1956), pp. 188–9. For a detailed discussion of the first movement of the 'Prague' Symphony including its ritornello component, see Elaine R. Sisman, 'Genre, Gesture, and Meaning in Mozart's "Prague" Symphony', in *Mozart Studies 2*, ed. Cliff Eisen (Oxford: Oxford University Press, 1998), pp. 27–84.

[51] In contrast to the concerto, chamber music was likened more often to conversational than to dramatic dialogue (see Chapter One). This suggests that a somewhat different understanding of dialogue is necessary for late-eighteenth-century chamber music than for the late-eighteenth-century concerto. Comparative work in this area, however, has yet to be undertaken. In any case, multi–voiced dialogue (assuming the definition established in Chapter Two for the time being) is more evenly distributed across the exposition, development and recapitulation sections of, for example, the first movements of Mozart's six 'Haydn' Quartets (1782–5) than it is in the first movement of the piano trio, K. 502/i. For late-eighteenth- and early-nineteenth-century descriptions of the string quartet in conversational terms, see Ludwig Finscher, *Die Entstehung des klassichen Streichquartetts*, pp. 285–8. For further discussions of conversational dialogue in chamber music, see Würtz, *Dialogué*; Wheelock, *Haydn's Ingenious Jesting with Art*, pp. 90–115; and Hanning, 'Conversation and Musical Style'.

apotheosis of relational development in the first movement of K. 491 prompted a general rethinking of relational development in Mozart's subsequent symphonic and chamber works, as well as in his later concerto writing. The extraordinary design of K. 491's recapitulation, bringing together all the important thematic material from the orchestral and solo expositions and combining the symmetrical arrangements of both in a *tour de force* of dialogic technique, offers something of an equivalent, among the concertos, to the famous coda from the finale of the 'Jupiter' Symphony (No. 41, K. 551). Just as the contrapuntal complexity of Mozart's symphonic writing reaches its zenith in the 'Jupiter' coda, with all the important motives and themes from the finale presented concurrently, so the elaborate dialogic interaction of Mozart's piano and orchestra in his Viennese piano concertos reaches its own climax in the recapitulation of K. 491/i.[52] It is perhaps significant, in light of the stylistic summits reached, that the remarkable K. 491 and 551 mark, respectively, the end of Mozart's four-year preoccupation with piano concertos (with a sharp decrease in productivity over the next five years) and the end of his symphonic composition altogether.

In 1799, after attending a performance of K. 491, Beethoven famously remarked to Johann Baptist Cramer: 'we shall never be able to do anything like that!'[53] Perhaps Beethoven was aware that, from the point of view of piano/orchestra dialogue in the concerto, K. 491/i was unique. This is not to devalue the achievement represented by either the earlier or the later concertos, but by gloriously realizing in K. 491/i the full potential of a pattern of intricate, elaborate and intense piano/orchestra interaction that had occupied him for the previous four years, Mozart had also sowed the seeds for the pattern's demise.

Whether Mozart was aware of it or not, his professional life was at a crossroads in the middle of 1786; thereafter – and in contrast to his first four years in Vienna – he would establish himself in the eyes of the Viennese musical public more as an operatic composer than as a composer (and performer) of instrumental music. His supreme achievement in the first movement of K. 491 was that, by extending his standard pattern of piano/orchestra interaction to its limit, he had put a crucial aspect of his piano concerto style at a crossroads as well.

[52] For a persuasive interpretation of the 'Jupiter' coda in terms of Kant's 'mathematical sublime', see Elaine R. Sisman, *Mozart: The 'Jupiter' Symphony* (Cambridge: Cambridge University Press, 1993), p. 79.

[53] See Elliot Forbes, ed., *Thayer's Life of Beethoven* (Princeton: Princeton University Press, 1967), p. 209. Also quoted in Maynard Solomon, *Beethoven* (New York: Schirmer, 1977), p. 97.

5

From Opera to Concerto to Opera (1780–1787)

The Inter-Generic Development of Dramatic Dialogue in Mozart's Works

In Chapters Three and Four, a theoretical and practical contextualisation of dramatic dialogue enabled us to paint a clear picture of the evolving nature of solo/orchestra relations in the first movements of Mozart's piano concertos. Without an assessment of how relational development in the piano concertos corresponds to that in opera, the dramatic genre to which Mozart was most intimately connected, however, this picture remains incomplete. Broad generic links between interaction in Mozart's concerto movements and operatic arias and ensembles have never been in question: both set a soloist (or soloists) against an accompanying orchestra; and both reconcile soloistic display with orchestral participation. More precise stylistic affinities, however, remain unsystematically explored. A comparison of dramatic dialogue in the two genres not only supports the musical manifestation of behavioural types identified earlier, but also traces an inter-generic development of dialogic techniques across Mozart's works.

While correlations between dialogic interaction in Mozart's concertos and operas have not yet received scholarly attention, structural, gestural and stylistic connections between the late-eighteenth-century concerto and opera have been explored thoroughly. Classical writers noticed general similarities between the two genres – Lacépède believed that the soloists' skills were revealed in similar ways, and Koch identified the concerto as an 'imitation [*Nachahmung*] of the aria'[1] – and drew specific parallels between the *opera seria* aria and the concerto.[2] Many twentieth-century writers have followed suit, identifying structural similarities between aria form and first-movement concerto form, as well as widespread stylistic and gestural parallels between late-eighteenth-century operas and concertos (Mozart's in particular).[3]

[1] Lacépède, *La Poétique de la Musique*, p. 341; and Koch, *Musikalisches Lexikon*, col. 351.

[2] See Jutta Ruile-Dronke, *Ritornell und Solo in Mozarts Klavierkonzerten* (Tutzing: Hans Schneider, 1978), pp. 41–6; and Stevens, 'Theme, Harmony and Texture', pp. 26–7.

[3] The literature on these parallels is considerable. For an account of the *da capo* aria's influence on the mid-century instrumental concerto, see Ortrun Landmann, 'Einige Ueberlegungen zu den Konzerten "nebenamtlich" komponierender Dresdener Hofmusiker in der Zeit von etwa 1715 bis 1763', in *Die Entwicklung des Solokonzertes im 18. Jahrhundert: Studien zur Aufführungspraxis und Interpretation von Instrumentalmusik des 18. Jahrhunderts*, ed. Eitelfriedrich Thom (Magdeburg:

The presence of dialogic similarities in concerto movements and operatic numbers, however, are only partially explained by common stylistic, structural and gestural properties. In order to compare dialogue in Mozart's operas and concertos more fully, we must account not only for exchange between the soloist and the orchestra in arias (the principal focus hitherto in comparing the operas to the concertos) but also for that between characters in ensembles and between the orchestra and characters in ensembles. Although general similarities between the formal structures of operatic numbers and concerto movements often point towards close correspondences in relational development (among the on-stage characters and/or between the characters and the orchestra), these similarities are not the only important ones. The overall 'trajectories' of relational development in the first movements of Mozart's piano concertos, although closely bound up with the formal structure of the movements (as shown in Chapters Three and Four), need not be thought of *exclusively* in structural terms: the 'shapes' of relational development in operatic numbers and concerto movements are often similar irrespective of structural correlations. In any case, the inconclusive nature of structural parallels between Mozart's own *buffa* arias and concerto movements[4] necessitates extending dialogic connections beyond the formal realm.

Whatever the relationship between Mozart's operatic and concerto dialogue, there is one significant difference, namely the presence of textual *and* musical dialogue in opera. These types of dialogue are semi-autonomous, as the appearance of one does not assume the appearance of the other. Therefore, manifestations of musical dialogue in Mozart's concertos and operas – adopting the definitions established in Chapter Two for both genres[5] – can be compared,

Blankenburg, 1983), pp. 57–73. A number of scholars have argued for formal connections between the late-eighteenth-century aria and the concerto. See in particular, Tovey, *Essays in Musical Analysis: Vol. 3, Concertos*, pp. 6–16; Forman, *Mozart's Concerto Form*, Introduction, pp. 11–23; Ruile-Dronke, *Ritornell und Solo*; Charles Rosen, *Sonata Forms* (New York: Norton, 1980), Chap. 4 'Aria' and Chap. 5 'Concerto', pp. 27–95; Ratner, *Classic Music*, pp. 297–305; Robert Levin, 'Mozart's Piano Concertos', in *The Mozart Compendium*, ed. H. C. Robbins Landon, pp. 263–4; Konrad Küster, *Formale Aspekte des ersten Allegros in Mozarts Konzerten* (Kassel: Bärenreiter, 1991), pp. 224–8; and, most recently, Martha Feldman, 'Staging the Virtuoso: Ritornello Procedure in Mozart, from Aria to Concerto', in *Mozart's Piano Concertos*, ed. Neal Zaslaw (Ann Arbor: University of Michigan Press, 1996), pp. 149–86. For stylistic and gestural parallels, see Istvan Kecskeméti, 'Opernelemente in den Klavierkonzerten Mozarts', *Mozart-Jahrbuch 1968–70*, pp. 111–18; Hutchings, *A Companion to Mozart's Piano Concertos, passim*; Forman, *Mozart's Concerto Form, passim*; Reinhard Strohm, 'Merkmale italienischer Versvertonung in Mozart's Klavierkonzerten', *Analecta Musicologica* 18 (1978), pp. 219–36; Marius Flothuis, 'Bühne und Konzert', *Mozart-Jahrbuch 1986*, pp. 45–58. Wye Jamison Allanbrook considers *opera buffa* gestures in Mozart's piano concertos, most notably gestures that relate to endings, cadences and finales; see 'Comic Issues in Mozart's Piano Concertos', in *Mozart's Piano Concertos*, ed. Zaslaw (Ann Arbor: University of Michigan Press, 1996), pp. 75–105. Allanbrook also touches on parallels between opera and concerto in 'Mozart's Tunes and the Comedy of Closure', in *On Mozart*, ed. James M. Morris (Cambridge: Cambridge University Press, 1994), pp. 169–86.

[4] See Webster, 'Are Mozart's Concertos "Dramatic"?', especially pp. 111–30.

[5] The fact that much of Reicha's discussion of dialogue (particularly in the *Art du compositeur dramatique*) is aimed specifically at opera justifies adopting definitions established in Chapter Two for Mozart's operas as well as his concertos.

at least initially, without recourse to the textual dimension of operatic dialogue. That said, musical dialogue in Mozart's operas often coincides with textual dialogue, reinforcing dramatic (including relational) development in the process. Ultimately, comparisons between musical dialogue in Mozart's operas and concertos are convincing (albeit in different ways, as we shall see) whether or not textual and musical dialogue coincide.

Although an examination of every type of multi-tiered dialogue in Mozart's operas – textual, musical and non-musical (in *Die Entführung* and *Die Zauberflöte*) in literal and metaphorical guises – would be a pre-requisite for establishing a thoroughly comprehensive understanding, such theorizing is unnecessary for the comparative task at hand. Musical dialogue – indeed interaction in general – in Mozart's operas exists in a continuum, ranging from those arias, duets, and ensembles that feature musical dialogue in abundance, to those in which it is almost non-existent.[6] This observation is not intended to impart a qualitative judgement about individual operatic numbers; nor is it intended to indicate that numbers in which dialogue plays a peripheral role are intrinsically less 'dramatic' than those in which it plays a prominent role. In the context of opera/concerto parallels, however, it is a comparison of dialogue-oriented operatic pieces with their concerto counterparts that uncovers the inter-generic trajectory of Mozart's dramatic dialogue.[7]

A methodological issue directly relevant to the comparative study at hand and, more specifically, to a postulation of inter-generic dramatic dialogue, is how the dramatic component of concerto and opera dialogue is distinct from that of dialogue in other instrumental genres, such as the symphony and the string quartet. To be sure, the presence of a prevailing soloist (or soloists) and an orchestra distinguishes a concerto and an operatic number from a symphony or a chamber work. But this does not *in itself* establish distinct types of dramatic dialogue. When late-eighteenth-century theoretical descriptions are taken into account, however, differences between the nature of dialogue in the concerto, symphony and string quartet become more readily apparent. As we have seen in Chapter One, the string quartet was likened to intimate conversation – which in turn carried connotations of an equality of participation among interlocutors – rather than dramatic dialogue. Although dialogue in the symphony like dialogue in the concerto was compared to dramatic exchange, and the orchestras of both the symphony and the concerto likened to the Greek

[6] In a similar vein, James Webster remarks that 'Mozart's operas exhibit a continuum of instrumental usage, from plain interjections to full-fledged agents'. See Webster, 'The Analysis of Mozart's Arias', p. 126.

[7] Although dialogue between the piano and the orchestra in individual Mozart concerto movements also exists in a continuum, this continuum is considerably more constricted than the operatic one. The discrepancy between a duet or ensemble that features perpetual musical dialogue (usually motivated by the text) and an aria, say, that features little to none, has no parallel in Mozart's piano concertos. Thus, the difference in quantity between dialogue in K. 415/i and 491/i, movements at either end of the concerto spectrum, is considerably less extreme than the difference between dialogue in, for example, arias and ensembles at either end of the corresponding operatic spectrum.

Chorus,[8] the effects of the drama in each genre were perceived very differently. The symphony's 'quality of massed expression', for example, distinguished it in a fundamental way from the concerto.[9] Whereas communal expression characterised the symphony for late-eighteenth-century writers, expression *split* between the solo and orchestral forces – whether in a co-operative or a competitive context – remained a central component of critical discourse on the concerto (see Chapters One and Three). Above all, relations among participants comprised the essential drama of concerto dialogue, to an extent that could not have existed in symphonic dialogue, given that the symphony spoke to late-eighteenth-century theorists with a 'communal voice'.[10] In contrast, of course, literal and musical relations among individual on-stage interlocutors are *always* a focal point of Mozart operas, providing the life-blood of the drama. Thus, in the theoretical context of character relations, as well as in the generic and expressive context of a soloist and orchestra, it is Mozart's operatic and not his symphonic dialogue that most closely resembles concerto dialogue.

The ensuing study compares dialogic confrontation and co-operation in Mozart's arias and ensembles from *Idomeneo* (1780–1), *Die Entführung aus dem Serail* (1782), *Le nozze di Figaro* (1786) and *Don Giovanni* (1787) to similar behaviour between the piano and the orchestra in Mozart's Viennese concertos, K. 413–491 (1782–6).[11] Even without historical attention to concertos and operas of Mozart's predecessors and contemporaries, these works not only offer a unique opportunity for identifying and explaining Mozart's inter-generic dramatic dialogue, but also enable an assessment of its development over a protracted period.[12] Representing a broad alternation in compositional emphasis

[8] See Chapter One above for the concerto, and Bonds, 'The Symphony as Pindaric Ode', in *Haydn and His World*, ed. Sisman, p. 147, for the symphony.

[9] Bonds, 'The Symphony as Pindaric Ode', in *Haydn and His World*, ed. Sisman, p. 148.

[10] Ibid., p. 150.

[11] For present purposes dialogue in operatic recitatives will not form part of my investigation. Recitative dialogue is appreciably different stylistically from dialogue in operatic arias, duets and ensembles, and from piano/orchestra dialogue in Mozart's concertos. With negligible instrumental participation for the most part, dialogue in recitatives requires a different set of criteria in regard to interactional relations among interlocutors.

[12] To be sure, valuable recent work on concerto and operatic traditions has increased our appreciation of Mozart's stylistic debts to his predecessors. For Mozart's concertos, see Jane R. Stevens, 'The Importance of C. P. E. Bach for Mozart's Piano Concertos', in *Mozart's Piano Concertos*, ed. Zaslaw, pp. 211–36; and Derr, 'Some Thoughts on the Design of Mozart's Opus 4', pp. 187–210. For Mozart's operas, see: Mary Hunter and James Webster, eds., *Opera Buffa in Mozart's Vienna* (Cambridge: Cambridge University Press, 1997); Mary Hunter, *The Culture of Opera Buffa in Mozart's Vienna: A Poetics of Entertainment* (Princeton: Princeton University Press, 1999); John Platoff, 'Musical and Dramatic Structure in the Opera Buffa Finale', *Journal of Musicology* 7/2 (1989), pp. 191–230; Platoff, 'Tonal Organization in "Buffo" Finales and the Act II Finale of *Le nozze di Figaro*', *Music & Letters* 72/3 (1991), pp. 387–403; Platoff, 'The Buffa Aria in Mozart's Vienna', *Cambridge Opera Journal* 2/2 (1990), pp. 99–120; Platoff, 'How original was Mozart? Evidence from *Opera Buffa*', *Early Music* 20/1 (1992), pp. 105–17. For the purposes of determining Mozart's stylistic *development*, however, interrelationships among his own works take precedence.

from opera (1780–2) to concerto (1782–6) to opera (1786–7), they neatly encompass Mozart's first putatively 'mature' operas (*Idomeneo* and *Entführung*), his most productive period of concerto composition, and his most exquisitely crafted operatic masterpieces (*Figaro* and *Don Giovanni*).

The make-up of operatic interlocutors in our study will be determined according to the type of number under discussion. Dialogue in duets, trios, quartets and other ensembles will account for the musical and dramatic development of relations among characters, as well as the orchestra's role in reinforcing such developments; dialogue in arias will relate only to solo/orchestra interaction.[13] After examining dialogic confrontation and co-operation separately, stylistic information on operatic and concerto interaction gleaned from that investigation, as well as stylistic conclusions on Mozart's piano concertos drawn from Chapters Three and Four, will be used to establish inter-generic developments in Mozart's dramatic dialogue.

Dialogic Confrontations in *Entführung*, *Figaro*, *Don Giovanni* and Mozart's Piano Concertos

Entführung[14]

Most of the characteristics of piano/orchestra confrontation in Mozart's great four-year sequence of Viennese Piano Concertos (1782–6) are presaged by characteristics of character confrontation in *Die Entführung aus dem Serail* (1782), the opera that immediately precedes them. Above all, Mozart uses tonal devices – modulatory sequences and major/minor shifts for example – to accentuate dialogic confrontations among his operatic characters, in the process establishing stylistic and procedural precedents for piano concerto movements such as K. 450/i and 482/i.

The *Lied* and Duet No. 2 from *Entführung* (Belmonte and Osmin) illustrates how tonal procedures play a crucial role in emphasizing confrontation between characters. At the beginning of the number, Osmin ignores Belmonte's two spoken attempts to attract his attention and to ask him about Pascha Selim. He obstinately repeats his sung theme in full after both of Belmonte's spoken interjections (bars 20–36 and 37–53, corresponding to bars 3–19), but is forced to pay attention to Belmonte and abandon his repetitive presentation when

[13] To be sure, arias are often addressed to an on-stage or off-stage character, although the addressee in such cases cannot be described as an active interlocutor. This kind of 'dialogue' will not form part of my investigation.

[14] Given that *Idomeneo* relies on an alternation of recitatives and arias, and features only three ensembles (the type of operatic number in which confrontation is most prevalent), I have limited my discussion here to *Die Entführung*. Although Elettra in particular is an agent of dramatic conflict in *Idomeneo*, the conflicts are mostly internal ones, and do not involve her direct interaction with other characters. See Craig Ayrey, 'Elettra's First Aria and the Storm Scene', in Julian Rushton, *W. A. Mozart: Idomeneo* (Cambridge: Cambridge University Press, 1993), p. 152.

Belmonte *sings* for the first time in bar 54, dialoguing the 'Trallalera' material. In textual terms, Belmonte's dialogue is a direct, confrontational (and successful) attempt to engage Osmin in discourse ('A pox on you and your song! I'm tired of your singing; just listen to a word!').[15] In musical terms, too, Belmonte's dialogue is confrontational; it changes the tempo abruptly from *Andante* to *Allegro* (an attribute of oppositional dramatic dialogue, according to Reicha[16]) and, questioning the authority of Osmin's G minor, begins the first modulation of the number (B♭ is confirmed in bar 68). Indeed, Osmin sticks resolutely to G minor for the first fifty-three bars and – symbolic of his stubborness – only moves on tonally when prodded by Belmonte. In short, Belmonte's dialogue challenges Osmin at the *musical* level to abandon his persistent attachment to G minor as well as at the verbal level to engage in discourse.

This passage from the *Entführung* duet establishes a procedural precedent for the tonal *impasse* between the piano and the orchestra in the solo expositions of K. 482/i and 450/i. Just as Osmin shuns dialogue with Belmonte in bars 1–53 and remains intently fixed on G minor, so the piano in the solo exposition of K. 450/i eschews dialogue with the orchestra almost completely, bringing initially at least an harmonic stasis and absence of directional thrust to the music, an agenda with which the orchestra (judging by its outburst in bars 86–7) clearly does not agree (see Chapter Three and Examples 5 and 6, pp. 58 and 59). Equally, the confrontational dialogue in bars 53–9 of the duet, and analogous dialogues in bars 216–22 of K. 482/i and 152–6 of K. 450/i (see Examples 2 and 4, pp. 54 and 57) alter their respective state of affairs in regard to tonal procedure. After the initial modulation to B♭ in the duet, for which Belmonte's contribution in bars 53–9 acts as a catalyst, the music turns away decisively from G minor, passing through E♭ (bar 76), F (bar 89), A minor (bar 103), C major (bar 111), C minor (bar 114), G minor (bar 129), E♭ (bar 152) and B♭ (bar 164) on route to D in bar 176. Similarly, bars 152–6 of K. 450/i, which precipitate a sequential modulation from F minor to C minor to G minor, spell the end for the piano's harmonic stasis, and lead eventually (in the recapitulation) to a 'correction' of the static pedal from the beginning of the solo exposition. Bars 216–22 of K. 482/i also initiate a more active role for the orchestra in the modulatory process of the movement.

Dialogic confrontations in the first movements of piano concertos such as K. 450 and 482 are also foreshadowed by other tonally-oriented dialogic confrontations in *Entführung*. Later in the Duet No. 2, after Osmin's initial criticism of Pedrillo for example, Belmonte explains 'Ihr irrt, ihr irrt, ihr irrt, es

[15] Unless otherwise indicated, English translations of text from Mozart's operas are taken from booklets accompanying the following recordings: *Mozart: Idomeneo. Sir Colin Davis, Bavarian Radio Symphony Orchestra.* Philips, 422 537–2 (Complete Mozart Edition, vol. 37); *Mozart: Die Entführung aus dem Serail. Sir Colin Davis, Academy of St. Martin in the Fields.* Philips, 422 538–2 (Complete Mozart Edition, vol. 38); *Mozart: Le nozze di Figaro. Bernard Haitink, London Philharmonic Orchestra.* EMI, 7 49753 2; *Mozart: Don Giovanni. Lorin Maazel, Orchestra of the Théâtre National de l'Opéra, Paris.* CBS Masterworks, M3K 35192.

[16] See Reicha's musical examples of dialogue, *Traité de mélodie*, vol. 2, p. 63 (No. 4).

ist ein braver Mann' ('You're wrong, he [Pedrillo] is an honest man'), to which Osmin replies 'So brav, so brav, so brav, dass man ihn spiessen kann' ('So honest that I'd impale him on a spit'). Osmin repeats Belmonte's strident *forte* phrase almost note for note (bars 111–17, see Example 27[17]), shifting the music from C major to C minor and 'taking up his opponent's words' in a confrontational manner characteristic of *stichomythia* (short, alternating statements). Pedrillo and Belmonte contradict Osmin in a similar fashion in the Trio

Example 27. Mozart, *Die Entfuehrung aus dem Serail*, No. 2, Duet, bars 111-17.

No. 7, 'Marsch, Marsch, Marsch'. Although the ensemble's key signature changes from C minor to C major immediately before Osmin's 'Marsch, fort, fort, fort, fort, fort' (bars 98–9), neither his vocal line, nor the accompanying orchestral instruments feature an all-important E *natural*, and thus do not verify the modal shift. The first E naturals coincide with Belmonte's and Pedrillo's subsequent 'Platz, fort, fort, fort, fort, fort' (bars 100–3) giving the firm impression that contradiction of Osmin's preceding statement is tonal as well as textual. As observed in Chapter Three, confrontational modal shifts of a comparably forceful kind to those in Nos. 2 and 7 of *Entführung* occur in dialogue between the piano and the orchestra in bars 126–8 of K. 482/i and bars 152–6 of K. 450/i (and also bars 107–10 of K. 467/i, see Chapter Six, p. 154). Equally, two other confrontational dialogues between Belmonte/Pedrillo and Osmin in the trio ('Don't come any nearer'/'Stand away from the door'; and 'March! Be off with you!'/'Make way!'), featuring a circle of 5ths (F–B♭–E♭–A♭, bars 22–6) and a spiralling, descending progression (bars 41–6) respectively, foreshadow the sequential and modulatory components of the confrontational dialogues in the development sections of K. 482/i (bars 216–22, Example 2, p. 54), K. 491/i (bars 330–45, Example 25, p. 90), and K. 449/i (bars 188–203, see Example 15, p. 68).

Mozart's musical representations of textual confrontations between characters

[17] Musical examples are not annotated in as much detail in Chapter Five as in Chapters Three and Four. For the most part, only dialogue between the vocalists and the orchestra is annotated; dialogue among the vocalists is deemed self-evident.

in *Entführung* are not, of course, limited to the procedures described above. In some cases, such as the beginning of the B section of the Duet No. 9, 'Ich gehe, doch rate ich dir' (bars 56–74), where Blonde dialogues the oboe's rather than Osmin's version of the melody and Osmin's melody is itself dialogued by the bassoon, confrontation takes a form that has no parallels in Mozart's piano concertos. Here, the orchestra, by dialoguing with the two characters independently, accentuates the absence of dialogue between the characters themselves and also the oppositional nature of their respective sentiments (Osmin: 'O Englishmen! What fools you are to let your women have their way'; Blonde: 'A girl born to freedom will never slavishly take orders'). In other cases, Mozart does not retain musical characteristics of confrontational dialogue throughout a particular confrontation. After the C major/C minor dialogue between Belmonte and Osmin in No. 2 (bars 111–17), for example, textual confrontation is rife, although tonal and harmonic illustrations of it (disjunctions, modal shifts, modulatory progressions etc.) are few and far between.

Nevertheless, *Entführung*'s striking musical manifestations of dialogic confrontation explained above all occur at pivotal dramatic and/or musical moments in their respective ensembles. Belmonte's musical interjection in bars 53–9 of No. 2 is his first in the ensemble, forcing Osmin to pay attention to him and to abandon his hold on G minor; furthermore, Belmonte's C major/ C minor confrontation with Osmin (bars 111–17) comes soon after the first mention of Pedrillo, and begins a significant escalation (from a dramatic, if not a musical, perspective) in their confrontation. Belmonte's and Pedrillo's modal contradiction of Osmin in the Trio No. 7 is the moment of most far-reaching significance for the ensemble's tonal and dramatic trajectory, the moment at which the tonic C minor is usurped for the first time by the key that will bring the piece to a close, C major, symbolizing their on-stage 'victory' over Osmin (i.e. getting past him and entering Pascha Selim's house). Just as Mozart's most musically explicit dialogic confrontations in *Entführung* underscore the dramatic significance of particular moments, so the most powerful piano/ orchestra confrontations in his concertos, especially those at the beginning of the development sections of K. 450/i and 482/i, emphasise the dramatic nature of relational development in individual movements.

Figaro and Don Giovanni

Although tonality and harmony provide a backdrop for character confrontations in *Entführung*, their role is more pronounced in this respect in the Viennese piano concertos (for example K. 449, 450, 467, 482, 491) and in ensembles (especially the finales) from *Figaro* and *Don Giovanni*.[18] In addition,

[18] Dialogic confrontation in textual terms is standard practice in late-eighteenth-century *opera buffa* finales. As John Platoff points out, librettists provide 'an active dialogue followed by an expressive tutti' and, over the course of the finale, 'escalate an already existing dramatic conflict into a crisis'. See Platoff, 'Musical and Dramatic Structure', pp. 213, 223.

Figaro and *Don Giovanni* feature a number of examples of the kind of Reicha-esque confrontational dialogue witnessed in the Viennese piano concertos, in particular K. 491.

In a large number of the *Figaro* and *Giovanni* ensembles that include textual confrontations in dialogue, Mozart turns tonality – in the form of modulation, or key confirmation – into a central component of the confrontation process, and a vital musical manifestation of the dramatic structure. In the first Allegro section from the Act 2 Finale of *Figaro*, for example, the Count – furious at the Countess for concealing Cherubino in the closet – completely dominates the tonal direction of the music. He begins the process of modulating to the dominant B♭ in bars 13–17; affirms V/V in the strongest possible terms (against a crescendo to *forte*) in bars 31–4; asserts V/ii in bar 63 after an antecedent-consequent dialogue with the Countess and subsequently confirms the key (bar 64); puts an emphatic end to a quick-fire dialogue about the Countess's guilt with an ostentatious, recitative-like affirmation of dominant harmony (bars 80–1), and a confirmation of the return to E♭ (bar 83). Correspondingly, in the second Allegro of the Act 2 Finale – in which the Count, learning of his mistake, seeks forgiveness from the Countess for his suspicions – Susanna and the Countess are in control tonally, providing all the authoritative perfect cadences in the middle of the trio. While the Count moves to the dominant F in bars 176–91 – he is only partially penitent at this stage, saying 'if I've done you wrong I beg your pardon, but playing such jokes is cruel, after all' – the perfect cadence confirmation is carried out by Susanna and the Countess (bars 191–5). Subsequently, as the Count makes bungled attempts both to apologise to, and to express his love for, the Countess, Susanna and the Countess dictate the music's tonal course, underscoring V–I perfect cadences in F major (bars 197, 199), G minor (bar 211), E♭ (bars 218, 226) and a modulation to A♭ (bar 234). Only unconditional penitence ('Confused, repentant, I've been punished enough, have pity on me') enables the Count to participate freely again in perfect cadence tonal confirmations (for example, A♭ in bars 242 and 253, F minor in bar 259 and E♭ in bars 263 and 279). In the ensuing quick-fire dialogue (see Example 28), the Countess barks 'Ungrateful!' at the Count and contradicts the prevailing B♭ major tonality with a move to B♭ minor (bar 301). The Count's final, decisive statement ('Look at me! I was wrong and I repent!', bars 301–6, Example 28), accentuated by a German augmented 6th–V–diminished 7th–V progression, is a wonderful representation of his penitence. He does not contradict the Countess's disgruntled move to B♭ minor as she had contradicted his B♭ major; instead, he includes a D♭ in a prominent melodic position (bar 305), as if to acknowledge *musically* the Countess's digression to the minor and, by implication, the source of her disgruntlement.[19]

[19] For a splendid analysis of the entire Act 2 Finale of *Figaro*, containing a plethora of trenchant observations on character relations etc., see Wye Jamison Allanbrook, *Rhythmic Gesture in Mozart: 'Le nozze di Figaro' and 'Don Giovanni'* (Chicago: University of Chicago Press, 1983), pp. 119–36.

Example 28. Mozart, *Le nozze di Figaro*, Act 2 Finale, bars 297-306.

Connections between tonal processes and dramatic structures are as rife in the confrontations of *Don Giovanni* as they are in the confrontations of *Figaro.* In the Andante Maestoso section of the Act 1 Finale, for example, Don Giovanni is confronted by Donna Anna, Donna Elvira and Don Ottavio. The accusers' control of the situation is mirrored by their tonal control. Don Giovanni's suggestion of F major (bar 514) is immediately negated by Elvira's D minor (bars 514–15); thereafter, Don Giovanni can only submit to the will of the group, echoing Elvira's D minor (bar 515) and Don Ottavio's B♭ (bar 516) before falling silent. In the ensuing Allegro section (bar 533ff.), Anna, Elvira, Zerlina and Masetto repeatedly interrupt Leporello/Don Giovanni, starting their phrases before Leporello and Don Giovanni have finished theirs (bars 543, 548, 550, 552). The interruptions reach their zenith in bars 571–7 (see Example 29) and 600–6, when the group replace the C major harmony to which Don Giovanni and Leporello are heading with diminished harmonies (bars 571, 575, 600, 604). In the Finale to Act 2, Don Giovanni also loses the upper hand in the affirmation of tonalities, as if to symbolise his impending defeat. Although he responds confidently to the Commendatore's invitation to dine, cadencing in G minor in bars 515–16, and affirms that 'there is no repentance' modulating from G minor to D minor (bars 528–30), he subsequently relinquishes control; in the sequential exchange 'Repent!' 'No! – E♭–B♭7–e♭-diminished–c–D7–g–E♭ (augmented 6th)–A7–d–B♭ (augmented 6th)–diminished–A7 (bars 538–48) – it is the Commendatore, not Don Giovanni, who presents the root position

Example 29. Mozart, *Don Giovanni*, Act 1 Finale, bars 568-77.

chords of the local tonics and who provides the ostentatious and authoritative confirmation of D minor (bars 549–54) leading into the concluding allegro section (bar 554ff.).[20]

Given the vast literature on the interrelationships between musical and dramatic processes in Mozart's operas,[21] the correlations described above

[20] For more detailed discussions of harmonic and tonal processes in regard to confrontation in this finale, see Glenn Stanley, 'The Second-Act Finale Confrontation between Don Giovanni and Il Commendatore: Structural Coherence and Dramatic Intensification', *Mozart-Jahrbuch 1991*, pp. 879–87; and Allanbrook, *Rhythmic Gesture*, pp. 287–319.

[21] See, most recently, the provocative essay by Jessica Waldoff and James Webster, 'Operatic Plotting in *Le nozze di Figaro*' in *Wolfgang Amadè Mozart: Essays on his Life and Music* (Oxford: Clarendon Press, 1996), pp. 250–95. Waldoff and Webster expand the notion of 'plot' to encompass the 'dynamic of text, action and music': 'Anything that happens can be understood as an operatic event: an action in recitative, a contemplative aria, a complex ensemble; a horn call, a melisma, a reminiscence; a seduction, a duel, an act of forgiveness. Even as these events constitute the operatic plot, all are constituted in text, action and music'. (p. 255)

must be regarded as typical manifestations of Mozart's operatic *modus operandi*. More remarkable, however, are the musical and procedural similarities between the character confrontations in these operas and the piano/orchestra confrontations in Mozart's preceding concertos. At a general level we have seen in Chapter Three that tonal 'authority' is a source of relational unease in the solo exposition sections of K. 450/i and 482/i (leading to dialogic confrontations at the beginning of the development sections), just as tonal 'authority' is the provenance of a particular operatic character in confrontation with another character or group of characters at a particular stage in the plot.[22] More specifically, musical manifestations of relational tension between the piano and the orchestra in Mozart's concertos are strikingly similar to such manifestations among his operatic characters in *Figaro* and *Don Giovanni*. The powerful alternation of contrasting material in equal two-bar units invoking Antoine Reicha's paradigm of confrontational dialogue in the development section of K. 491/i – itself foreshadowed in Mozart's earlier concertos (see Chapter Four) – is closely paralleled by the forceful alternation of strongly contrasting, equal-length segments in Mozart's operatic confrontations. The opposing group's most intense interruptions of Don Giovanni and Leporello in the Act 1 Finale of *Don Giovani*, where ascending unison quaver scales in the two voices, oboes and lower strings are pitted against a harmonised sequence of descending crotchet chords in five voices and the full orchestra, consist of alternating (and overlapping) two-and-a-half bar units (bars 569–77 and 598–606, see Example 29 above); Donna Anna's, Zerlina's, Ottavio's and Masetto's two most emphatic denials of Donna Elvira's request for mercy on behalf of Don Giovanni (Leporello in disguise) in the Act 2 Sextet (see Example 30) contrast *piano*, sparsely-scored one-bar chromatic descents (bars 86, 94) with *forte*, fully-orchestrated one-bar diatonic descents (bars 87, 95), in the process thrusting Elvira's V/g harmony to VI on both occasions, and resolving it authoritatively to G minor two bars after the second such exchange (bar 98); and Don Curzio's and the Count's confrontation with Susanna/Figaro/Marcellina/Bartolo in the Act 3 Sextet of *Figaro* juxtaposes dynamically, texturally, instrumentally and rhythmically contrasting one- and two-bar (overlapping) units (bars 111–124; see Example 31 for bars 111–15). The kind of modulating, quick-fire dialogic confrontation between the piano and the orchestra heard at the beginning of the development section of K. 482/i (see Chapter 3, Example 2, p. 54) also appears in confrontational dialogues between operatic characters in *Figaro* and *Don Giovanni*. The confrontation between the Commendatore and Don Giovanni in the Act 2 Finale of *Don Giovanni*, for example, contains a spiralling, modulatory sequence (as outlined above); the earlier duel between the Commendatore and Don Giovanni in Act 1, scene 1 – carried out musically on behalf of the

[22] For an essay that argues for tonal 'command' and 'tonal duelling for the Count's authority' (p. 174) in the context of the Act 1 trio from *Figaro* ('Cosa sento'), see David Lewin, 'Musical Analysis as Stage Direction', in *Music and Text: Critical Inquiries*, ed. Steven Paul Scher (Cambridge: Cambridge University Press, 1992), pp. 163–76.

Example 30. Mozart, *Don Giovanni*, Act 2 Sextet, bars 86-98.

Example 31. Mozart, *Le nozze di Figaro*, Act 3 Sextet, bars 111-15.

two characters as it were through dialogue between the first violins/cellos and the basses – spirals downwards in a circle of 5ths (A7–D7–G7–C7–F7; bars 168–72); Elvira's confrontation with Don Giovanni ('You brute, I don't believe you'/'Ah, you must believe me') in bars 46–50 of the Act 2 Trio, No. 15 underscores a terse modulatory progression: C–diminished–a–diminished–D6–V7/A; and the altercation between the Count and the Countess immediately prior to the reprise of *Figaro*'s Act 2 Trio moves from dominant to tonic against the backdrop of one-bar dialoguing segments and changes of harmony every two bars (V–V7/V–V7–I6/4–V7–I, bars 63–71), intensified by *fortepianos* and tremolos in the strings.

In addition to musical similarities between confrontations in Mozart's operas and concertos, there are strong procedural links between concerto movements and operatic ensembles in which confrontations play a crucial role. As explained in Chapter Three, the dialogic confrontations at the beginning of the development sections of K. 450/i and 482/i are, at one and the same time, products of relational tension from the solo exposition, catalysts for later piano/orchestra collaboration, and indicators that relations develop gradually, not abruptly, across complete movements. Dialogic confrontations in the ensembles of *Figaro* and *Don Giovanni* fulfill analogous, multi-tiered functions. This is especially evident in the Act 3 Sextet from *Figaro*, which solidifies perhaps the single most important relational twist in the opera – the realization that Figaro is Marcellina's and Bartolo's son.[23] The confrontation between Don Curzio/

[23] Charles Rosen analyses this number, especially its formal and motivic content, to illustrate the 'adaptability of the sonata style to opera' (p. 290), thus providing a more generic link between this sextet and Mozart's instrumental compositions than is offered here. See *The Classical Style*, pp. 290–95.

Count and Susanna/Figaro/Marcellina/Bartolo (bars 111–122, see Example 31 above for bars 111–15) in this ensemble realises tensions latent in the musical differentiation of the two character groups earlier in the number, as do the piano and orchestra's dialogues in the context of their respective movements at the beginning of the development sections of K. 450/i and 482/i. In bars 18–40, the Count and Don Curzio dialogue with each other (textually and musically), as do Marcellina, Bartolo, and Figaro; in bars 55–72, Don Curzio, the Count and Susanna (who is as yet unaware of the revelation that Figaro is Marcellina's and Bartolo's son) sing sharp, dotted rhythms, predominantly in quavers and semiquavers to almost identical words of fury ('I'm/He's boiling, I'm/he's raging with fury; an old woman/destiny has done this to me'), while Bartolo, Marcellina and Figaro sing more flowing and graceful melodies to the same expression of joy.

In the subsequent confrontation (bars 111–22, Example 31), this musical and verbal differentiation – Susanna is now on the side of Bartolo, Marcellina and Figaro – is intensified considerably: the statements are separated and more acutely contrasted from a musical perspective; and the words of the two groups are more closely matched, with one crucial difference underscoring the opposing sentiments of the two groups ('My soul can barely resist any longer the *fierce torment* of this moment' in contrast to 'My soul can barely resist any longer the *sweet delight* of this moment'). While there is no *verbal* dialogue in the strictest sense, there is certainly a dialogue of contrary *sentiments*, with 'fierce torment' set against 'sweet delight'. In this way, Mozart's operatic characters engage in a 'passionate dialogue' of 'feelings' akin to Heinrich Koch's theoretical description of the solo/orchestra interaction in the late-eighteenth-century concerto (although Koch does not account, admittedly, for strongly contrasting feelings as such in the concerto). In any case, there are strong connections between this operatic confrontation and the kind of confrontation witnessed in Mozart's piano concertos. We have already observed, for example, the similarity between this particular dialogue in the Act 3 Sextet and Antoine Reicha's paradigm of confrontational dialogue – most clearly exemplified in the piano concerto genre by bars 330–45 from K. 491/i; in addition, this operatic confrontation connects the *stichomythia* technique of 'taking up . . . an opponent's words', such as that identified in bars 216–22 of K. 482/i, with an *actual* 'taking up of an opponent's words' ('di questo momento' and 'quest'anima appena register or sà' in bars 113–20).

Dialogic procedures in the Act 3 Sextet are also similar, in more general respects, to dialogic procedures in those piano concerto movements combining co-operation and competition. Just as piano/orchestra dialogues at the beginning of the development sections of K. 450/i and 482/i act as catalysts for co-operative dialogue later in the movements, so textual and musical dialogue between Susanna and the other characters – straightforward three-note imitations on 'His mother' and 'His father' in bars 80–94 – acquaints her with the relational twist in the plot, and provides the catalyst for her later musical alignment (in the confrontation, for example) with the joyful Marcellina,

Bartolo and Figaro rather than the angry Count and Don Curzio. Equally, the eventual assimilation of co-operative dialogue between the piano and the orchestra in K. 450/i and 482/i finds a parallel in the gradual assimilation of the Count and Don Curzio's confrontational material into the musical fabric of the ensemble. While the Count and Don Curzio's first two statements alternate strictly with the statements of Figaro/Susanna/Marcellina/Bartolo (bars 111–15, Example 31), their third is overlapped by two beats (bars 116–17) and their fourth juxtaposed with the end of the group's preceding phrase and the beginning of the next (bars 119–21). Crucially, the orchestral support for the Count's and Don Curzio's confrontational material disappears after bars 119–21 and the interjections stop. Although for the remainder of the sextet their material remains rhythmically distinct from that of the other characters (and the orchestra) and continues to express 'fierce torment' as opposed to 'sweet delight', the musical contrast is by no means as remarkable as in the dialogic confrontation. In fact, the dotted-quaver/semiquaver rhythms characteristic of their material earlier in the ensemble and in the confrontation, progressively diminish (two in bar 124, one in bar 127) and then disappear altogether. Thus, musical relations between Mozart's operatic characters, like those between his concerto 'characters', evolve in stages, rather than in the abrupt manner of a much-derided *coup de théâtre.*

The Act 2 Trio in *Figaro* (No. 13, Susanna/Count/Countess), like the Act 3 Sextet, follows a similar dialogic trajectory to another piano concerto that combines co-operation and competition, K. 449/i. In dramatic terms, the trio exhibits only the very slightest of 'resolutions' – the Count is initially obstinate in his demand to open the closet, but by the end agrees with the Countess (he is unaware of Susanna's presence) that a scandal must be avoided – in contrast to more emphatic resolutions in K. 449/i (see Chapter Three). Yet Mozart combines a quick succession of relational unease and resolution to similar effect in both the concerto movement and the operatic ensemble. In the first section of the trio, the Count and Countess engage in a 4 + 4-bar dialogue in which the phrases are set in dynamic, rhythmic and textural opposition (bars 14–22), and an overlapping three-way dialogue (with Susanna) where the music digresses uncertainly to the dominant minor (bars 23–34);[24] the more co-operative split-theme and antecedent-consequent dialogues are sung only by the similarly-minded Susanna and Countess (bars 36–40 and 55–61). As we have already noticed, the lead into the reprise is also marked by a confrontational dialogue between the Count and Countess (bars 63–71). Initially in the reprise the Count and Countess intensify their opposition (bars 78–89, corresponding to 14–22), with the Count effecting a digression to A♭ – he 'must go the Countess one better'[25] – and thus lending added weight to the opposition between his phrases and those of the Countess. Later however, at the point at

[24] 'Uncertainly', as it is difficult to pinpoint whether the modal digression occurs at the Count's entry in bar 29 or the Countess's in bar 31.

[25] See Allanbrook, *Rhythmic Gesture*, p. 118.

which material from the end of the first section (bars 45–61) is extended to conclude the number (bars 109–46) and the shared desire to avoid scandal is expressed, all three characters unite in a *tour de force* of co-operative dialogue. The passage in which Susanna's partially chromatic quaver ascent (bars 115–17) grows from the full orchestra's (and the Count's/Countess's) preceding chromatic oscillation (bars 114–15) corresponds to bars 50–3 in the first section; but the Count's chromatic ascent (G–G♯–A, bars 119–21), which dialogues with Susanna's line, and the subsequent three-note vocal imitations (Count, Countess, Susanna, bars 122–4) are new additions. The dialogue becomes still more elaborate in the final bars (see Example 32): the dialogue of chromatic material (bars 129–32, corresponding to bars 114–17) is extended to Susanna's and the Count's melodic lines (bars 135–6, 139–40) and to the E–E♭–E movement in the oboe (bars 140–2); and the concluding vocal melody is dialogued, for the first time, by all three singers (Susanna, bars 134–6; Countess, bars 138–40; Count, bars 142–4). In short, Mozart delicately balances musical expressions of relational unease and *slight* resolution in the reprise of the Act 2 Trio, just as he uses confrontational interaction in conjunction with – and ultimately as a reinforcement of – co-operative piano/orchestra dialogue in the corresponding section (i.e. the recapitulation) of K. 449/i.

Dialogue and Co-operation: *Idomeneo*, *Entführung*, *Figaro*, *Don Giovanni* and Mozart's Piano Concertos

Idomeneo and Entführung

As we observed in Chapter 4, the reinforced co-operation model of piano/orchestra relations (intimate dialogue, opposition, reinforced intimate dialogue, coinciding with the solo exposition, development and recapitulation sections) established itself firmly in the first movements of the Viennese piano concertos of 1782–6 and led to a high degree of sophistication in dialogic interaction. Although the dialogic refinement and intricacy apparent in the reinforced co-operation model of Mozart's concertos are rivalled on a consistent basis only by arias and ensembles in *Figaro* and *Don Giovanni* (see below), they are foreshadowed in isolated arias and ensembles from *Idomeneo* and *Entführung*.

Although *Idomeneo* on the whole features far fewer interactional subtleties than Mozart's later concertos and operas, several of its arias highlight types of intricate dialogue that resurface in subsequent works. In Elettra's aria 'Idol mio', No. 13, for example, solo/orchestra dialogue elegantly bridges the gap between the 'exposition' and the 'recapitulation',[26] in the same way as piano/orchestra dialogue creates smooth segues into the recapitulations of K. 413/i (bars

[26] Julian Rushton discusses aria forms in *Idomeneo* and their relationships to sonata structures in *W. A. Mozart: Idomeneo*, pp. 99–105.

Example 32. Mozart, *Le nozze di Figaro*, Act 2 Trio, bars 129-46.

229–36), 450/i (bars 189–97), 456/i (the bassoon's chromatic ascent passed to the oboes, flute, and bassoon in bars 229–37), 459/i (bars 241–8), and 595/i (bars 231–44). The closing figure of the aria's 'exposition' (bars 63–4) is dialogued by the second violin (bar 64) and then the first violin (bar 65), as the music modulates back to the tonic G; Elettra's melody at the beginning of the 'recapitulation' (bar 66) continues the dialogue and completes a graceful transition between sections. Elettra's later aria, No. 29a, 'D'Oreste d'Aiace', also includes a glimpse of dialogue characteristic of the piano concertos, on this occasion the kind of self-perpetuating dialogue best illustrated by the piano and orchestra in K. 459/i. (See the discussion of this movement in Chapter 6, pp. 164–6.) Expressing her utter despair that the gods have made Idamente king and Ilia his wife, Elettra dialogues with the orchestra on her concluding words, 'or a sword shall end my pain' (bars 39–49, see Example 33). Elettra's two-bar phrase (diminished 7th–B♭7, bars 39–40) is dialogued sequentially by the winds (diminished 7th, bars 41–2), who are answered in turn by Elettra's cadential figure (I6/4–V7, bar 43). The confirmation of E♭ is sidestepped in bar 44, in favour of a repetition of this pattern (bars 44–9) now cadencing in E♭ (bar 49). The bassoons and second violins then take up a three-bar chromatic descent (E♭–D–D♭–C, bars 49–51) that dialogues the chromatic descents in the cellos and basses from the preceding exchange (B–B♭–A, bars 39–41 and 44–6): dialogue, as it were, begets dialogue.[27] Finally, No. 24, in which the Chorus and the High Priest reflect sorrowfully on Idomeneo's vow to sacrifice to Neptune the first person he sees (i.e. his son Idamente) after surviving the storm, follows a procedure for introducing the soloist that becomes standard practice in the Viennese piano concertos. As we have seen in Chapter Four, Mozart often introduces the piano into the solo expositions of the first movements of his concertos in a dialogue with the orchestra that elaborates corresponding dialogue from the orchestral exposition. He engages in a similar procedure for the introduction of the High Priest into No. 24 of *Idomeneo.* Initially, the Chorus takes part in an antecedent-consequent dialogue with the winds (bars 11–15). This dialogue reappears among the winds and the flute/first violins at the entrance of the High Priest, but with an added twist: the High Priest provides a second consequent concurrently with the original consequent (bars 25–6, 27–8) that, in fact, better complements the antecedent than the original consequent. (The High Priest's consequent is almost identical rhythmically to the antecedent, replacing the crotchet at the end of the antecedent with two quavers.)

In spite of the precedents in *Idomeneo* for various dialogic procedures common to piano/orchestra interaction in the Viennese piano concertos, there are few precursors in the opera – with the possible exception of rudimentary instances in 'Idol Mio', No. 13, and the High Priest/Chorus ensemble, No. 24 – for the reinforced co-operation paradigm of solo/orchestra relations (i.e. intimate dialogue – opposition – reinforced intimate dialogue). In the 'recapitulations' or reprises from *Idomeneo*'s arias, Mozart rarely adds much to the solo/orchestra dialogue from earlier sections, a common feature of the first movements of his Viennese piano concertos as we have seen in Chapter Four. The arias No. 2 'Non ho colpo' (Idamente), No. 4 'Tutti nel cor vi sento' (Elettra), No. 7 'Il padre adorato' (Idamente), No. 10 'Se il tuo duol' (Arbace), No. 19 'Zeffiretti lusinghieri' (Ilia), No. 29a 'D'Oreste d'Aiace' (Elettra) and No. 30a 'Torna la pace' (Idomeneo) are typical in this respect.

Solo/orchestra dialogue in *Entführung*'s arias and dialogue between singers in

[27] At the reappearance of this passage in C minor (bars 93–103) the harmonic pattern is modified (bars 93–6 corresponding to bars 39–42 include two bars of diminished harmony, one-and-a-half bars of C minor, and two beats of VI) and the accompanying chromatic descents are omitted.

Example 33. Mozart, *Idomeneo*, No. 29a 'D'Oreste', bars 39-51.

its ensembles offer closer parallels with piano/orchestra dialogue in the Viennese piano concertos than the corresponding numbers in *Idomeneo.* This is particularly true of the centrepiece of *Entführung*, Constanze's aria 'Martern aller Arten'. Since the aria is cast in an adapted concerto form, it is a natural place in which to look for interactional parallels with Mozart's concertos.[28] In addition, several thematic foreshadowings of the Viennese piano concertos (for example, bars 19–21 of 'Martern' are invoked in bars 7–8 of K. 467/i and bars 19–20 of 482/i, and bars 24–5 of 'Martern' in bars 115–16 of K. 414/i) suggest the possibility of other connections as well. In fact, thematic and procedural affinities between this aria and Mozart's subsequent Viennese piano concertos are numerous. The semiquaver scales in K. 414/i dialogued between the piano and the orchestra from the first theme to the orchestral tutti (bars 76–82, see Example 19, p. 83) and then from the end of the solo exposition to the beginning of the development (bars 141–5), are anticipated by similar scalic dialogue in 'Martern', first among the instrumental soloists immediately before

[28] See Feldman's 'simplified representation' of the form of 'Martern aller Arten' in 'Staging the Virtuoso', in *Mozart's Piano Concertos*, ed. Zaslaw, p. 172. (My analysis adopts Feldman's sectional designations.) Thomas Bauman states: '"Martern aller Arten" moves into clear dramatic focus if we hear it not as an expression of Constanze's defiance itself but of her struggle for this new-found spirit of resolve, a struggle which encompasses both proud derision and earnest pleading'. He then asks rhetorically: 'If so, what better vehicle than the trappings of the concerto?' See Bauman, *Die Entführung aus dem Serail* (Cambridge: Cambridge University Press, 1987), p. 81.

the second theme (bars 87–90) and then (as in K. 414/i) from the end of the solo exposition to the beginning of the 'middle ritornello' (bars 113–30). The second theme of the aria (bars 24ff and 93ff) also anticipates thematic material and dialogic procedures from the first movements of the Viennese piano concertos. The repeated falling thirds in crotchet-quaver rhythms, the thematic presentation in thirds, and the split-phrase dialogue embedded in an antecedent-consequent dialogue (bars 93–100, see Example 34) all reappear in the second theme of K. 459/i (bars 131–8, see Example 53 in Chapter 6, p. 167),[29] while the melodic and textural thirds coupled with split-phrase dialogue re-emerge among the winds in bars 28–32 of K. 467/i. The solo flute and oboe's subtle elaboration of the second bar of the consequent also foreshadows the piano's elaboration of the consequent to the main theme of K. 453/i. Just as bars 29 and 98 of 'Martern aller Arten' draw the solo flute and oboe closer to the clarinets and bassoons than at the corresponding point of the antecedent (by virtue of descending scales that reappear in bars 30 and 99), so bars 80 and 81 of K. 453/i bring the piano closer to the echoed material in the flute and oboe (bar 82) than at the parallel moment of the antecedent, through semiquaver elaborations (see Chapter 4, and Example 17, p. 80).

Example 34. Mozart, *Die Entfuehrung aus dem Serail*, No. 11 ('Martern aller Arten'), bars 93-100.

[29] The theme from K. 459/i is presented in 6ths, that is, inverted 3rds.

In addition to specific connections with the Viennese piano concertos, 'Martern aller Arten' – featuring four instrumental soloists, a vocal soloist and a full, accompanying orchestra – anticipates their high level of dialogic activity to a greater extent than any other aria in Mozart's pre-Viennese operas. The 'introductory ritornello' includes: split-theme dialogue (bars 4–19) between the soloists; split-theme and antecedent-consequent dialogue between the soloists and the orchestra (bars 24–31); overlapping dialogue in which the oboe and cello soloists copy the texture and contour of the strings' writing while the flute and violin soloists dialogue ascending arpeggios (bars 30–5); octave-ascending semiquaver scales that are imitated among the soloists and themselves echo the preceding octave ascent in the violins (bars 36–42); a staccato figure dialogued between violin/cello and oboe/flute soloists (bars 46–8); and semiquaver patterns passed among the soloists (bars 57–9). In turn, Constanze, the instrumental soloists and the orchestra elaborate dialogue from the 'introductory ritornello' in the 'solo exposition', as do the piano and the orchestra in the solo expositions of the concertos (see Chapter Four). After the second theme (bars 93–100, Example 34), for example, Constanze and the solo violin take up the concluding figure from the consequent (bars 99–100 imitated in bars 100–1) almost unchanged, and are imitated in diminution by the turn-like semiquavers (bar 102) in the solo flute and oboe; the pattern is then repeated with Constanze and the solo oboe answered by the solo flute and violin (bars 102–4). Constanze subsequently modifies the semiquaver motif, preserving the original oscillation and turn-like writing (bars 106 and 108), while accompanying figurations are simultaneously passed from the solo cello to the solo violin (bars 105–8). Also, the imitation of running semiquavers in the 'solo exposition' is extended considerably from the 'opening ritornello'; they are now passed freely among the instrumental soloists and Constanze at the end of the section (bars 113–27) and are taken up by the first and second violins at the beginning of the ritornello (bars 129–32), effecting a smooth transition to the ritornello. In short, Constanze – like the piano soloist in the majority of the solo expositions from the first movements of Mozart's concertos – is gracefully integrated into the dialogic fabric of the piece, and helps to add subtlety on occasion to dialogue from the 'opening ritornello'.

While 'Martern aller Arten' is exceptional in *Entführung* for its length and its extraordinary orchestration, it is by no means the only number in the opera to foreshadow interactional procedures from the Viennese piano concertos. The Quartet No. 16 (Blonde, Constanze, Belmonte, Pedrillo), for example, uses intimate and oppositional musical dialogue to underscore evolving on-stage relations between the characters, tracing a musico-dramatic pattern analogous to the reinforced co-operation pattern of piano/orchestra relations in the concertos. The tonal scheme of this ensemble and the broad development in the relations between the characters in the plot (the first reconciliation of the two pairs of lovers) coincide as follows:

Allegro [Joy and hope among all four characters]: D–A (bar 47)–D (bar 60)
Andante [Pedrillo and Belmonte doubt Blonde's and Constanze's fidelity; their doubts are alleviated]: g (bar 90)–c (bar 103)–B♭ (bar 112)–c (bar 124)–E♭ (bar 143)–b♭ (bar 156)–d (bar 167)–c (bar 174)–B♭ (bar 180)–g (bar 187)
Andantino [Pedrillo and Belmonte are happy; Blonde and Constanze are a little annoyed at their suspicions]: A (bar 193)
Allegretto [Pedrillo and Belmonte ask for forgiveness from Blonde and Constanze and it is eventually granted]: A–D (bar 251)
Allegro [The couples are joyfully reconciled and together praise love]: D

In the first *Allegro* section the joyous mood is accentuated by musical dialogue between the characters (split-theme, antecedent/consequent and imitation for Constanze and Belmonte in bars 10–23, 33–41 and 41–4 respectively, and thematic dialogue for Pedrillo and Blonde in bars 48–59), and between the four characters together and the orchestra (alternation of one-bar units in bars 70–74, 79–83). The *Andante* again features musical dialogue between the singers (those who are engaged in literal dialogue and those who are not). However, dialogue is situated for the most part in modulatory passages (for example, Belmonte and Constanze in bars 92–107, Pedrillo and Blonde in bars 118–27, and among all four characters in bars 168–87) in which tonal 'disagreements' accentuate on-stage relational uncertainty, and/or in passages immediately preceding abrupt, unprepared modulations (for example to E♭ in bar 143 and D minor in bar 167, prefaced by dialogue in bars 126–39 and 157–64 respectively).

While we have already observed similarities between tonal 'disputes' in Mozart's operatic and concerto confrontations, we can also draw attention to a specific procedural parallel – which has ramifications for character relations – between an evolving harmonic progression preceding the abrupt modulations in the *Andante* section of the *Entführung* quartet and an harmonic progression emerging over the course of the first movement of Mozart's Piano Concerto No. 17 in G, K. 453. Bars 96–7, 141–2, 165–6 of the quartet comprise augmented 6th–V progressions implying g, g and B♭ respectively, but moving suddenly instead to c, E♭ and d in the last two instances after ostentatious pauses. A different combination of characters carries the progression and the subsequent modulation on each occasion (Belmonte and Constanze; Constanze and Belmonte/Pedrillo; Constanze and Blonde), symbolising the relational confusion on stage. The augmented 6th–V progression reappears at the point at which all four characters sing together (bars 191–2), 'correctly' resolved for the first time (to A at the beginning of the *Andantino*, bar 193) by the orchestra. Although only Belmonte and Pedrillo, now convinced of the innocence of their partners, are happy at this stage (Constanze and Blonde are annoyed at Belmonte's and Pedrillo's suspicions), their intimate *musical* bond with Constanze and Blonde is re-established through the 'correct' completion of the augmented 6th–V–I progression (see Example 35), a symptom of relational unease in its earlier, incomplete incarnation. The bond among the group is then consolidated by collective dialogue with the orchestra (bars 193–6 [winds], extended in bars 197–204 [voices]). In fact, the orchestra plays a vital role in the process of musical reconciliation, stepping in for the singers as it were (bar 193) in order to ensure the 'correct' resolution to the augmented 6th–V progression.

It is perhaps not unreasonable to suggest that the orchestra at this juncture fulfils the kind of role specified by eighteenth-century writers such as Gluck, Grétry, Adam Smith and Ginguené (see Chapter 1); namely, expressing the true feelings of the characters more accurately than the characters themselves (especially the reconciliation not yet articulated verbally by Constanze and Blonde). In any case, the free, unencumbered dialogue in the final *Allegro* section (bar 258ff.) affirms the unambiguously joyous musical and dramatic reconciliation of the two couples. Moreover, an emphatic augmented 6th chord reappears towards the end of the ensemble in bar 348 and, again resolving to the 'correct' key (augmented 6th–V–II7–V6/5–I–vi–ii6/5–V–I in D, bars 348–54, see Example 36), strongly invokes the earlier resolution to the augmented 6th–V progression. As in bars 191–3, the chord is rendered conspicuous by musical pauses; in addition, it appears in conjunction with dialogue between the orchestra and the collective group of singers (antiphonal alternation of minims in bars 337–41 and 345–8), just as the augmented 6th–V–I progression in bars 191–3 immediately precedes dialogue between the orchestra and the collective group.

The first movement of K. 453, like the Act 2 quartet in *Entführung*, highlights an evolving augmented 6th progression that has important relational implications, in this case for the piano and the orchestra. In bars 48–9 Mozart colours the tonic G with a V–♭VI cadence, reconfirming G via a ♭VI–vii6/5 of V–I6/4–vi–ii–V–I progression (bars 53–7). The theme from bar 49 in modified form is treated sequentially at the beginning of the development section (B♭, bar 184; A minor, bar 192); in turn, ascending and descending figures related motivically to the woodwinds' writing at the beginning of the development reappear in the piano at the end of the section (bars 219–22). These bars are preceded by a variation of the harmonic progression from bars 53–7: the dominant (bar 219) follows vii6/5 of V–German augmented 6th (bars 217–18), rather than ♭VI–vii6/5 of V harmony (bars 53–4); and the German augmented 6th–V progression is repeated in the piano (bars 222–3), while the woodwind sound octave pedal Ds. Thus, the piano synthesises the motivic element from bar 184ff. with the harmonic progression from bars 53–7, altering the latter in such a way as to show that ♭VI harmony has the potential to function as fully-fledged German 6th harmony. In fact, when the orchestra's theme from bar 49 reappears immediately before the cadenza (bars 319–27), the diminished harmony of bar 54 is replaced by an emphatic and authoritative German 6th (bars 323–4). The piano and the orchestra have therefore grasped the potential of ♭VI to function as a German 6th from a kind of long-range, piano/orchestra 'dialogue' of thematic and harmonic material over the course of the movement (orchestra, bars 49–57; piano, bars 217–25; orchestra, bars 319–27).

Ultimately, the evolution of the augmented 6th progression in both the

Example 35. Mozart, *Die Entfuehrung aus dem Serail*, No. 16 (Quartet), bars 188-204.

Example 36. Mozart, *Die Entfuehrung aus dem Serail,* No. 16 (Quartet), bars 345-58.

Entführung quartet and the first movement of K. 453 helps to reinforce the bond between characters, literal and metaphorical characters alike. As we observed in Chapter 3, the piano and the orchestra strengthen their union in the recapitulation of K. 449/i by meeting this self-imposed challenge to their co-operation in a forceful and convincing fashion. Equally, the test of the lovers' commitment to each other in the *Andante* section of the *Entführung* quartet – conveyed musically in part by the unresolved augmented 6th–V progressions – in the end intensifies their intimate relations; they are forced to reconsider and then to demonstrate their love and commitment, and cannot simply take it for granted, as they had at the beginning of the ensemble. While there is little by way of confrontation as such in K. 453/i, the evolving long-range 'dialogue' strengthens the co-operation of piano and orchestra in a way similar to the evolving progression in the quartet; it enables the piano and the orchestra to reinforce co-operative behaviour over a protracted period. The fact, moreover, that both the *Entführung* quartet and the piano concerto K. 453/i reserve their most forceful and emphatic augmented 6th progressions until the end of their respective pieces, further accentuates the teleological nature of their processes of relational reinforcement. The operatic and concerto characters give more intense, dynamic and decisive demonstrations of the strength of their bond to one another at the end of their pieces than they could possibly have given at the beginning.

Although the Act 2 Quartet has strong similarities in terms of the musical manifestations of relational development to one Mozart piano concerto in particular, another number in *Entführung* foreshadows relational procedures in the reinforced co-operation movements of the Viennese piano concertos more generally. Belmonte's aria No. 15, 'Wenn der Freude Tränen fliessen', brings dialogue techniques from stanzas 1 and 2 (*Adagio*) together at the beginning of stanza 3 (*Allegretto*, see Example 37), much as the piano and the orchestra integrate dialogue from the orchestral and solo expositions at the beginning of the recapitulations of K. 414/i, 449/i, 456/i and 459/i (see Chapter Four).[30] Stanza 1 (bars 1–36) features three instances of dialogue: the main theme (bars 9–20) elaborates and extends the violin's introductory statement (bars 1–9), although voice/orchestra dialogue is obscured by the violin's performance throughout both statements; the winds echo Belmonte's and the strings' cadential figure (bars 19–20 corresponding to bars 8–9), but are interrupted by Belmonte's exclamation 'Ach Constanze!'; and the full orchestra and Belmonte ('lohnt für wahr nicht Crösus' Pracht') dialogue three- and four-note figures (bars 26–8). In stanza 2 (bars 62–83), Belmonte and the strings echo the winds (not vice versa), with Belmonte's exclamation 'Ach Constanze!' contributing to (rather than interrupting) the exchange (bars 72–4); the dialogue on 'lohnt für wahr' (bars 76–9), however, is curtailed by another interjection from Belmonte (bar 79). The beginning of stanza 3 (Example 37) brings together full-theme and echo dialogue, the two types heard in Stanzas 1 and 2. As at the beginning of stanza 1, the voice/strings theme (bar 96ff.) is preceded by a full statement (bar 84–96), but the dialogue now rendered more explicit by the strict separation of the winds and the voice/strings. Similarly, the echo in the clarinets and bassoons (bars 108–9), corresponding to the earlier clarinet echoes (bars 8–9 and 19–20) and the voice/strings echoes from stanza 2 (bars 72–4), is no longer interrupted by Belmonte. Thus, Mozart invokes dialogic procedures from stanzas 1 and 2 in stanza 3, rendering voice/orchestra dialogue itself more exact, just as he synthesises dialogue from the orchestral and solo expositions in the recapitulations of his Viennese piano concertos, often elaborating the earlier dialogue in the process.

To be sure, the dialogue process in 'Wenn der Freude Tränen fliessen', culminating with the exchange at the beginning of stanza 3, would have been designed in part to reflect the nature of the text. Whereas the first half of the first two stanzas concern the sentiment of love in general and the second half feelings for Constanze in particular (No. 2), the third *combines* a general sentiment (the 'pain separation causes') with a specific concept ('us never meeting again' [*uns niemals wiederfinden*]), just as musically it combines the reappearance of the two types of dialogue from stanzas 1 and 2 with a specific

[30] There are significant discrepancies between the version of this aria in the *Neue Mozart Ausgabe* and the version in the commonly used Dover edition (a reprint of the *Breitkopf und Härtel* version from 1868). My bar numbers refer to the former, although I discuss only three stanzas (bars 1–36, 63–83, 84–174, excluding 125–57) in accordance with the typical performance convention for this aria.

Example 37. Mozart, *Die Entfuehrung aus dem Serail*, No. 15 ('Wenn der Freude'), bars 84-109.

procedural invocation of the beginning of the aria. However, there are indications elsewhere in *Entführung* that Mozart might not have been concerned *exclusively* with textual matters when altering musical dialogue in reprise, recapitulation or finale sections of his arias. Belmonte's aria No. 4, 'O wie ängstlich' and Constanze's arias No. 6, 'Ach ich liebte', and No. 10, 'Traurigkeit ward mir zum Lose', for example, do not feature the kind of textual directionality witnessed in 'Wenn der Freude Tränen fliessen': the characters express personal sentiments throughout each aria (Belmonte yearning for Constanze in No. 4; Constanze explaining her initial happiness in love and the pain of separation in No. 6 and voicing her sorrow and longing in No. 10), rather than a combination of personal sentiments and more general proclamations. Nevertheless, Mozart still adds dialogic subtleties to the final sections of these arias, thereby elaborating the relationship between the singer and the accompanying orchestra in spite of no obvious textual reasons for so doing. The aria No. 10 begins with a two-bar phrase (i–augmented 6th–V) presented by the winds and repeated in the strings/voice (bars 1–4). Although the same pattern occurs at the beginning of the reprise (bars 67–70), a new dimension is added: it is preceded by Constanze's repeated statements of the head motif (bars 63–6), which extend the dialogue by four bars, smooth the division between sections and – by providing V–i inflections (to C minor and D minor) rather than progressions from i to V – complement the original motif in an effective manner by reversing its harmonies. Like No. 13, 'Idol Mio', from *Idomeneo*, this procedure of inter-sectional dialogue foreshadows similar procedures in piano concerto movements such as K. 413/i, 450/i, 456/i, 459/i and 595/i. In the recapitulation of No. 6, the echoes from Constanze to the winds are altered (bars 99–101, corresponding to bars 33–5 in the exposition), and dialogue added first in bars 109–12 (initially involving the strings and winds; subsequently including Constanze, who, together with the winds, augments and elaborates the four-note repeated figure in bars 111–12, beat 1) and then in bars 115–19 (a theme split between Constanze and the winds). Lastly, the reprise of No. 4 adds a demisemiquaver dialogue (bars 70–4), in which Constanze and the orchestra combine trill-like and scalic figures, as well as echoes of Constanze and the strings in the winds (bars 85–7 and 99–101). Thus, the technique of elaborating voice/orchestra dialogue in the final sections of these three arias foreshadows – albeit in a more rudimentary fashion than the Act 2 Quartet and Belmonte's aria 'Wenn der Freude Tränen fliessen' – the technique of elaborating piano/orchestra dialogue that becomes a vital component of the reinforced co-operation paradigm in the Viennese piano concertos.

Figaro and Don Giovanni

Duets: 'Là ci darem la mano' (Don Giovanni, Zerlina) and 'Che soave zeffiretto' (Countess, Susanna)

As we have seen in Chapter Two, the 'dialogued duet' was firmly established in the operatic repertory by the middle of the eighteenth century, and frequently discussed in French theoretical literature from the second half of the eighteenth century. Patterns of dialogue and unification were standard practice in *opera buffa* duets. Typically, these duets would involve co-operative motivations – most frequently love, friendship and common goals[31] – providing an immediate point of comparison with the majority of Mozart's piano concerto movements.

[31] See Platoff, 'How Original was Mozart?', p. 109.

The duets 'Là ci darem' (*Don Giovanni*) and 'Che soave zeffiretto' (*Figaro*), two of the most popular numbers from their respective operas, are especially ripe for comparison with reinforced co-operation movements from Mozart's piano concertos. 'Là ci darem' follows the standard *buffa* duet progression 'from an intial dialogue [bars 1–49], with the two singers alternating, to passages of simultaneous, largely homophonic singing [6/8 section, bar 50ff]'[32] in which shared feelings are expressed, and is a paradigmatic example of a gradually tightening musical and dramatic bond between the characters. 'Che soave zeffiretto', following a similar pattern through intricate alternation, imitation, overlapping and unification of the voices, is one of the subtlest duets in *Figaro* and, from the perspective of character interaction, one of the most emphatically and unambiguously co-operative. In addition, the role of the orchestra as a fully-fledged interlocutor in both duets provides another point of comparison with Mozart's Viennese piano concertos.

Although musical manifestations of Don Giovanni's successful wooing of Zerlina in the vocal writing of 'Là ci darem' – shorter and shorter alternating phrases, overlapping phrases and finally phrases sung together – have been well documented,[33] less attention has been paid to the orchestra's contribution to the bonding process. To a large extent, of course, the developing musical relationship between the voices and the orchestra takes a back seat to the developing musical and dramatic relationship between Don Giovanni and Zerlina. Nevertheless, the orchestra plays a pivotal role in supporting the evolving relationship between the characters, and in establishing and reinforcing an intimate musical relationship with the singers. While Don Giovanni and Zerlina dialogue a full theme in the A section (bars 1–18), the winds provide one-bar dialogic segues between phrases that also subtly echo vocal material. In bars 4–5, 8–9 and 12–13, for example, the bassoon, oboe and bassoon echo the stepwise ascents in the vocal lines of bars 3, 7 and 11 respectively, and the winds together segue neatly from the end of one vocal phrase to the beginning of the next; in the final bar, the violins, flute and oboe echo Zerlina's A–C♯–A (bars 17–18, beat 1). The orchestra continues its dialogic echoes and segues in the B section (bars 19–29), while the vocal theme is split into alternating 2 + 2 + 2 + 4-bar phrases: the contour of the violins' motif in bar 22 echoes that of Zerlina's semiquavers in the preceding bar (A♯–B–C♯–B–A♯ and G♯–A–B–A–G♯); and the stepwise descent joining the B and A′ sections in the winds and violins (bar 29) complements the stepwise ascent in the first bar of the main theme (bar 30). Voice/orchestra dialogue returns as an echo/segue in the A′ section (bars 33–4, corresponding to bars 4–5), but is made more elaborate in the final bars (46–9, see Example 38). Here, the strings engage in intimate dialogue with Don Giovanni, joining one vocal note to the next (F♯–D, G♯–E, A–F♯) through overlapping quavers on the second beats of each bar. This also produces a split-

[32] See Platoff, 'How Original was Mozart?', p. 109.

[33] See, for example, Allanbrook's typically insightful analysis of the duet in *Rhythmic Gesture in Mozart*, pp. 262–7.

theme effect, and leads directly to the crucial moment when Zerlina complies with Don Giovanni's request ('Andiam', bars 48–9).

Example 38. Mozart, *Don Giovanni*, No. 7 ('La ci darem'), bars 46-49.

Thus, the orchestra play a pivotal role in the musical reinforcement of this duet's dramatic process. On the one hand, the subtle dialogic segues in the A section 'predict' the overlapping (and subsequent joining) of the dramatic characters; on the other hand, the voice/orchestra dialogue at the end of the A′ section (bars 46–9) *continues* the process of musical overlapping, momentarily replacing the second singer, as it were. The orchestra's intervention at this the most important dramatic juncture of the duet (bar 49) offers further evidence of their significant role in realizing dramatic development.

In addition to contributing fully to the dramatic momentum of the duet, the orchestra – together with the singers – engage in musical procedures akin to dialogic procedures in the Viennese piano concertos. Segues, for example, effect a close bond between the singers and the orchestra in the A section of the duet, as they do for the piano and the orchestra in the solo exposition of K. 488/i; equally, the duet uses its dialogic procedure to smooth the transition to the reprise, in a similar fashion to concertos such as K. 413/i and 459/i at the moment of recapitulation.

It is to the second movement of K. 449, however, that 'Là ci darem' is most comparable. Like the duet, the concerto movement combines echo/segue and thematic dialogue in the context of an ABA′ structure.[34] In the A section, the first violins echo the piano's B♭–C and A♭–B♭ leaps (bars 32 and 34) from the 'transition', and the first and second violins echo the piano's stepwise ascents from the 'second theme' (bars 42 and 44). The B section, to all intents and purposes a transposition of the A section, follows the same pattern, but now treats the main theme as an antecedent-consequent dialogue between the strings and the piano (bars 52–9). Thus, the B sections of both the duet and the concerto movement split thematic material between the 'characters' for the first time (Don Giovanni and Zerlina, and the piano and the orchestra) and retain

[34] In his tabular categorization of the formal types of the second and third movements of Mozart's piano concertos, James Webster lists K. 449/ii as a hybrid of concerto, rondo, and ABA form. See Webster, 'Are Mozart's Concertos "Dramatic"?' p. 113. I shall preserve this hybrid quality by referring to traditional sonata designations (transition, second theme, etc.) within an ABA′ context, and shall call the section preceding the entrance of the soloist (bars 1–22) the 'orchestral introduction'.

the A section's orchestral echoes/segues. In the A′ section, Mozart again splits the main theme between the strings and the piano, bringing together the orchestral version from the 'orchestral introduction' (bars 80–3, corresponding to bars 1–4) with the more ornate style of the piano statement from the A section (see bars 84–9 and bars 23–30), and again incorporates echoes into the 'second theme', on this occasion in the piano (bars 99 and 101). The reprise also restates material from the 'orchestral introduction' (bars 11–22) for the first time (bars 90–3 and 112–19), subjecting it to the two types of dialogue, echo and thematic (in bars 91, 93 and 112–19 respectively), that dominate piano/orchestra interaction in the movement.[35] These two types are then fused exquisitely in the concluding bars (see Example 39): the figure from bar 22, subsequently used as echo material in the A section (bars 32, 34), reappears in an antecedent-consequent dialogue that continues to preserve a kind of echo effect in the piano (bars 119–23).

Example 39. Mozart, Piano Concerto K. 449, 2nd Movement, bars 119-23.

The second movement of K. 449 and 'Là ci darem', like a number of the first movements of Mozart's piano concertos, utilise specific dialogic procedures in order to establish and reinforce intimate relations between the soloist(s) and the orchestra. Both pieces, moreover, combine echo/segue and thematic procedures in new instances of dialogue at the end of the reprise sections, thus bringing these sections to an impressive close through a blending of the two techniques.

As in 'Là ci darem' and K. 449/ii, parallels between dialogue in Mozart's exquisite duet 'Che soave zeffiretto' from *Figaro* and the second movement of his Piano Concerto No. 19 in F, K. 459, underscore the similarly dramatic nature of reinforced intimate relations among Mozart's operatic and concerto characters. Although the pieces are different from a structural perspective – K. 459/ii is an intricate slow-movement sonata form with an added orchestral exposition and 'Che soave zeffiretto' a pastorale, with a modified reprise – they

[35] In spite of the first violins doubling the piano in bars 116–19, I have characterised bars 112–19 as strings-piano dialogue. The piano states a more syntactically 'appropriate' answer to bars 112–15 than the first violins, preserving the original register and arpeggiated accompaniment.

are similar from a procedural point of view. In bypassing a middle section, for example, both pieces move immediately from establishing intimate relations between the characters in the initial sections, to reinforcing intimate relations in the recapitulation and 'reprise' sections. In addition, both pieces create mellifluous, florid, and self-perpetuating dialogue between the soloist(s) and winds (in particular), which has few precedents or antecedents in Mozart's operatic and concerto repertories.

The second movement of the Piano Concerto K. 459 is a supreme example of pure, unadulterated co-operation between the piano and the orchestra that increases in intensity over the course of the movement. As in the first movement, the piano begins the solo exposition with a near-exact repetition of the main theme as presented by the orchestra in the orchestral exposition (bars 26–30, see Example 40, corresponding to bars 1–5). The subsequent dialogue (bar 31ff., Example 40) immediately demonstrates the piano and orchestra's sensitivity towards each other's preceding material, thus establishing an intimate bond between them. The winds, for example, adopt the piano's turns, even though the turns are not part of the original presentation in the orchestral exposition. The piano (right hand) then begins in bar 34 exactly where its oboe and bassoon interlocutors leave off (D, F), preserving both the winds' textural thirds and the turn figures (bars 36 and 37) to produce an extremely smooth dialogic segue between the head motif and the 'new' transitional material (winds, bar 34–5, piano bar 35ff.). (This procedure is strikingly similar to the procedure at the corresponding moment in the transition section from the solo exposition of the first movement [bars 106–111], where imitative entries and an overlapping A″ in the flute and piano also effect a smooth dialogic segue; see Example 52 in Chapter 6, p. 166.) The piano and orchestra follow the same pattern in the second theme section: after a 4 + 4-bar dialogue (bars 44–51), the piano picks up the first violin's semiquaver B–D–G–D accompanying figure from bar 51 to initiate the ensuing phrase (bar 52, see Example 41), again using dialogue to segue neatly from one passage to the next. Finally, the split-theme dialogue at the end of the solo exposition (bars 79–82) continues to illustrate the piano and orchestra's sensitivity towards each other's material. Just as the winds embellish their part of the second antecedent and consequent with semiquavers (bars 81 and 82, beat 1), so the piano follows suit with triplet semiquavers (bars 81 and 82, beat 2).

The recapitulation of K. 459/ii reinforces co-operative interaction between the piano and the orchestra by adding new dialogue, and by ending with a dialogic *tour de force.* In bars 102 and 133–6, for example, piano/orchestra dialogue is created from previously undialogued material, the solo exposition's segue technique now reappearing in new contexts. The piano's semiquavers in the bars preceding the second theme (99–101, corresponding to 40–2) include chromatic descents (D–C♯–C) that are passed to the winds (G–F♯–F–E) and then lead directly into the reprise of the second theme (bar 103ff.). Later, the winds dialogue the beginning of the piano's theme from bar 74 (bars 133–6), and the piano in turn embellishes a fragment of the oboe's melody (F–E–A, bars

Example 40. Mozart, Piano Concerto K. 459, 2nd Movement, bars 26-37.

135, beat 2 – 136, beat 1 elaborated into G♯–B–A–C semiquavers, bars 136–37) as a segue to its cadential phrase. Bars 146–9 again cast in dialogue material not treated in this way earlier in the movement (the antecedent-consequent at the end of the orchestral exposition in bars 21–5); moreover, the piano's second consequent (bar 149), provides a rhythmic segue to the ensuing semiquaver

Example 41. Mozart, Piano Concerto K. 459, 2nd Movement, bars 50-53.

scales. (See Example 58 in Chapter 6, p. 175, for bars 146–59.) The final ten bars (150–9) feature imitations of these semiquaver scales among the piano and the winds, and overlap with a kind of antecedent-consequent exchange (bars 154–8) in which the piano brings the strings' phrase to a tonal close (I–vi–ii6/5–V7–vi answered by V6/V–I6/4–V7–I).

Musical dialogue among the Countess, Susanna and the orchestra in 'Che soave zeffiretto' is as fluid and self-perpetuating as dialogue between the piano and the orchestra in K. 459/ii, and equally representative of co-operative intent.[36] From the perspective of the plot, there can be few more co-operative ventures in Mozart's entire operatic repertory: the Countess and Susanna share wholeheartedly in their desire to trap the Count, with the Countess dictating a letter (to be sent by Susanna) to this effect.[37] The common cause of the characters is supported musically by diverse dialogue among the Countess, Susanna and the winds. In the first section (bars 1–36), Susanna imitates the winds (bars 2–3) and vice versa (bars 27–8); the winds imitate the Countess (bars 6–7) and she likewise mimics Susanna (F–C, C–F, bars 10–11), both in such a way as to segue smoothly between phrases; themes are repeated in dialogue (bars 1–6, 29–32) and split between interlocutors (bars 14–17); beginnings of phrases 'grow' from the ends of preceding phrases (the stepwise ascent in bars 17–18 and the chromatic ascent in bar 21); and the voices join together as is typical in *buffa* duets (bars 34–6). In the 'reprise' (bars 37–61), thematic repetition in dialogue is elaborated through an overlapping of individual statements (bars 37–43, 45–9); imitation extends to 'accompanying' figures (the oboe's repeated quavers in bars 50–1 imitating the Countess's and Susanna's oscillating semiquavers in bars 48–9); the voices join together for a longer period of time than in the previous section (bars 50–6, 60–1); and a new type of dialogue, an antecedent-consequent, is heard between Susanna and the Countess (bars 56–60). Thus, even in this ostensibly 'simple' duet, dialogue is gently intensified in the reprise.

As with 'Là ci darem' and K. 449/ii, the general parallels between 'Che soave zeffiretto' and K. 459/ii testify to the analogous nature of dramatic interaction in Mozart's operas and concertos rather than to hard-and-fast connections between the specific pieces. Just as the reinforcement of co-operative relations in K. 459/ii involves the piano and the orchestra adding new dialogue to the recapitulation in such a way as to highlight the same segue technique that underscored interaction in the solo exposition, so the intensification of musical

[36] James Webster and Jessica Waldoff also draw attention to the remarkably subtle interaction among Susanna, the Countess and 'a third, equally essential agent' (the oboe-bassoon pair), focussing on bars 1–18. See Waldoff and Webster, 'Operatic Plotting', in *Wolfgang Amadè Mozart*, ed. Sadie, pp. 270–2. See also Allanbrook, *Rhythmic Gesture*, pp. 145–8.

[37] Reinhold Schlötterer postulates that Mozart modified Da Ponte's text for 'Che soave zeffiretto' in order to represent the Countess's dictation of the letter to Susanna. See 'Das Duettino "Che soave zeffiretto" in *Le nozze di Figaro*', in *Festschrift Rudolf Bockholdt zum 60. Geburtstag*, eds. Norbert Dubowy and Soren Meyer-Eller (Pfaffenhofen: Ludwig, 1990), pp. 233–46.

dialogue among the Countess, Susanna and winds in the 'reprise' of 'Che soave zeffiretto' involves interlocutors elaborating specific dialogic procedures from earlier in the duet. Although the intimate dialogue characteristic of the duet can be explained as an extremely refined musical reaction to the dramatic situation and pastoral atmosphere, the process of dialogic intensification in the 'reprise' cannot.[38] In dramatic terms, the reinforcement of relations in 'Che soave zeffiretto' – like the analogous procedure in K. 459/ii – has a specifically *musical* interactive dimension.

Trio: 'Ah, taci, ingiusto core' (Don Giovanni, Donna Elvira, Leporello)

Like 'Là ci darem' and 'Che soave zeffiretto', the Act 2 Trio from *Don Giovanni* ('Ah, taci, ingiusto core') demonstrates striking similarities with Mozart's reinforced co-operation movements.[39] The exposition of the trio, for example, introduces each of the three soloists in dialogue with the orchestra (bars 1–4, 14–15, 16–17), just as the solo expositions of Mozart's concertos introduce the piano in dialogue with the orchestra; the development section coincides with the principal moment of relational tension (see above), as do the development sections, by and large, of Mozart's first movements; and the recapitulation elaborates voice/orchestra dialogue from the exposition in much the same way that recapitulations of piano concerto movements elaborate piano/orchestra dialogue from the solo expositions (see Chapter Four).

In addition to the overt procedural parallels between 'Ah, taci' and Mozart's piano concertos outlined above, there are also more covert connections between this operatic ensemble and individual concerto movements. As in K. 488/i (see Examples 21–3, p. 87) and K. 449/ii, for example, dialogic segues in the trio's exposition demonstrate the orchestra's lively interaction with the soloists (see bars 4, 8, 12, 22, 26). In addition, semiquaver motifs in the winds, imitated by Leporello and Don Giovanni (bars 14–17), provide smooth segues between vocal material, preserving the fluidity of the melodic line. A similar combina-

[38] For a discussion of the pastoral atmosphere of the duet, see Allanbrook, *Rhythmic Gesture*, pp. 145–8. Webster and Waldoff state that Susanna and the Countess 'merge into a single persona, beyond class' in the second half of the duet, but do not go into musical detail on this point. See 'Operatic Plotting', in *Wolfgang Amadè Mozart*, ed. Sadie, p. 274.

[39] My discussion of 'Ah taci' will follow the lead of critics such as Joseph Kerman and Julian Rushton in adopting sonata form designations. See Joseph Kerman, *Opera as Drama* (Berkeley: University of California Press, 1988 [rev. edn]), pp. 63–8; and Rushton, *W. A. Mozart: Don Giovanni* (Cambridge: Cambridge University Press, 1982), p. 92. John Platoff, among others, has recently warned against characterising operatic numbers in this way, as 'musical demarcation of [sonata form] divisions may not be crucial in an operatic number'. See 'The buffa aria', pp. 99–120, at p. 119. The onset of 'exposition', 'development' and 'recapitulation' sections of 'Ah taci', however, closely correspond to changes in the action on stage: Donna Elvira addresses Leporello and Don Giovanni from the balcony in the exposition; Don Giovanni tries to persuade Donna Elvira of his love for her in the development; and all three characters express their feelings in the recapitulation. In this context, sonata designations seem appropriate. For a recent discussion of sonata procedures in *Figaro, Don Giovanni* and *Così*, see Tim Carter, 'Mozart, Da Ponte and the Ensemble: Methods in Progress?', in *Wolfgang Amadè Mozart: Essays on his Life and Music*, ed. Sadie, pp. 241–9.

tion of imitation and smooth segue characterises the dialogue between Don Giovanni and the first violins in bars 53–4: the rhythm and melodic shape of Don Giovanni's closing gesture and the violins' initial figure gracefully merge the end of the development and the beginning of the recapitulation (bar 53–4), just as piano/orchestra dialogue in bars 189–97 of K. 450/i (see Example 10, p. 63), bars 241–53 of K. 459/i (Chapter 6, Example 54) and especially bars 231–45 of K. 595/i elegantly bridges the corresponding sectional divide in Mozart's piano concertos.

As well as effecting a smooth sectional transition, musical dialogue in the trio's recapitulation reinforces relational development between Don Giovanni, Donna Elvira and Leporello. The voices unite for much of the recapitulation, a standard practice in a *buffa* ensemble but one that also reflects in this instance a *slight* development in terms of character relations in the plot.[40] (Donna Elvira disparages Don Giovanni's protestations of love in the development section, but asks the gods to 'protect my trusting heart' in the recapitulation.) Whereas the three voices are introduced separately in dialogue with the orchestra in the exposition, they are reintroduced *together* in dialogue with the orchestra at the beginning of the recapitulation (bars 54–6). A procedure from the exposition is therefore modified in such a way as to accentuate the relational development. In a similar vein, dialogue between the orchestra and the voices in bars 67–70 elaborates the corresponding dialogue from the exposition (bars 14–17): the winds now perform their semiquaver figure in thirds in order to accommodate the new combined presentations in thirds by Elvira and Don Giovanni and by Don Giovanni and Leporello (bars 68–9).

Although the elaborations of voice/orchestra dialogue in the recapitulation of the trio reinforce the slight dramatic development in the plot, they also correspond in musical terms to procedures in the piano concertos. As we have seen in Chapters Three and Four, the recapitulations of movements such as K. 414/i, 449/i, 456/i, and 459/i commence with piano/orchestra dialogue that invokes – procedurally and thematically – the beginnings of *both* the orchestral and solo expositions. Similarly, the beginning of the recapitulation of 'Ah, taci' not only restates the main theme from the opening, but also invokes the exposition's *procedure* of introducing the characters in dialogue with the orchestra, now presenting the singers as a single unit rather than as three separate individuals.

Arias: 'Batti, batti' (Zerlina), 'Voi che sapete' (Cherubino), 'Deh vieni' (Susanna)

The evolving relationships between the vocal soloists and the orchestra in the arias 'Batti, batti' (*Don Giovanni*), 'Voi che sapete' (*Figaro*) and 'Deh vieni' (*Figaro*) follow trajectories similar to the evolving relationship between the

[40] As Allanbrook points out, the trio 'sets up a situation which is not intended to have its culmination until the painful sextet (II, 6) when Elvira discovers her "lover" is not Don Giovanni, but Leporello'. See *Rhythmic Gesture*, p. 250.

piano and the orchestra in the reinforced co-operation concerto movements. Co-operation as such between the soloist and the orchestra is of more direct significance in a concerto movement than in an operatic aria, because there is no text to divert attention away from solo/orchestra interaction. Nevertheless, the orchestra, actively participating in dialogue with the singer in these arias, acts as a sensitive *confidante* to the character, emphasising this role more and more as the arias progress.[41]

'Batti, batti' is characterised by dialogue between Zerlina and the orchestra, in which Zerlina's line adapts itself subtly to orchestral material. (For bars 16–28, see Example 42.) In bars 16–24, for example, an antecedent in the violins (bars 16–18, repeated in 20–22) is answered by a consequent in the winds and the voices/strings (bars 18–20, 22–4), split in such a way as to segue delicately from one interlocutor to the next by reversing the C–B semiquavers (bars 19, 23). The subsequent bars merge accompaniment and melody through dialogue (bars 24–7). Here, the obbligato cello's 'accompanimental' figures halt momentarily for the first time, producing an overlapping dialogue with Zerlina's 'melodic' material. Dialogue between Zerlina and the orchestra is most exquisite, however, in the transition to the reprise and the beginning of the reprise itself (bars 34–40, Example 43). The falling semiquavers in the winds (bars 35–6) are passed to the strings/voice, with the interlocutors overlapping for one crotchet (bar 36, beat 2), and lead directly into the reprise; Zerlina and the strings then elaborate the main theme in the style of the winds' falling semiquavers (bars 37–8). Just as piano/orchestra dialogue in Mozart's concertos brings together the beginnings of the orchestral and solo expositions at the commencement of the recapitulation, reinforcing co-operation between the interlocutors in the process (see, for example, K. 414/i, 449/i, 456/i, 459/i), so voice/orchestra dialogue in 'Batti, batti' brings together specific techniques – overlapping dialogue and the smooth segue – at the beginning of the reprise, reinforcing the intimacy of voice/orchestra relations. Although the process in 'Batti, batti' does not appear to have been motivated by *textual* considerations (bars 36–7 mark the beginning of a straightforward textual repetition), it acts as an important indicator of relational reinforcement, one that coincides – as in Mozart's reinforced co-operation concerto movements – with the beginning of the reprise.

[41] James Webster describes the orchestra's role in Pamina's aria 'Ach ich fuhls' from *Die Zauberflöte* in a somewhat similar way. Building on the theories of Edward Cone (*The Composer's Voice* [Berkeley, 1974]), Webster writes: 'the two agents, Pamina and the orchestra, are complementary: her primary mode of expression is despair, intermingled however with symptoms of shock; theirs is shock punctuated by brief outbursts of despair. Each incorporates and reflects the nature of the other'. In its postlude, the orchestra 'transforms her disjointed utterances into a complex, coherent gesture, appropriate to her inner nobility and the high purposes of the opera'. See Webster, 'Cone's "personae" and the Analysis of Opera', in *College Music Symposium* 29 (1989), pp. 44–65, at pp. 49, 50. For the important role of the orchestra in several numbers from *Zauberflöte*, see Thomas Bauman, 'At the North Gate: Instrumental Music in *Die Zauberflöte*', in Daniel Heartz, *Mozart's Operas*, ed. Bauman (Berkeley: University of California Press, 1990), pp. 277–97.

Example 42. Mozart, *Don Giovanni*, No. 12 ('Batti, Batti'), bars 16-28.

Example 43. Mozart, *Don Giovanni*, No. 12 ('Batti, Batti'), bars 34-40.

In 'Voi che sapete' and 'Deh vieni' from *Figaro*, the reinforcement of close relations between the singer and the orchestra stems from the progressive refinement of specific dialogic procedures, the segue and the echo, rather than from a joining of dialogic procedures (as at the beginning of the reprise in 'Batti, batti'). The orchestra's segues between Cherubino's phrases in 'Voi che sapete', for example, bare a closer resemblance to the preceding and/or ensuing material in the later part of the aria than in the earlier part. Whereas the orchestral segues in bars 16 (section A), 24, 28, 32 (section B) are loosely derived from preceding material – in bars 16 and 32 the flute/oboe and oboe invert Cherubino's immediately preceding stepwise ascent and arpeggiated figures respectively – the later segues in bars 40, 54, 56 (section B), 65 (A′) are integrated more closely into the melodic fabric. The flute in bar 40 not only imitates Cherubino's falling arpeggio but also pre-empts his subsequent E♭–C quavers (bar 40, beat 2 – 41 beat 1); the flute and oboe in bars 54 and 56 anticipate Cherubino's stepwise-rising sequence by ascending chromatically from B♭–C and C–D respectively; and the clarinet in bars 65–6 (C–C♯–D) foreshadows Cherubino's subsequent chromatic ascent (D–E♭–E in bar 66) and also segues neatly from the final note of the preceding vocal phrase (C) to the first note of the next (D). In addition, the winds' echo of Cherubino's concluding cadence (bars 77–9) expands the brief two-note echo from the corresponding moment in the A section (bar 20). The overall impression in the B and A′ sections of 'Voi che sapete', then, is that the orchestra has become increasingly sensitive to melodic material sung by the soloist.

The orchestra in Susanna's 'Deh vieni', as in Cherubino's 'Voi che sapete', actively engages with the soloist by seguing between vocal phrases.[42] In some instances, segues proceed directly from the last note of the preceding vocal phrase to the first note of the subsequent phrase (for example, the F–B♭ stepwise ascent in the oboe in bars 9–10, the repeated Cs in the flute in bar 23, and the arpeggios from C–B♭ and A–G in the flute in bars 26–7 and 29–30);[43] in others instances, they relate motivically to surrounding material (for example, the ascending F-major arpeggios in the oboe and bassoon in bars 15–16 after Susanna's descending F-major arpeggio in bar 14, and the E–G–E movement in the oboe in bar 20 before the E-G that opens Susanna's phrase in bars 20–21). Although voice/orchestra dialogue with the stepwise semiquaver motif (heard only in the winds in bars 5 and 18–19) is initially conspicuous by its absence, it surfaces towards the end of the aria: Susanna picks up the motif in bars 39 and 43 (in response to the winds in bars 36–7) and passes it back to the winds in bar 44, where it is now inverted.[44] Thus, the orchestra's procedure of inverting vocal

[42] For Webster and Waldoff, 'Deh vieni', like 'Dove sono' and 'Che soave zeffiretto', contains 'persona-like interactions between voice and wind'. See 'Operatic Plotting', in *Wolfgang Amadè Mozart*, ed. Sadie, pp. 272–3. (Several of my observations coincide with their remarks.)

[43] I begin bar numbering at the onset of the aria, not at the onset of the recitative, as in the commonly-used Dover edition of *Figaro*.

[44] Webster describes the process of interchange with the ascending semiquaver figure as 'a double rapprochement between soloist and orchestra'. See 'Are Mozart's Concertos "Dramatic"?', in *Mozart's Piano Concertos*, ed. Zaslaw, p. 122.

material in the context of dialogic segues (for example, the ascending and descending arpeggios in bars 14–15 and 24–6) also extends to material previously in the orchestral domain only.

Voice/orchestra dialogue in 'Deh vieni' and 'Voi che sapete' functions in an analogous way to piano/orchestra dialogue in the reinforced co-operation movements of Mozart's piano concertos.[45] Just as the most intricate piano/orchestra dialogue in movements such as K. 414/i, 449/i, 453/i, 456/i, 459/i, 488/i, 491/i is reserved until the recapitulation, lending a teleological quality to the development of solo/orchestra relations, so the increased integration of dialogic segues into the melodic fabric of 'Voi che sapete' and the addition of subtle semiquaver dialogue in 'Deh vieni', both reserved until the later stages, lend a teleological quality to the development of solo/orchestra relations in these arias. Co-operation between the piano and the orchestra is reinforced as a result of this process in the concertos, while the orchestra's role as a sensitive *confidante* is progressively strengthened in the arias.

Developments in Mozart's dramatic dialogue, 1780–7

Our comparisons of dialogic confrontation and co-operation in Mozart's operas and Viennese piano concertos, together with our stylistic investigations of the piano concertos in Chapters Three and Four, enable us to draw historical and stylistic conclusions about the inter-generic development of Mozart's dramatic dialogue in the period 1780–7.

Although we have established precedents in *Entführung* for confrontational procedures evident in the Viennese piano concertos (tonal impasses, modal shifts, modulatory dialogues), we witness only in *Figaro* and *Don Giovanni* the rugged intensity of the famous confrontation from K. 491/i (bars 330–45). As observed in Chapter Four, the K. 491/i confrontation is of great stylistic significance in the context of Mozart's piano concertos; it is foreshadowed by confrontations in Mozart's preceding Viennese concertos, but supersedes them in raw, interactional passion. Equally, the K. 491/i confrontation unleashes a heightened level of *operatic* character conflict in *Figaro* and *Don Giovanni.* The alternation of strongly contrasting, equal-length units, along the lines prescribed by Reicha for confrontational dialogue, makes its first emphatic appearances in Mozart's operas in the Act 3 Sextet of *Figaro*, and the Act 1 Finale and Act 2 Sextet of *Don Giovanni* (see above). Given the new and strikingly powerful effect of these confrontations in both Mozart's concertos and operas, and the close proximity in their composition (K. 491 was completed on 24 March 1786 and *Figaro* first performed on 1 May 1786), they forcefully demonstrate Mozart's inter-generic approach to confrontational dramatic dialogue. (Also, the fact that

[45] On parallels between the moment of recapitulation in K. 467/ii and modulatory procedures in 'Voi che sapete' see Webster, 'Are Mozart's Concertos "Dramatic"?', in *Mozart's Piano Concertos*, ed. Zaslaw, pp. 127–31.

they appear in the very different contexts of piano/orchestra dialogue and dialogue among operatic characters attests to the malleability of the technique itself.) Even if bars 330–45 of K. 491 were not ringing in Mozart's ears when he came to compose the Act 3 sextet (or, just possibly, vice versa[46]), it is highly likely that he would have had similar confrontational effects in mind for each piece.

If K. 491/i, the Act 3 sextet from *Figaro* and the Act 1 finale and Act 2 sextet from *Don Giovanni* demonstrate climactic moments in the evolution of Mozart's confrontational dramatic dialogue, another work, K. 449/i, can lay equal claim to a pivotal stylistic significance in regard to dialogic confrontation. The development section of K. 449/i offers not only the earliest precedent in Mozart's piano concertos for the stark oppositional dialogue that culminates in bars 330–45 of K. 491/i (see Chapter Four), but also the first example of genuinely confrontational interaction of any kind in Mozart's concertos. As explained in Chapter Three, K. 449/i follows a trajectory from co-operative dialogue in the exposition to competitive dialogue in the early part of the development and ultimately to co-operative dialogue punctuated by moments of competition in the recapitulation. The sheer intensity and dramatic fervour of the orchestra's forceful interruptions of the piano in bars 234 and 319, coupled with the ingenious dialogic resolutions of the relational abrasions, are unrivalled in Mozart's earlier piano concertos.

Our understanding of the stylistic significance of K. 449/i's dialogic confrontations in Mozart's *œuvre* is enhanced by consideration of the movement's protracted genesis. As Alan Tyson discovered in his study of paper types, Mozart began work on K. 449/i not in 1784 as is commonly believed (it was entered into the *Verzeichnüss* on 9 February 1784), but rather in 1782, alongside the 'subscription' concertos, K. 413, 414, 415. According to Tyson, Mozart composed as far as bar 170 (two bars after the piano's cadential trill at the end of the solo exposition), put the concerto aside and resumed work at the beginning of 1784, concurrently with his concertos K. 450, 451 and 453.[47]

Both written and musical evidence and more specific evidence of dialogic confrontation support an interpretation of K. 449/i as a hybrid of the 1782 and spring 1784 concertos. Mozart recognised, for example, that K. 449 and the K. 413, 414, 415 set, similarly scored for two oboes, two horns and strings, could be performed 'a quattro', that is, without the oboes and the horns.[48] He considered K. 449 different at a basic level from the three 'grand concertos',

[46] According to Alan Tyson, the Act 3 sextet was written on a paper type that is also found in Acts 1 and 2 of *Figaro*, making it likely that this was one of the earliest numbers composed in Act 3. See Tyson, *Mozart: Studies of the Autograph Scores* (Cambridge, Massachusetts: Harvard University Press, 1987), pp. 119–20.

[47] Tyson, *Mozart: Autograph Scores*, pp. 19, 53.

[48] See Emily Anderson, *The Letters of Mozart and His Family* (New York: Norton, 1985 [3rd edition]), p. 877, for the 'a quattro' reference to K. 449; and Otto Erich Deutsch, *Mozart: A Documentary Biography*, trans. Eric Blom, Peter Branscombe, Jeremy Noble (Stanford: Stanford University Press, 1965), p. 212, for a similar reference to K. 413, 414, 415, in Mozart's 'musical announcement' in the *Wiener Zeitung* of 15 January 1783.

K. 450, 451 and 453: 'The one in E♭ [K. 449] does not belong at all to the same category. It is one of an entirely special manner, composed rather for a small orchestra than for a large one'.[49] Procedural similarities with K. 414/i reinforce K. 449/i's connection to the 1782 concertos. The piano and the orchestra in both K. 414/i and 449/i disturb the musical flow at the end of the development/ beginning of the recapitulation in similar ways: in K. 414/i, pauses in successive bars (194–55) – the second leading to a general pause – prevent a smooth segue to the return of the main theme; in K. 449/i, the piano's chromatic ascent and its forceful interruption by the orchestra's rendition of the main theme, create an abrupt and uneasy transition from the development to the recapitulation (see Chapter Three). Furthermore, the two ruptures themselves hint at how co-operative dialogue between the piano and the orchestra will be restored: in K. 414/i, a progression from the piano and the orchestra together (bar 194), to the piano alone (bar 195), to the orchestra alone (bar 196), although not in itself constituting dialogue, at least initiates an alternation of forces that will generate dialogue at the beginning of the recapitulation;[50] in K. 449/i, the disruptive chromatic ascent in the run-up to the recapitulation is immediately reassimilated as a co-operative element in the orchestra's split-theme dialogue with the piano (see Chapter Three).

In spite of procedural similarities between K. 414/i and 449/i, there is no mistaking the later concerto's increase in confrontational intensity. In this respect, K. 449/i is much more akin to the concertos from the spring of 1784 (K. 450, 451 and 453) than to the 1782 set. K. 449/i and 451/i incorporate confrontational interaction to similar effect at the beginning of their development sections (see Chapter Four), and K. 450/i includes an important confrontational dialogue at the same juncture (see Chapter Three). Moreover, the dramatic intensity of bars 234 and 319–20 of K. 449/i, unmatched in the 1782 concertos, is rivalled by bars 86–7 of K. 450/i, and the ingenuity of relational resolution through dialogue in bars 242ff. and 328 of K. 449/i is rivalled by the exquisite three-way dialogue in the transition from the development to the recapitulation of K. 450/i.

It is perhaps significant that Mozart stopped work on K. 449/i in 1782 at the end of the solo exposition. Could he have been unsure of exactly how to proceed, of how to achieve a more powerful and succinct contrast to the collaborative dialogue from the solo exposition than at the corresponding moment in his earlier concertos? In any case, when he resumed work on K. 449/i two years later he introduced not only a new type of confrontational dialogue into his piano concertos (the stark alternation of the piano and the orchestra in bars 188–203), but also a new level of dramatic and dialogic intensity. (In so doing, he maintained procedural links between K. 449/i and

[49] Anderson, *The Letters*, p. 877. (Translation slightly amended.)

[50] In addition to dialogue created by alternating semiquaver ascents and arpeggio figures (bars 212–18) which correspond to the beginning of the solo exposition (bars 80–6), the main theme is dialogued between the strings and the piano for the first time in the movement (bars 196–203, 204–12).

414/i.) Undoubtedly, the end of Mozart's hiatus in composing his Viennese piano concertos (1782–4) coincides with his most significant stylistic 'advances' in dramatic dialogue therein.

While there are no direct precedents in *Die Entführung* and *Idomeneo* for K. 449/i's remarkable technique of immediately following a confrontation with a dialogic resolution, there *are* operatic precedents (as discovered earlier in this chapter) for confrontational procedures featured in Mozart's next concerto, K. 450/i. The tonal *impasse* between the piano and the orchestra in the solo exposition, the modal shift to designate confrontation, and the eventual 'correction' of harmonic stasis are all foreshadowed in *Die Entführung*.

Two additional factors, specific to Mozart's concertos, also have a direct bearing on K. 450/i, the first of his movements to trace a relational progression from competition in the solo exposition to fully-fledged co-operation in the recapitulation. First, the emergence of this type of relational trajectory is intrinsically linked to the initial appearances in his concertos of confrontational dialogue. Unlike K. 413, 414 and 415, K. 449/i and 450/i both incorporate confrontational dialogue, K. 449/i effecting a movement away from the dialogic co-operation of the solo exposition at the beginning of the development, and K. 450/i taking tentative steps towards resolving the uneasy piano/orchestra relations from the solo exposition at the corresponding moment. Although devised for a reinforced co-operation movement (K. 449/i), confrontational dialogue in the concertos is reserved almost exclusively thereafter for movements that do not follow the reinforced co-operation pattern (K. 450/i, 467/i [see the discussion of this movement in Chapter 6, pp. 154–6] and 482/i; bars 330–45 of K. 491/i are an obvious exception).

Second, it is not coincidental that K. 450/i, the earliest of Mozart's 'competitive' movements, is also the first to make prominent use of the woodwinds, and part of the first work Mozart described as a 'grand concerto' (*grosses Konzert*) featuring a large accompanying orchestra.[51] The emergence of the winds as a distinct interlocutor in its own right enables Mozart to accentuate differences in relational behaviour in the first two sections: the strings and woodwinds collaborate freely through dialogue in the orchestral exposition; in contrast, the piano and the strings/winds engage in very little dialogue in the solo exposition, the piano's harmonic stasis creating uneasy solo/orchestra relations. Moreover, the emergence of the winds facilitates an especially effective resolution to relational tension: the piano and the orchestra establish a state of

[51] See Mozart's letter to Leopold (26 May 1784), in Anderson, *The Letters*, p. 877. As Irving R. Eisley points out: 'The new concertato orchestra [i.e. with an elevated role for the woodwinds] appears abruptly, with little or no hint to be found in the earlier concertos, in the B♭ concerto, K. 450'; see 'Mozart's Concertato Orchestra', *Mozart-Jahrbuch, 1976–7*, p. 9. Mozart performed K. 450 at the Burgtheater, Vienna, on 1 April 1784 and possibly at the Trattnerhof, Vienna, on 24 March 1784. For a full list of public concerts in Vienna from 1760 to 1810 and works performed at them, see Mary Sue Morrow, 'Appendix One: Public Concert Calendar', in *Concert Life in Haydn's Vienna: Aspects of a Developing Musical and Social Institution* (Stuyvesant, New York: Pendragon, 1989), pp. 237–364.

co-operation through subtle, three-way dialogue in the transition from development to recapitulation (strings-piano-winds, bars 189–98), fortifying co-operation with three-way dialogue in the recapitulation itself (strings-piano-winds, bars 249–64).

Thus, in developing the 'competitive' type of piano concerto movement for K. 450/i, Mozart draws on confrontational interactive techniques from both opera and concerto. Building on established confrontational procedures in *Die Entführung* and a newly discovered confrontational intensity in K. 449/i, Mozart forges a new type of relational trajectory, with a progression from competition to co-operation at its core. In this respect, the confluence of operatic and concerto procedures exemplifies Mozart's inter-generic approach to confrontational dramatic dialogue.

Just as inter-generic stylistic development has been found in confrontational dialogue – from tonal procedures in *Die Entführung* (1782) to the increased intensity of K. 449/i (1782–4) and K. 450/i (1784), culminating in the altercations of K. 491/i (1786), *Figaro* (1786) and *Don Giovanni* (1787) – it can also be established, albeit in a more general way, in co-operative dialogue. As we have seen, there are precedents in *Idomeneo* and especially *Die Entführung* both for the general pattern of reinforced co-operation that dominates the first movements of Mozart's 1782–6 concertos and for specific dialogic procedures that become commonplace (long-range 'dialogue', the elaboration of orchestral dialogue by the soloist, inter-sectional dialogue, and the synthesis of dialogue and/or dialogic procedures in the reprise). Also, 'Martern aller Arten' from *Die Entführung*, with its whole host of thematic and procedural foreshadowings of the Viennese piano concertos, was clearly a special source of inspiration for Mozart when he came to compose his concertos. In addition, there are numerous dialogic similiarities between *Figaro*/*Don Giovanni* and Mozart's preceding concertos, suggesting a similar cross-fertilization of dramatic dialogue.

In spite of the affinities that all four Mozart operas share with concerto dialogue, Mozart's operatic orchestra consistently demonstrates a more sophisticated level of involvement in dramatic dialogue in *Figaro* and *Don Giovanni* than in *Idomeneo* and *Die Entführung*. The subtlety and intricacy of orchestral participation in 'Là ci darem', 'Che soave zeffiretto', 'Ah, taci' and 'Batti, batti' described above, is rivalled only by that of 'Martern aller Arten' from *Die Entführung*. In this respect, the increasingly active orchestral participation in dialogue with the soloists in *Figaro* and *Don Giovanni* is consistent with orchestral participation in Mozart's piano concertos reaching its apotheosis in 1786 with K. 491/i. Although the extraordinary heights achieved by piano/orchestra dialogue in K. 491/i forced Mozart to re-think his relational paradigm of reinforced co-operation in the first movements of his final three piano concertos (see Chapter Four), the same cannot be said for the corresponding paradigm in *Figaro* and *Don Giovanni*. For it is in these operas – in their arias, duets and ensembles alike – that dialogic collaboration between Mozart's soloist(s) and orchestra is most often akin to dialogic collaboration between the piano and the orchestra in his preceding Viennese concertos. We can therefore conclude that Mozart adapted his extraordinarily refined approach to co-operative piano/orchestra interaction from his 1782–6 concertos, albeit in a fairly general way, to the musical and dramatic demands of voice/orchestra interaction in *Figaro* and *Don Giovanni.*

Procedural affinities between Mozart's concerto movements and operatic numbers – for both dialogic co-operation and confrontation – underscore ostensibly classical modes of dramatic thought in both genres. As observed in Chapter 3 in particular, Mozart's piano and orchestra engage in rigorous *processes* of exchange that audiences must follow closely in order to grasp *how* states of co-operation are attained or reinforced. Musical interaction among the soloists in Mozart's operas and between the soloist(s) and the orchestra is similarly demanding: listeners must understand the full *musical* significance of, for example, characters clashing forcefully in the Act 3 sextet of *Figaro* by realizing tensions latent in the differentiation of the two character groups earlier in the number, of a repeated augmented 6th–V progression eventually resolving 'correctly' in the *Entführung* quartet, and of the orchestra playing a crucial supporting role in 'Là ci darem', before they are able to grasp the complete dramatic significance of Mozart's interactional processes.

Ultimately, Mozart's carefully crafted inter-generic dialogic processes engage his piano concertos and operas from the 1780s in their own kind of 'dialogue'. Techniques and patterns of dialogue in the Viennese piano concertos are informed by similar techniques and patterns in *Idomeneo* and *Die Entführung*, and, in turn, inform dialogue in *Figaro* and *Don Giovanni.* By adding to his interactional repertoire over time, Mozart develops and reinforces the inter-generic quality of his dramatic dialogue, a quality transcending fundamental differences in the make-up of concerto and operatic interlocutors. Moreover, just as musical dialogue in both genres is nothing if not dynamic, so the relationship between Mozart's concertos and operas is itself a vibrant one, each genre drawing inspiration from the other. Formal and gestural parallels between Mozart's operas and concertos cannot in themselves characterise the vitality of this reciprocal process; the energy and verve of Mozart's dramatic dialogue, however, captures the real spirit of stylistic confluence.

An important historical conclusion can be drawn from a re-evaluation of dialogue, one of the most significant components of Mozart's dramatic style, in terms of inter-generic development. Of course, Mozart's position as the pre-eminent musical dramatist of the late eighteenth century has never been in question. It has emerged, however, that in order to understand the full theoretical and practical significance of this position we must comprehend the dramatic achievements of his piano concertos as well as of his operas. Only from an explanation of similarities in the interactions within Mozart's operatic and concerto works will we begin to appreciate that Mozart's dramatic genius depends fundamentally on a vivid 'dialogue' between his works in both genres.

6

Dialogue and Drama in Mozart's Three-Movement Concerto Cycles

My final chapter attempts to answer two related questions. How does the drama of piano/orchestra dialogue in Mozart's concertos, examined systematically only in first movements thus far, play out over the course of a three-movement cycle? And, how might interpretations of these cycles in dialogic terms shed light on the potential of Mozart's piano concertos to fulfil functions analogous to spoken plays? For a long while a topic of relatively unsystematic speculation, cyclicity in late-eighteenth-century music – and its related practice of through-composition – has recently received rigorous attention at the hands of James Webster, who has reshaped the musicological community's understanding of Haydn's stylistic development in general and the coherence of individual works in particular, through 'multivalent' analyses of formal, structural, developmental, instrumental and registral elements of Haydn's works.[1] Piano/orchestra dialogue, although less able to effect *overall* coherence in a multi-movement work, along the multivalent lines followed by Webster, is nevertheless the key to developing an historical understanding of the *dramatic* coherence of Mozart's concerto cycles – since piano/orchestra relations, articulated through dialogue, are central to the late-eighteenth-century dramatic experience of these works (see Chapter One).[2] Moreover, dialogue, by virtue of its proven ability to enforce relational change in the first movements (either reinforcing co-operation or resolving confrontation) will be in a privileged and powerful position *vis-à-vis* the development of piano/orchestra relations in the second and third movements of the cycle as well. Equally, dialogue's status as 'the comfortable middle ground between what was too simple, too unpolished . . .

[1] Webster, *Haydn's 'Farewell' Symphony and the Idea of Classical Style: Through-Composition and Cyclic Integration in His Instrumental Music* (Cambridge: Cambridge University Press, 1991). Although he uses 'through-composed' to denote 'dynamic or gestural phenomena (run-on movements, recalls, unresolved instabilities, lack of closure, and so forth' and 'cyclic integration' and 'organization' to signify 'aspects of musical construction and technique (commonalities of material, tonal relations, and the like)', he counsels that 'these domains cannot be meaningfully dissociated, and the reader must not expect total consistency of usage' (pp. 7–8).

[2] In any case, Webster concedes that 'Only a small minority of [Haydn's] works are overtly through-composed, in the manner of the Farewell Symphony. More common is to find tangible links between only two movements, or within only one musical domain (motives, tonality, gesture)'. See *Haydn's 'Farewell' Symphony*, p. 174.

and too complicated, unnatural and affected'[3] makes it a particularly effective means for conveying the dramatic coherence of a late-eighteenth-century concerto to listeners of varying musical aptitudes.[4]

The issue of coherence in late-eighteenth-century instrumental music that is specifically dramatic, with a corollary of dramatic clarity, is not new to the secondary literature. David P. Schroeder's *Haydn and the Enlightenment: The Late Symphonies and Their Audience*, for example, assumes a link between the dramatic nature of Haydn's works – especially the 'London' symphonies – and their intelligibility and interest to contemporary audiences.[5] Following a common critical argument (discussed in relation to the concerto in Chapter Three) that drama in instrumental music is manifest in conflict – the 'dramatic duality of themes', 'dramatic polarities', and the 'fusion of dramatic polarities' and 'opposites central to dramatic process', for example[6] – Schroeder identifies 'dramatic problems' in individual movements from Haydn's *oeuvre* and traces their subsequent resolutions. His analyses of the 'London' symphonies, however, do not evaluate resolutions to these 'problems' in the second, third and fourth movements of the cycles in addition to the first movements, a profitable extension above all because recalcitrant material or gestures introduced in the first movements are sometimes integrated into a smooth musical fabric only later in the work.[7] The fact that Haydn intended at least one entire symphony, No. 60 *Der Zerstreute*, as a musical representation of a contemporary spoken play (Regnard's *Le distrait*) further emphasises the potential value of examining the drama of his symphonies in the context of multi-movement cycles.[8]

In contrast to the dramatic element in Haydn's symphonies, the relational drama in individual movements of Mozart's piano concertos can be regarded in one sense as more complete and self-contained. As we observed in Chapters Three and Four, the piano and the orchestra in the recapitulations of Mozart's first movements reinforce co-operative dialogue from the solo exposition, or resolve relational tensions from the solo exposition and development, or

[3] Hanning, 'Conversation and Musical Style', *Eighteenth-Century Studies*, p. 524. Although Hanning's comment refers specifically to the *style dialogué* (which plays only a small part in Mozart's piano concertos, as noted in my Introduction), it can be taken as a general indication of dialogue's broad appeal.

[4] Maynard Solomon characterises the late-eighteenth-century concerto as 'a genre that temporarily united several different audiences into a unique, amalgamated one'. See Solomon, *Mozart: A Life* (New York: HarperCollins, 1995), p. 293.

[5] See Schroeder, *Haydn and the Enlightenment*, pp. 5, 42, 178 and *passim*.

[6] Ibid., pp. 67, 135, 137, 137.

[7] I have explored this point in relation to the disruptive unison gestures in bars 1, 6, 81 and 86 from the first movement of Haydn's Symphony No. 102, and their eventual assimilation in the minuet and trio, in 'Dialogue and Drama: Haydn's Symphony No. 102', *Music Research Forum* 11/1 (1996), pp. 1–21, at pp. 6–21.

[8] For probing consideration of the correlations between Haydn's symphony and Regnard's play, see Robert A. Green, 'Haydn's and Regnard's "Il Distratto": A Re-examination', *Haydn Yearbook* 11 (1980), pp. 183–95; and Sisman, 'Haydn's Theater Symphonies', *Journal of the American Musicological Society* 43, pp. 292–352, at pp. 311–20.

(exceptionally in K. 449/i) integrate confrontational interaction into the reinforcement of co-operation. It would be a mistake, however, to interpret these reinforcements and resolutions as final and conclusive acts in the relational drama. For as we shall see, Mozart's second and third movements, by reshaping and transforming earlier dialogic procedures, sometimes strengthen the resolution of first-movement confrontation or reinforce co-operative interaction still further. In this respect, the process-orientated dramatic theory of the late eighteenth century – in which conveying the means of character and plot-related development is privileged over and above surprising the spectator – offers a particularly rich insight into the dramatic workings of Mozart's concertos; since the eventual outcome of Mozart's relational drama is not really in doubt, given the proliferation of overtly co-operative piano/orchestra dialogue in the finales in general, the listener can turn his or her attention exclusively to interactive processes.

In order to evaluate the dramatic nature of Mozart's three-movement concerto cycles, cyclic dialogic procedures are first examined separately, and then situated in the context of contemporary theoretical commentaries on the aims and objectives of complete dramas and late-eighteenth-century concertos. Ultimately, similarities between the theoretical objectives of late-eighteenth-century concertos and classical plays – active audience engagement, edifying effects and broad appeal for listeners and spectators of varying aptitudes – enable analytical commentary to convey with accuracy the dramatic intensity and enormous dramatic potential of Mozart's complete concertos.

Reinforced Resolution to Confrontation

As explained in Chapters Three and Four, the piano and the orchestra sometimes introduce conflicting agendas in the solo exposition and development sections of Mozart's first movements, creating relational tension that is later resolved through dialogue in the recapitulation. In the second and/or third movements of these concertos – especially K. 450, 451, 482 and 595 – Mozart refers back to the earlier confrontations in various ways, finally reinforcing the sense of relational resolution.

The sonata-rondo finale to K. 450/iii[9] ends with a strong invocation of the initial source of tension between the piano and the orchestra in the first movement – the ostentatious piano entry that forces the orchestra into a back-seat role – and an emphatic reinforcement of the resolution to that tension. Bars 295–316 (Example 44) contain several overt references to bars 53–70 from the first movement (see Examples 5 and 9, pp. 58 and 61). The antecedent-consequent dialogue between the piano and the winds (bars

[9] James Webster, in his tabulation of the formal types of the second and third movements of Mozart's piano concertos, calls this movement a 'concerto-rondo' on account of its 'synthesis of ritornello form and sonata-rondo, analogous to concerto form as synthesis of ritornello form and sonata form'. See Table 1 in Webster's 'Are Mozart's Concertos "Dramatic"?' p. 113.

Example 44. Mozart, Piano Concerto K. 450, 3rd Movement, bars 295-316.

295–303), for example, is motivically and procedurally very similar to the antecedent-consequent dialogue between the winds and strings in bars 53–7 of the first movement: both antecedents are four-beat arpeggiated B♭ chords, played in octaves; both consequents are four-beat conjunct phrases articulating V–I harmonies. The subsequent static B♭ harmony (bars 303–13), with its semiquaver figurations in the piano and its registral ascent to F''' (bars 313–14), recalls the same distinctive characteristics from bars 63–70 of the first movement. In the finale, however, there are also important adjustments to the earlier passage. The arpeggiated antecedent, for example, continues beyond the confines of the antecedent-consequent dialogue (see the horn and winds in bars 303–12), thus transcending the strict division between the corresponding material in the first movement. In addition, the registral peak (F'''), formerly an inconclusive point from which the piano immediately recedes (bars 68–70 in the first movement), now functions as an authentic climax: it is heard not just in the piano but in both the piano and the winds, and coincides with *tutti* V–I cadences (bars 313–15) as opposed to unaccompanied, static B♭ harmony. The extended tonic harmony is, in any case, more syntactially appropriate to the end of the work than to the moment at which the piano and the orchestra prepare harmonically for the return of the main theme in the solo exposition of the first movement.

As observed in Chapter 3, relational tension between the piano and the orchestra in the solo exposition of K. 450/i is resolved later in the movement, with one source of tension – the piano's pedal contributing to the harmonic stasis at its point of entry – recast in an harmonically 'correct' fashion in the recapitulation. Bars 295–316 of the finale reinforce relational resolution by invoking the uneasy piano passage from the first movement in specific terms, in the process recasting several elements in a more co-operative light. Mozart's concluding bars thus provide not only an effective final showpiece for the piano's virtuosity (the semiquaver figurations), audible to one and all, but also a more sophisticated, subtly altered re-enactment of the piano's entry into the first movement, upon which only the initiated listener will reflect. By positioning this passage at the end of the finale, Mozart brings his concerto full circle. Initially a source of relational unease, the passage now constitutes a final affirmation of piano/orchestra collaboration. In short, we learn retrospectively that co-operation (in the finale passage) is latent even in relational unease (at the piano's entry in the first movement).

The finales of K. 451 and K. 595, like the corresponding movement of K. 450, invoke confrontational interaction from the first movements, while in the process reinforcing the co-operative bond between the piano and the orchestra. Bars 157ff. from the C ('development') section of the sonata-rondo K. 451/iii, for example, follow a very similar interactional pattern to bars 187ff. from the development section of K. 451/i. In both passages, co-operative dialogue gives way to opposition, with the piano drawing on earlier arpeggiated figurations in order to distance its own material from that of the orchestra. The piano's triplet arpeggios interpolated into the dialogue with the orchestra in bars 191–2 of K. 451/i dominate the texture (bars 199–214), effectively precluding further dialogue. Similarly, the piano modifies its falling semiquaver arpeggios from bars 155–6 of K. 451/iii to produce alternating oppositional dialogue with the orchestra (bars 172–87) and semiquaver flourishes (bars 188–205) that again prohibit additional dialogue.

If anything, piano/orchestra opposition is more pronounced in the finale than in the first movement: contrasting material, in which the piano alone leads the music to E minor and C major in bars 178 and 184, alternates strictly (bars 172–88) in a very similar manner to the contrasting material in confrontational dialogue in the development sections of K. 449/i and 491/i (see Chapter Four). Equally, resolution to the relational unease is more intense and concise in the finale. The C ('development') section concludes with a brief, *stichomythia*-like dialogue (bars 206–13, Example 45) based on the head motif of the main theme. In spite of initial harmonic and melodic contradictions among the participants (oboe [C♯], flute [C♯m], piano [diminished on C♯], bars 206–11), the final entry in the violins (bars 212–13), accompanied *forte* by the rest of the orchestra who render the harmony V7/D, forcefully affirms the piano's preceding C♯–E–G–E phrase. Thus, co-operation between the piano and the orchestra is re-established and relational unease resolved through the dialoguing of a segment (the main theme's head motif) that had featured in the preceding rift.

As in K. 451, Mozart takes specific confrontational characteristics from the development section of K. 595/i and integrates them into K. 595/iii. The beginning of the development of K. 595/i highlights indecisive and disjunctive three-way dialogue with its 'incorrectly' resolved diminished chord (bars 194–7) and its harmonic contradictions (bars 200–4, see Chapter Four). Piano/orchestra dialogue in K. 595/iii also draws attention to these procedures, recasting them, however, in a more co-operative light. In bars 79–90, for example, diminished chords (E–G–B♭–D♭ and F♯–A–C–E♭) are presented by both the piano and the orchestra rather than the orchestra alone, in an harmonically fluid, not disjunctive, dialogue that nevertheless resembles the

Example 45. Mozart, Piano Concerto K. 451, 3rd Movement, bars 206-15.

earlier dialogue in its quick succession of two different diminished chords (bars 190, 194–6 [first movement] and 80–3 [finale]) and its exchange of short, clearly defined segments. Bars 186–96, like bars 79–90, negate the harmonic disjunction from the beginning of the development section of the first movement in the process of invoking the earlier passage. One- and two-bar segments dialogued again in clearly defined units among the three interlocutors take the music smoothly from E♭ (the key of the rondo return beginning in bar 182) to V/B♭, via a systematic, sequential alternation of local tonics in major and minor modes (E♭–e♭–D♭–a♭–E♭–b♭); a coherent modulatory process replaces disjunctive modulation.

In Chapter Four we explained that the oppositional effects from the development sections of K. 451/i and 595/i are resolved later in their respective movements as the piano and orchestra recapture the intimacy of their dialogue from the solo exposition. The invocation of, and adjustment to these specific procedures in K. 451/iii and 595/iii thus reinforce relational resolution across the broader time frame of a three-movement cycle. This reinforcement is especially pronounced in K. 451/iii, as a result of the musical intensification of both the relational conflict and its resolution.

The resolution to piano/orchestra confrontation in K. 467/i, as in K. 450/i, 451/i, and 595/i, is also reinforced in the finale in the context of thematic and procedural allusions to the earlier movement. The solo exposition of K. 467/i combines confrontational and co-operative behaviour. Nowhere is this more evident than at the initial appearance of the soloist (Example 46), where the oboe, bassoon, flute and piano enter at two-bar intervals (bars 68, 70, 72, 74) and the piano elaborates the woodwinds' head motif in semiquavers (bar 74–5). With its inconspicuous entrance as part of a dialogue, the piano first co-operates with the orchestra in its dominant preparation for the return of the main theme. Moreover, the strings continue the piano-orchestra dialogue by reducing the piano's figurations to repeated quavers (bars 74–6). In the ensuing bars (76–9), however, the piano usurps the arrival of the tonic and the restatement of the main theme by extending its semiquaver elaboration to create a virtuosic and ostentatious ascent to a climactic F‴. Just as the piano's intricate elaborations in bars 76–9 effectively prohibit further dialogue, so they also shift the focus of the dominant build-up from the return of the main theme (bar 80) to the striking fermata in bar 79. (Most solo performers add a brief cadenza here, thereby adding further emphasis to this moment.[10]) Thus, the piano's contribution to the dialogue is at least in part self-serving and not exclusively collaborative. Relational ambiguity is, in fact, a feature of dialogue in the solo exposition as a whole, since a moment of confrontation is interspersed with demonstrations of co-operation. Although the piano and the orchestra co-operate freely on a number of occasions – splitting the main theme in bars 80–91, passing the secondary theme back and forth in bars 128–40 and exchanging the main theme's head motif in bars 143–8) – on another occasion their dialogue is more fraught. In bar 109 (in the transition) the piano contradicts the orchestra's immediately preceding affirmation of the dominant, shifting the music abruptly to the dominant minor. This dialogue in turn leads to thematic stasis rather than productive exchange: the piano bides its time, elaborating a central pitch D (bars 110–14) and a descending scale (bars 115–17), absorbed (as in bars 75–9) by the intricacies of its own writing rather than by its interaction with the orchestra.

Whereas specific manifestations of piano/orchestra tension in the solo

[10] Mozart's autograph score of K. 467 (held at the Pierpont Morgan Library in New York City) gives no indication that a brief cadenza should be performed. See Wolfgang Amadeus Mozart, *Piano Concerto No. 21 in C Major, K. 467: The Autograph Score* (New York: Dover, 1985), p. 7. Mozart did write brief cadenzas on other mid-movement fermatas (see, for example, K. 414/i, bar 194 and K. 415/i, bar 198), however, thus suggesting that one on bar 79 of K. 467/i is not inappropriate.

Example 46. Mozart, Piano Concerto K. 467, 1st Movement, bars 68-81.

exposition – the piano's ostentatious overshadowing of the orchestra's presentation of the main theme and its modal contradiction of the full orchestra – are eliminated from the recapitulation of the first movement, thus settling the earlier relational ambiguity in favour of co-operation, they are resolved in a more direct fashion in the finale. In bars 58ff., for example, the piano and the orchestra allude to the G major/G minor confrontation, but now in the context of co-operative dialogue. As in the first movement, the piano states arpeggiated minims in octaves, again answering a scalic octave figure marked *forte* in the orchestra (bars 52–6). No longer contradicting the modality of the orchestra's preceding statement, however, the piano's C–E–G arpeggio is dialogued by the horn (bars 60–6), in contrast to the G minor arpeggio from the first movement. In addition, this passage leads not to thematic self-absorption on the part of the piano as in the first movement, but rather to a co-operative three-way dialogue (strings-woodwinds-piano, bars 74–86). The concluding chromatic descent of the piano's preceding phrase (bar 72) subtly predicts both the chromatic ascent of the main theme (bar 65) and the piano's chromatic descents (bars 86–95) at the beginning of the ensuing modulatory passage that culminates in the confirmation of the dominant (bars 109–10).[11] Equally, the piano makes two references to its initial entry in the first movement, de-emphasizing relational unease in the process. Immediately before the tonic return of the main theme in the exposition (A′ in sonata-rondo terminology), for example, the piano's repetition and liquidation of a three-beat semiquaver motif ascending to a fermata on an F‴ and V7/C harmony (bars 169–77, Example 47) and accompanied by repeated quavers in the strings, explicitly invokes bars 74–9 from the first movement. But the absence of initial dialogue with the orchestra as a *raison d'être* for this passage, together with the fact that the piano's virtuosic elaborations and brief cadenza in bar 177 detract (if anything) from the piano's *own* presentation of the beginning of the main theme (bar 178ff.) rather than from an orchestral presentation, gives little indication of relational unease.

Moreover, in a later passage from the C/development section (bars 269–76, Example 48), the piano finally assimilates a build-up sequence very similar to bars 74–9 from the first movement into an exclusively co-operative dialogue with the orchestra. Although the piano writing, consisting of a three-beat figure growing out of dialogue with the orchestra (bars 264ff.) that is repeated and liquidated in a progressive ascent, invokes the initial first-movement entry thematically and procedurally, the effect is very different from a relational perspective. Instead of usurping the piano with a flamboyant fermata and cadenza-like flourishes, the piano now uses its dialogued material to confirm F

[11] This entire passage is reworked in the recapitulation. Whereas the scalic orchestral figures preceding the piano's arpeggiated statement and the three-way exchange of the main theme are omitted, the dialoguing of the piano's statement itself is extended, in a slightly modified form, to the bassoons and strings (see bars 333–45).

Example 47. Mozart, Piano Concerto K. 467, 3rd Movement, bars 169- 81.

without further ado (bars 275–7) and to lead immediately to a protracted dialogue with the winds (bars 278–95).[12]

The second movement of K. 482, like the finales of K. 450, 451, 467 and 595, recasts a source of confrontation from the first movement in such a way as to reinforce, rather than obscure, the intimacy of piano/orchestra relations. The piano and the orchestra fail to see eye-to-eye in the solo exposition and the beginning of the development section of K. 482/i, resulting in modal and tonal disputes in bars 126–9 and 216–22 (see Chapter 3, pp. 53–5). Tonal 'opposition' between the piano and the orchestra is extended to the individual formal sections of K. 482/ii. Following the orchestra's initial presentation of the theme section in C minor (bars 1–32), the piano and the orchestra adhere to minor and major keys respectively for their alternate presentations of the A1, B, A2 and C sections.[13] Although direct manifestations of tonal confrontation – ostentatious harmonic gestures and tonal/modal change allied with dynamic change – are not evident in the second movement in the same way as in the first, the distinct tonal 'worlds' inhabited by the piano and the orchestra serve as a general reminder of the more explicit tonal confrontations in the first movement. In the A3 and Coda/B sections, however, the piano and orchestra engage in dialogue for the first time since bars 1–64, each taking up thematic material and tonalities associated with the other party in the A1, B, A2 and C sections. The orchestra presents material derived from the A section in C minor (bars 145–64), and the piano presents material from the B section (bars 193ff.), twice

[12] Even if the piano's modal contradiction of the winds in bars 264–7 (A to a) is taken as an indication of relational unease, the unease is immediately negated by the winds' and piano's restatements of the motif in A minor (bars 268–70).

[13] I have followed Elaine R. Sisman's interpretation of this movement as a rondo-variation (A, A1, B, A2, C, A3, Coda/B). See Sisman, *Haydn and the Classical Variation*, p. 228.

Example 48. Mozart, Piano Concerto K. 467, 3rd Movement, bars 264-77.

hinting at C major (bars 201, 205) in recognition perhaps of the major modes of the preceding orchestral B and C sections. The A3 and Coda/B sections, moreover, are cast almost entirely in co-operative dialogue (split themes in bars 145–56, 157–60, 165–85, 201–9 and a full theme in bars 186–201): thus, they succinctly re-establish intimate relations between the piano and the orchestra, and firmly set aside the spectre of tonal confrontation from the first movement.

Recurring Dialogic Procedures in the First and Second Movements of Mozart's Piano Concertos

The recurrence of specific dialogic procedures across Mozart's three-movement cycles is a standard feature of his piano concertos. Although these cyclical procedures take a variety of forms, they serve in each case to reinforce the dialogic co-operation established between the piano and the orchestra in the first movement. The slow movements of Mozart's piano concertos, often different from their preceding first movements in affective terms, nevertheless exhibit striking dialogic parallels with them. As we shall see, dialogues themselves may be reshaped from one movement to the next, but interactive patterns and procedures are invariably retained.

Several of Mozart's piano concertos simultaneously demonstrate specific *and* general dialogic connections between individual movements. In K. 453/ii, for example, both the elaboration of dialogue from the orchestral to the solo exposition and the evolution of a long-range 'dialogue' across the movement as a whole invoke K. 453/i. In the solo exposition of K. 453/i the piano and the orchestra embellish previously introduced dialogue, creating a more elaborate bond between these two forces than between the orchestral interlocutors in the earlier section (see Chapter 4, p. 80). The same process is evident in the solo exposition of K. 453/ii. The winds' internal dialogue from the orchestral exposition (bars 8–13), reappearing in bars 42ff., is extended by the piano so that it may be dialogued with the subsequent second theme (bars 54ff.). The outlined stepwise descent D–C–B in the winds' imitated motif (bars 42–6, beat 1), lengthened across four bars (E–D–C–B in the right hand, bars 47–50) to inflect to C, b, and a on route to the dominant G (bar 50), uses the motif's semitone auxiliary-note gesture (D♯–E, bar 51) to generate turn-like figures (bar 51); both of these elements dialogue elements of the ensuing second theme (the semiquaver turns in bars 55–7 and the rising semitones in bars 59–61). Just as the piano elaborates the main theme of the first movement in such a way as to draw it closer to the echoed material in the winds (see bars 79–83) than at the corresponding juncture of the orchestral exposition, so the piano embellishes and elongates the material from bar 8ff. of the second movement in bar 46ff., bringing it into closer relation with the material from bar 54ff. than in the orchestral exposition.

Moreover, at a broader level of long-range 'dialogue', K. 453/ii demonstrates a procedural similarity with the augmented 6th progression that emerges gradually in K. 453/i (see Chapter 5, p. 124). From the beginning of the solo exposition of K. 453/ii onwards piano/orchestra interaction evolves steadily across the four presentations of the main theme. With the shift from dominant harmony to minor V after a pause (bars 34–5), the presentation of the main theme in the solo exposition demonstrates potential for dialogic opposition, a potential realised at the beginning of the development (bars 64–74). Here, the main theme is again interrupted by a pause (bar 68), with the harmonies on either side of the pause (V/G, d) corresponding to the major/minor shift in the solo exposition. On this occasion, however, dialogic opposition is made explicit: the winds (by themselves) end on a D major chord and are followed by the piano (by itself) beginning on the corresponding minor chord (d), an harmonic shift that underscores confrontational dialogue, according to Reicha's criteria (see Chapter 2).[14] Whereas the presentation at the beginning of the recapitulation follows a similar procedure to that of the solo exposition (the harmonic shift is now from V to ♭III), the final presentation is different, resolving the relational tension from the beginning of the development by splitting the theme

[14] In her analysis of this movement, Susan McClary misses the significance of the new dialogic manner in which the theme is presented at this juncture. Instead, she comments subjectively that 'the piano is no longer concerned with public display (to say nothing of the facile escapism offered by the orchestra), but rather with genuine expressions of loss'. See 'A Musical Dialectic from the Enlightenment: *Mozart's Piano Concerto in G Major, K. 453*, Movement 2', p. 148.

between the winds and the piano (bars 123–30, Example 49), uninterrupted by pauses for the first time in the movement. Instead of enacting harmonic and modal contrast, the piano now begins *exactly* where the winds leave off harmonically and melodically (i.e. on subdominant harmony and the flute's A″, bar 127), ensuring a smooth and co-operative exchange of material.[15] Thus, the piano and the orchestra progress systematically in their interaction over the course of the movement, presenting the theme together (i.e. without dialogue), later engaging in confrontational dialogue, and finally producing co-operative dialogue.[16] While the long-range 'dialogue' in K. 453/i features neither confrontation nor immediate dialogue between the piano and the orchestra, it does follow a similar teleological course to the evolving dialogue in K. 453/ii: both procedures recur at crucial formal junctures of their respective movements (the beginnings and ends of sections); both develop gradually, strengthening the bond between the piano and the orchestra by progressing to a point of resolution; and both culminate either immediately before (K. 453/i) or immediately after (K. 453/ii) the cadenzas of their respective movements. Girdlestone's general assessment thus seems accurate: 'Far from contrasting

[15] Girdlestone remarks that 'the opening strain . . . has at last found its answer. . . . [T]he question dies away, trusting and peaceful'. See *Mozart and His Piano Concertos*, p. 251. Charles Rosen writes in similar fashion: '[the main theme] melts into the succeeding phrase and is resolved in one of the most expressive, and yet perhaps most conventional, phrases that Mozart could have written . . . moving chromatically through the subdominant into the piano's cadence'. See *The Classical Style*, pp. 224–5. McClary also remarks upon the reconciliatory nature of the final presentation of the main theme – 'with the acceptance of the discipline of the motto, the divisiveness between the group and the individual has been overcome' (p. 155) – but finds the ending ambivalent: 'To those who value social order and find subjective expressivity self-indulgent, the winning over of the soloist to the harmonious, positive world of the orchestra is a triumph . . . But to those who identify with the free agency of the individual voice up against a repressive social order, the harmonious closure at the end . . . must seem bitter' (p. 156).

[16] In McClary's attempt to interpret K. 453/ii as articulating 'a society/individual problematic' ('A Musical Dialectic', p. 156) in which Mozart 'harnesses both our tendency to identify with the soloist in a concerto and with our desire for closure and reconciliation in order to pull the dilemma deep down inside the listener' (p. 159), I think she overstates the claim for opposition between the piano and the orchestra over the course of the movement. It is difficult to hear the piano as either 'the individual voice, heroic in its opposition to the collective orchestral force' or 'principally as flamboyant, theatrical, indulgent in its mode of self-presentation' (p. 147) after the pauses in bars 33–4 at the beginning of the solo exposition, when it engages in co-operative dialogue with the winds a few bars later (42–7). Her two possible interpretations for the beginning of the recapitulation – either 'Just at the moment at which the soloist seemed hopelessly lost in despair, the orchestra valiantly salvages the situation, returns the piece to the comfort of "rationality"' (p. 151), or 'the organic necessities of the individual are blatantly sacrificed to the overpowering requirements of social convention' (p. 151) – are similarly problematic, since they are grounded in the dubious assumption that the 'inevitable' tonic 'was achieved irrationally, not by means of the pure, pristine logic of conventional tonality' (p. 151). Whereas the orchestra does indeed accomplish the tonal journey from V/C♯ to C major in quick time (bars 86–90), it uses a variation of the piano's concluding gesture (B♯–D♯–G♯) rather than contrasting material to do it, and is careful not to contradict the piano's V/C♯ harmony in the initial bar (86).

with [the first movement], this second movement carries on its thought, emphasizing it and bringing out its essential elements'.[17]

Example 49. Mozart, Piano Concerto K. 453, 2nd Movement, bars 123-30.

As in K. 453, the first and second movements of K. 488 feature similar recurring dialogic procedures and similar overall relational trajectories. Whereas succinct dialogic segues and a single full-theme dialogue (the second theme, bars 99–114) dominate piano/orchestra interaction in the solo exposition of K. 488/i (see Chapter Four, pp. 64–7), these two types of dialogue mix more freely in the recapitulation. The progression towards a more equal blend is encapsulated by dialogue at the crossover between the solo exposition and the development, where a new theme is introduced in the strings (bars 143–8, see Example 50). Charles Rosen has rightly pointed out that this theme is distinctive and original, as it is 'both an end and a beginning: a final cadence for the *tutti* and the opening of the development'.[18] Its most striking feature, however, is its mode of presentation, which concisely unites the dialogic segue and the dialogued theme (see Example 50). On the one hand, the full theme is dialogued in bars 149–56; on the other, the piano begins its statement by picking up (and inverting) the strings' semiquaver scalic descents from bars 140–3. At the beginning of the recapitulation the twofold presentation of the main theme foregoes the subtle dialogic segue from bar 74, dialoguing the main theme between the orchestra and the piano instead, and thereby invoking the fully dialogued periods from the orchestral exposition (see bars 1–18 and 198–213). Equally, the theme from bar 143 – originally presented by the piano in a highly decorated fashion – is finally heard in its original form in the piano and passed in its entirety to the woodwinds (bars 261–75); once again the earlier dialogic segue is omitted. (This process is represented diagrammatically in Figure 4.)

Just as the intricate piano/orchestra exchange at the end of the solo exposition and beginning of the development of K. 488/i (bars 141–56) is a catalyst for equalizing the emphasis on dialogic segues and full-theme dialogues, so the piano/orchestra exchange at the corresponding point of K. 488/ii (the beginning of the B section, in the context of an ABA′ structure) has a similar function. A

[17] See Girdlestone, *Mozart and His Piano Concertos*, p. 246.
[18] Rosen, *The Classical Style*, p. 243.

Example 50. Mozart, Piano Concerto K. 488, 1st Movement, bars 141-56.

new theme in the relative major is introduced in the winds (I–V, bar 35–8) and passed to the piano (I–I, bars 39–42). The semiquavers in the winds and piano (bar 38) effect a smooth dialogic segue between the two statements, and bear a strong resemblance to the segue in bar 74 of the first movement: the winds, oscillating chromatically, descend from E to B; and the piano, in complementary fashion, ascends chromatically from B to E.

In the earlier A section there is a dialogued segue but no dialogued full theme:[19] the final notes of the piano's presentation of the main theme (A–G♮–F♮, bars 11–12) pre-empt the beginning of the first violins' and clarinet's

[19] In spite of similarities between the orchestral theme in bars 12–20 and the piano material beginning in bar 20 – both begin with i–i-V-i harmony for example – the piano and the orchestra cannot be said to engage in thematic dialogue at this point. The piano features a repeated two-bar pattern (bars 20–2 and 22–4, beginning again in bar 24), whereas the orchestra's melody ascends sequentially (bars 12–14, 14–16 and 16–18).

subsequent theme (A–G♯–F♯, bars 12–13) in an almost identical fashion to the phrase endings in bars 86 and 119–20 of the first movement (see Chapter Four). However, in the A′ section following the pivotal B section dialogue (bars 35–42), the theme from bar 12 is also dialogued (orchestra, bars 68–76; piano, bars 76–84). The arpeggiated accompanying figurations passed from the second violins to the left hand of the piano ensure a smooth transition between the end of the orchestral statement and the beginning of the piano statement (bars 75–6, beat 1), extending the prevalent segue technique to this new thematic

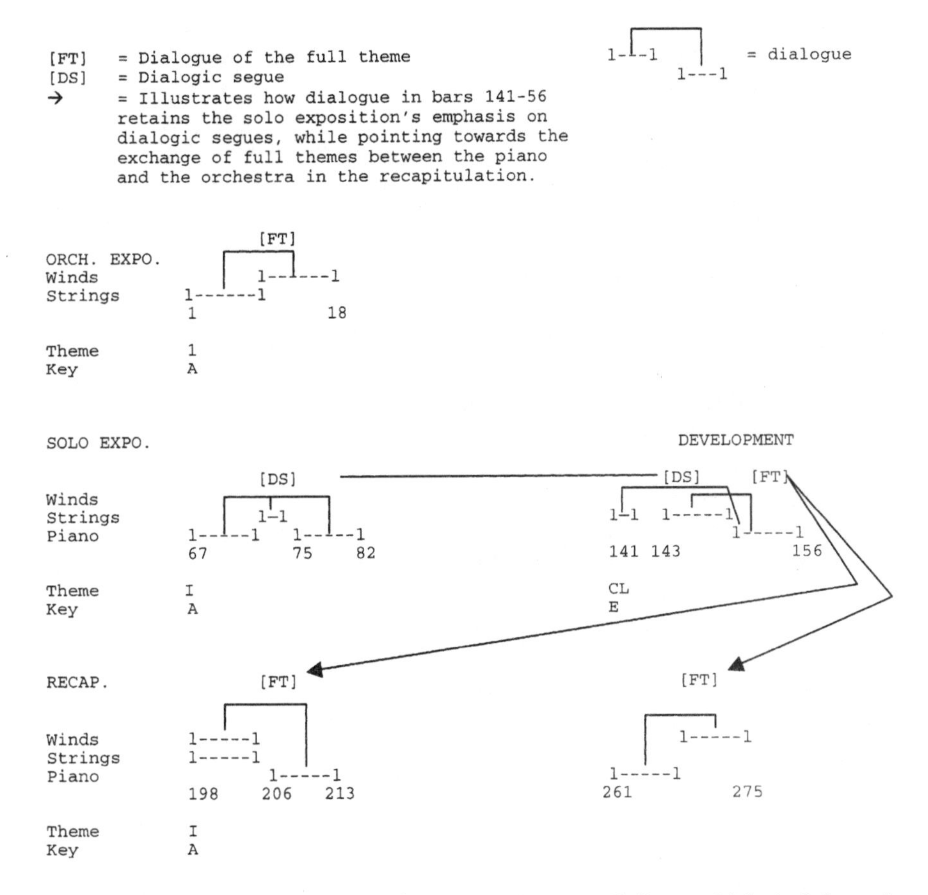

Fig. 4: Full theme Dialogue and Dialogic Segue in K. 488/i (first and 'closing' themes)

presentation.[20] Thus, in the same way as in the preceding movement in the cycle, the piano and orchestra in K. 488/ii progress towards an equal mixture of dialogic segues and dialogued themes in the reprise, again motivated by dialogue that combines both techniques at the beginning of the middle section.

Although other Mozart concertos are not as explicit as K. 453 and 488 in both repeating overall relational 'shapes' from movement to movement *and* bringing back specific dialogic procedures, they continue to feature highly developed cyclical procedures. For example, in K. 503/ii (concerto form, without a development section), Mozart exploits all six possible pairs of piano, winds and strings interlocutors (piano-winds, winds-piano, piano-strings, strings-piano, winds-strings, strings-winds) in a strikingly similar fashion to K. 503/i (see Chapter 4, pp. 94–5). The same four combinations heard in the solo exposition of K. 503/i reappear in the orchestral and solo expositions of K. 503/ii: the strings split a theme with the winds in the orchestral exposition (bars 16–19); the winds split part of the main theme with the piano at the beginning of the solo exposition (bars 27–30) and have their syncopated V7/F harmony imitated by the piano towards the end of the section (bars 63–5); the winds, in turn, imitate the piano shortly before the imperfect cadence in the main theme (bars 31–2) and repeat the piano's material from bars 51–3 in a slightly modified form (bars 54–6); and the strings are imitated by the piano (bars 63–5) and provide a three-quaver upbeat to piano material that precedes the second theme (see bar 38). Moreover, the same two combinations of interlocutors reserved until the development section of K. 503/i (piano-strings, winds-strings), are also reserved until the recapitulation of K. 503/ii: the piano's embellishments of the first bar of the main theme (bar 74) – ascending octave leaps followed by repeated notes – pre-empt the cellos' accompanimental figurations in bars 78 (see Example 51) and 80; and the strings (together with the piano and horns/bassoon) answer the winds (flutes, oboes, bassoons) in a short, thematic dialogue at the end of the movement (bars 102–8). Thus, the second movement of K. 503 closely follows the interactional scheme of the first, treating a recapitulation and not a development section as the place for weaving 'missing' dialogic combinations into the musical fabric.

Piano/Orchestra dialogue in the second movement of K. 459 also takes a procedural lead from dialogue in the first movement. (See the analysis of K. 459/ii in Chapter 5, pp. 133–5.) From the piano's perspective, the statements of the main themes at the beginning of both solo expositions – presented as a full-theme dialogue in the first movement (bars 72–87) and as a modified imitation of orchestral material in the second (bars 21–30) – are in each case near exact repetitions of statements from the beginning of the orchestral expositions (bars 1–8 in K. 459/i and bars 1–5 in K. 459/ii), setting the stage for the piano's and orchestra's extraordinary sensitivity to each other's material. Ensuing dialogue in the transition sections is also strikingly similar. The chain of imitative points in

[20] Dialogue of accompanimental material continues in bars 80–3, with the piano (left hand) and the bassoon sharing arpeggiated figurations.

Example 51. Mozart, Piano Concerto K. 503, 2nd Movement, bars 74-79.

the piano and the winds in the second movement (bars 31–4), with the piano picking up exactly where the oboe and bassoon leave off (bars 35) to ensure a smooth segue between thematic material, parallels the delicate synthesis of dialogic types in the first movement. At this juncture of the first movement, the piano enters as one of a succession of imitative interjections and seems to grow directly out of the flute's ascending half-step line (bar 111, see Example 52).

Comparable subtlety characterises the presentations of both secondary themes. The combination of thematic and segue dialogue in bars 44–52 of the second movement (see Chapter 5, p. 133) is, if anything, surpassed by the *tour de force* of full-theme, split-theme and imitative dialogue in bars 129–49 of the first movement (Example 53). The piano's E–C descent in the process of confirming the dominant C (bars 129^{4}–30^{1}) is imitated by the E–C movement in the first violins (bars 130^{4}–32^{1}) at the beginning of the secondary theme. The ensuing theme is delicately split between the strings and woodwinds (bar 130^{4}-38) and the entire period then presented by the piano (bars 139ff.).

Dialogue in the recapitulations of both movements also functions in similar ways. As we have seen, the piano and the orchestra demonstrate an increased sensitivity towards material presented by the other party in the recapitulation of K. 459/ii, creating dialogue from previously undialogued material. They do the same in the corresponding section of K. 459/i. First, the piano's statement of the main theme at the beginning of the recapitulation (bars 247–54), which dialogues with the full orchestra in bars 255–62, is pre-empted by a dialogue of the head motif between strings and woodwinds (bars 241–6, see Example 54). Unlike the corresponding moment in the solo exposition, the dialogued restatement of the main theme now grows directly from a preceding dialogue.[21]

[21] David Rosen makes a similar point in his recent discussion of K. 459/i. See '"Unexpectedness" and "Inevitability" in Mozart's Piano Concertos', in *Mozart's Piano Concertos*, ed. Neal Zaslaw, pp. 262–3. I do not agree with Rosen's assessment, however, that the piano's reappearance resolves a 'conflict' (p. 265) or 'quarrel' (p. 263) between the strings and the woodwinds. To be sure, the movement – in the six-bar dialogue – from A7 to the tonic (F) is a little uneven harmonically. But the strings and the woodwinds effect the modulation *together*, both parties contributing to the harmonic momentum.

Example 52. Mozart, Piano Concerto K. 459, 1st Movement, bars 106-112.

Second, Mozart introduces exquisite new dialogue in bars 338–48 (Example 55). The piano initially restates bars 171–2 from the solo exposition transposed into the tonic, and then turns immediately to a descending thirds motif, absent since the orchestral exposition (bar 43). The similarity between these two motifs is obvious: both comprise descending thirds (F–D–B♭–G), the first elaborating its descent with lower auxiliary notes. The ensuing dialogue between the piano and the orchestra (bars 341–5) replays the dialogue from bars 43–7 (woodwinds and strings). Whereas the piano's second and third entries (bars 342^4-43^3 and 344^4-45) cleverly combine the quaver rhythm of the motif from bars 338–9 and the melodic line of the motif from bars 340–1, the third entry adds an extra dimension to the dialogue: its octave figurations engage in dialogue with the ensuing octaves in the woodwinds (bars 348–52). In sum, the bonds between the piano and the orchestra in the first and second movements of K. 459 – already intimate in the solo expositions – are further strengthened in the recapitulations by dialogic interpolations that extend the give and take to material not previously treated in this way.

Even if not as pronounced in their cyclical tendencies as the first and second movements of K. 453, 459, 488 and 503, the slow movements of a number of Mozart's other Viennese concertos demonstrate to a lesser extent dialogic procedures consistent with those in the first movements. The piano and the orchestra in K. 414/ii and 451/ii, for example, engage in similar instances of dialogue to K. 414/i and 451/i. The soloist's distinctive preparation for, and dialogue with, ensuing *tutti* material in K. 414/i (see Chapter 4, p. 81), is also found in K. 414/ii: its conjunct semiquaver figurations in bars 46–7 and 90–4

Example 53. Mozart, Piano Concerto K. 459, 1st movement, bars 127-149.

2

Example 54. Mozart, Piano Concerto K. 459, 1st Movement, bars 241-50.

pave the way for the *tutti* interjections in bars 51–4 and 96–8 respectively. Equally, the introduction of thematic material at important formal junctures in dialogue with immediately preceding motifs pervades K. 451/i and 451/ii: the first theme, the V/V preparation for the secondary theme and the beginning of the development section in the first movement operate in this way (see bars 75–6, 116–20 and 185–9), as do the beginnings of the C and A″ sections in the second-movement rondo (bars 45–6 and 71–8). The first and second movements of K. 450 are dialogically similar in a more general respect. The gradual increase in dialogue over the course of K. 450/ii – the piano and orchestra alternate eight–bar statements in the theme and first variation sections, combine antecedent-consequent (bars 65–72) and alternate statements in the second variation, and mix two-quaver overlapping imitation (bars 95–8) and antecedent-consequent dialogue (bars 101–12) in the final 'Coda' section – broadly parallels the gradual increase in piano/orchestra dialogue across the solo exposition, development and recapitulation of the first movement, albeit without the relational progression from competition to co-operation.

Example 55. Mozart, Piano Concerto K. 459, 1st Movement, bars 338-53.

The Concerto Finales: Dialogic Culminations to Mozart's Three-Movement Cycles

Overall, the level of dialogic activity in Mozart's concerto finales is higher than in the other movements of the cycle. Finales, either in their entirety or in individual sections, often exploit or bring together earlier dialogic processes in order to create adept and effective conclusions. Although many of the standard procedures for articulating an 'apotheosis finale' in an instrumental cycle – 'run-on movements . . . the transformation of minor into major . . . prominent and unusual tonal relations . . . an impression of incompleteness or unfulfilled potential before the finale . . . [and] a mood of tension or irresolution'[22] – are not evident in Mozart's concerto finales, the combination in many of them of intricate procedural allusions to earlier movements and lively, unencumbered exchange lends them a powerful and poignant effect of culmination.[23]

As observed above, K. 453, 459 and 488 feature prominent recurrences of dialogic procedures across first and second movements. It is not surprising, therefore, that this trend continues in the finales. In K. 453/iii, for example, Mozart combines cyclic references to earlier movements with a teleological design. Each of the five variations highlights a slightly different approach to dialogue: the first features one-bar imitation from the piano to the strings (bars 25–8); in the second, statements are alternated between the winds and the piano, and internal dialogue appears later in the winds (bars 49–52); in the third, alternation between the winds and piano, and internal dialogue in the winds, is present throughout; the fourth (in the tonic minor) features alternation between the orchestra and the piano; and the fifth incorporates alternation between the orchestra and the piano and, at one point, a smooth dialogic segue through repeated Ds (bar 136).

The final *Presto* section brings back these dialogic types in quick succession – alternated statements (bars 171–221, 249–64), internal dialogue (bars 183–8, 202–11), segue between statements (the flute and piano in bar 256) and one-bar imitation (bars 213–16) – offering a neat summation of dialogue in the movement as a whole. Furthermore, the final bars of the *Presto* (bars 331–46, see Example 56) refer succinctly to dialogic procedures from the first and second movements. In general terms, an increase in the rapidity of piano/orchestra dialogue in this passage (4+2+4+2+1+1+1+1 bar units) relates to a similar increase at the end of the solo exposition of K. 453/ii (2+2+1 [the piano's triplet semiquavers continuing the winds' descending semiquavers] +half-bar units, in bars 54–61). More specifically, the final statement of the finale's main theme (bars 331–40, Example 56) encapsulates dialogue from the

[22] Webster, *Haydn's 'Farewell' Symphony*, p. 184.

[23] Webster's examples of 'finales as culminations' in Haydn's *oeuvre* are the fugal finales to the string quartets op. 20 and op. 54, no. 4. See *Haydn's 'Farewell' Symphony*, pp. 294–313.

main themes of the first *and* the second movements. On the one hand, the precise orchestral echoes – which copy and extend the piano's quaver figurations in bars 334–6 and 340–2 – invoke the meticulous echoes from the main theme's presentation in the solo exposition of the first movement. On the other hand, the modification of the final statement of the main theme, in the context of piano/orchestra dialogue, parallels the final statement of the main theme in the second movement: both are altered for the first time to tonally closed eight-bar units (bars 123–30 in the second and 331–4, 337–40 in the third movements).

Furthermore, the interpolated extended echo (bars 334–6) between the two halves of the finale's theme functions as a musically filled-in 'pause' that prolongs the tonic harmony from the end of the previous phrase; it thereby alludes to the distinctive *literal* pauses characteristic of the main theme of the second movement until the final statement. Mozart is able, therefore, to refer to the 'disrupted' and the 'resolved' versions of the main theme of the second movement at one and the same time! Likewise, by bringing together important interactional procedures from the first two movements of the concerto, he creates an exquisite conclusion to the work as a whole.

Whereas the end of K. 453/iii recalls specific procedures from earlier in the concerto, K. 488/iii convincingly exploits dialogic developments from its first two movements. An emphasis on full-theme dialogue – the type to which the piano and the orchestra progress in the first and second movements – is maximised in the finale. Each section in this sonata rondo features at least one dialogued full theme (A: bars 1–16, 106–29; B: 176–87; A′: 202–29; C: 262–85; A″: 330–45; B: 412–23; A‴: 441–56, 456–72, 481–96). The presence of three dialogued themes in quick succession in the final section not only makes for a forceful culmination to this process, but also for a joyous affirmation of the free, unencumbered spirit of piano/orchestra co-operation pervading the concerto as a whole.

As in K. 488/iii, the piano and the orchestra in K. 459/iii expand the closely co-operative relations established and reinforced in the first and second movements. Although dialogic interaction in the finale is not in general as intricate and sophisticated as earlier in the concerto, it nevertheless includes references to the first and second movements. For example, the presentation of the secondary theme (bar 203ff., Example 57), is almost a carbon copy of the presentation of the corresponding theme in the first movement. Although one is a full-theme dialogue (first movement, bars 131–49) and the other an antecedent-consequent (finale, bars 203–18), both are gracefully split between the strings and the winds in the first half of the dialogue, and answered by more elaborate piano writing in the second half. The piano's elaborations in both cases bring elements of the preceding orchestral material into closer thematic relation: in the first movement, the piano's embellishments of the oboe from bar 133 and the first violin from bar 135 (at bars 141 and 143 respectively, see Example 53 above) produce similar, conjunct figurations; in the finale, the semiquaver octave decorations of the violins' and flute's material from bars

Example 56. Mozart, Piano Concerto K. 453, 3rd Movement, bars 331-46.

205–6 (in bars 213–14) lead directly to the octave leap in bar 215 (corresponding to bar 207). Even the first violin's delicate imitation in the first movement of the E–C movement that concludes the piano's immediately preceding phrase (bars 129^4–32^1) is matched at the corresponding point in the finale: the turn figure completing the piano trill (bars 201–2) reappears in the first bar of the theme (bar 203).

Example 57. Mozart, Piano Concerto K. 459, 3rd Movement, bars 201-18.

Like its secondary theme, the closing material of K. 459's finale also demonstrates a deep-rooted (albeit more oblique) connection to the second movement. The final A″ section following the cadenza features constant dialogue between the piano and the orchestra (full theme, bars 454–70; split theme, bars 470–86;[24] alternated phrases, bars 486–502), with the interlocutors uniting – fittingly, given the descriptions of dialogue by eighteenth-century writers and Reicha – in the concluding bars (502–6). As Wye J. Allanbrook has shown, this section is an appropriate climax to the extended manipulation of the quaver motto across the movement, invoking 'obsessive' cadential formulations characteristic of *buffa* numbers (bars 470ff.).[25] Equally, dialogue in this section recalls the conclusion of the second movement (described in Chapter 5,

[24] Although strictly speaking there is no alternation in these bars, the quaver figures in the piano and subsequently the winds (bars 470–8 and 478–86) are more syntactically similar to the quavers and semiquavers preceding them than the crotchet-arpeggiated writing presented simultaneously.

[25] See 'Comic Issues in Mozart's Piano Concertos', in *Mozart's Piano Concertos*, ed. Zaslaw, especially pp. 92–7.

pp. 133–5). Both passages start, for example, with new dialogue, similar in function and style of presentation. Just as the finale's section features a self-contained antecedent-consequent statement of the main theme – the first of its kind in the movement[26] – dialogued by the orchestra, so the second movement's section (see Example 58) includes a self-contained, antecedent-consequent version of the main theme, heard in dialogue between the piano and the orchestra for the first time. The increase in the rapidity of dialogue in the finale passage (8+8, 2+2 and eventually 1+1) is also paralleled by increased intricacy in the second movement's passage: the straightforward antecedent-consequent, followed by the piano's rhythmic pre-empting of the semiquaver scales, lead to an overlapping of imitative and antecedent-consequent dialogue in the final bars (153–9, Example 58). To be sure, the lively banter of the *buffa*-like dialogue is far removed from the more refined dialogue at the corresponding point in the second movement, reflecting a broad distinction between the subtle and rarefied interaction of the second movement (and the first movement as well) and the more direct interaction of the third.[27] Yet the close procedural similarity between the dialogic culminations in the middle and finale movements ultimately underscores the rigour of relational development in K. 459 as a whole. Although the piano and the orchestra demonstrate a teleological relational development, carefully establishing and reinforcing dialogic co-operation in the first and second movements and reaping the rewards of their toil in the finale's uninhibited affirmation of co-operation, they never lose sight of different stages in this developmental process. By referring back to earlier dialogic procedures in the finale, the piano and the orchestra do not simply pay homage to the first and second movements; they actively build on its dialogic procedures to create a new atmosphere of unrestrained, irrepressible co-operation.[28] The point at which the co-operative spirit is ostensibly most different from earlier in the concerto – the brisk exchange in the final section – is, indeed, the point at which dialogic procedures are most similar.

A final climactic section in which the piano and orchestra demonstrate dialogic co-operation in a free, uninhibited fashion is a characteristic feature

[26] Allanbrook, 'Comic Issues in Mozart's Piano Concertos', p. 93.

[27] There is much straightforward and uncomplicated dialogue between the piano and the orchestra in this third movement, in addition to the subtler dialogue in the secondary theme section discussed above. The antecedent and consequent halves of the main theme are passed separately from the piano to the winds in bars 1–32 and 255–88, and the head motif among the strings, piano and winds in bars 166–82 and 354–69. (The main theme and the *buffa* motif are also dialogued, of course, in the final section.) The orchestra dialogue among themselves in three fugato passages (bars 32–50, 228–41 [doubled by the piano] and 288–345), adding to the spirit of free and open exchange, if not specifically to the spirit of piano/orchestra co-operation.

[28] Although arguing along different lines, Charles Rosen also recognises K. 459/iii as a stylistic culmination of the work as a whole: 'The first two movements . . . are already heavy with Baroque sequences and contrapuntal imitation, as if to prepare for the final Allegro assai, for the last movement is a complex synthesis of fugue, sonata-rondo-finale, and *opera buffa* style'. *Classical Style*, pp. 226–7.

Example 58. Mozart, Piano Concerto K. 459, 2nd Movement, bars 146-59.

not only of K. 453, 488 and 459 but of a number of Mozart's other concerto finales as well. In K. 413/iii, for example, the concluding section (bars 169ff.) is cast entirely in dialogue: the main theme is dialogued in its complete form for the first time (bars 169–84); material from the A′ *tutti* (bar 107) is passed from the orchestra to the piano (bars 184–201); the main theme is split between the orchestra and piano (bars 201–13); a 'new' concluding theme is dialogued between the violins and the left hand of the piano (bars 220–8); and short antecedents and consequents are exchanged between the piano and the strings at the close. The shortening of the dialogued units during the final section itself (8–bar, 4–bar, 2–bar and 2–beat units in bars 169–201, 201–20, 220–8 and 228–30 respectively) further reinforces the sense of climax. The final section of K. 537/iii also features perpetual dialogue between the piano and the orchestra: in bars 303–44, the piano and the orchestra closely follow the thematic presentation from the beginning of the movement (bars 1–42), now subjecting all of the material to dialogue; in bars 344–364, the orchestra completes the piano's phrases (344–56) and splits a repeated theme with the piano (356–64); and in bars 364–8, the piano manipulates its semiquaver figures to segue neatly to the orchestra's I6/4–V–I cadential gestures. As a result, the final section of K. 537/iii, like the corresponding section of K. 413/iii provides the pinnacle of dialogic activity in the movement as a whole.

As well as bringing finales to an effective close with rousing affirmations of piano/orchestra co-operation, dialogically climactic final sections often cast significant light on the relational development played out across three-movement cycles. We have already seen that the final sections of K. 453/iii, 459/iii and 488/iii play decisive roles in this respect, invoking dialogic procedures from earlier in their concertos in order to reinforce inter-movement relational consistency. The corresponding section of K. 449/iii is supremely effective in this respect. In both the first and second movements of this concerto, as discussed in Chapters Three and Five, the piano and the orchestra establish and reinforce intimate relations (albeit in different ways). They follow the same relational pattern in the finale, with the concluding 6/8 section of the movement playing a vital role in this process.[29] Although the piano and the orchestra in the first part of the 'recapitulation' up to the cadenza (bars 219–68) restate dialogue from earlier in the movement in slightly modified forms – bars 234–42 and 246–53 correspond to 151–4 and 113–22 respectively – they introduce a kind of 'new' dialogue after the cadenza that renders relations between them more elaborate than in the 'exposition'. The 6/8 section begins, in fact, with the finale's most intricate piano/orchestra dialoguing of the main theme (bars 269–300). At each of the previous appearances of the theme, a doubling and/or elaboration of the melodic line (bars 33–50, 91ff., 136–51, 219–34) obscures piano/orchestra dialogue. In the final 6/8 section, however, the full version of the theme is dialogued clearly: the antecedent-consequent from bars 1–16 is split between the piano and the winds/strings (bars 269–84); and the continuation in bars 17ff. passed from the piano to the strings to the piano (bars 285–300, see Example 59). The second of these two dialogues (see Example 59) is especially noteworthy, as in addition to the thematic exchange the piano takes up in bars 292–6 the repeated B♭s from bars 285–8 (strings), and delicately chromaticises its descending melodic line in bars 296–9, in response to the chromatic ascent outlined by the violins in bars 293–6 (E♭–E–F–F♯–G). Close piano/orchestra dialogue continues to prevail in the concluding bars: phrases are split into one-bar units among the upper strings and piano (308–12 and 312–16); and the final tonic chords are split between the solo piano and the orchestra (bars 320–1 and 321–2).

[29] I take this movement to be a kind of 'monothematic' sonata-rondo, divisible into the following sections: Exposition: A B (bar 91) A′ (bar 136); Development: C (bar 151); Recapitulation: A (bar 219) B (bar 269).

Example 59. Mozart, Piano Concerto K. 449, 3rd Movement, bars 285-300.

The final, 6/8 section of K. 449 lends an end-orientated trajectory to the development of piano/orchestra relations in the finale, one that parallels relational development in the first two movements. As in K. 459, this process is outwardly quite different in the finale, which contains neither the terse challenges to piano/orchestra co-operation from the development and recapitulation sections of the first movement, nor, for the most part, the rarefied dialogue of the second movement. Reinforced co-operation is, correspondingly, more straightforward and direct, with piano/orchestra dialogue elaborated in a single concluding section demarcated by the end of the cadenza and the new 6/8 metre. This overt procedural contrast between the finale and the earlier movements, however, ultimately underscores a profound connection. For in the finale section Mozart draws attention almost self-consciously to the reinforcement process, through ostentatious metrical, thematic and gestural devices (the new 6/8 time signature, the clear dialoguing of a new presentation of the main theme and the closing two-chord imitation respectively). It is as if he deliberately simplifies an initially cerebral and nuanced relational procedure for the benefit of his audience. Relational development is highly formalised in the first and second movements, closely tied as it is to structural organisation. Piano/orchestra confrontation, introduced in the development section of the first movement, for example, is succinctly resolved in a dialogue at the beginning of the recapitulation that brilliantly integrates thematic presentations from the beginnings of the orchestral and solo expositions, and is subsequently invoked (and forcefully resolved) immediately before the cadenza (see Chapter 3, pp. 64–8). Equally, piano/orchestra dialogue in the A′ section of the second movement includes all the principal thematic material from *both* the 'orchestral introduction' and A sections, thus effecting a kind of unification of these sections in the reprise. The process is less formalised, however, in the finale, as no attempt is made to systematically reinforce piano/orchestra co-operation through the articulation and resolution of confrontation, for example, or the recollection and development of earlier dialogic organisation. In the context of the concerto as a whole, therefore, the concluding section is a very effective *dénouement*, expounding the principal relational message of the work (the reinforcement of piano/orchestra co-operation) in a lively, upbeat manner.

The Drama of Mozart's Three-Movement Cycles

Following our analytical examination of dialogic processes in Mozart's three-movement cycles, we are in a position to evaluate the dramatic qualities of these complete works. The idea that a message of co-operation is continually reinforced over the course of a Mozart concerto does not necessarily rest easily with a generalised concept of the 'drama' therein. In order to show that the dramatic credentials of Mozart's concertos are actually considerably strengthened rather than weakened through such reinforcement, we must situate Mozart's dialogic processes in the context of the comparable, broad objectives of drama and the concerto, as understood by late-eighteenth-century musical and dramatic theorists.

As discussed in Chapter Three, eighteenth-century drama was required, at a basic level, to instruct its audience. In the first half of the eighteenth century, neo-classicists such as Gottsched stressed the didactic, moral mission of art. Later in the century, Lessing, although ideologically opposed to Gottsched, remarked in no uncertain terms that theatre is 'the school of the moral world'.[30] Schiller's opinion that the 'true function of art is to awaken free moral initiative in the individual' and J. M. R. Lenz's desire to train the audiences of his plays through a new kind of 'primitive theatre' also connect late-eighteenth-century drama to moral instruction.[31]

Enlightenment writers often linked the edifying nature of drama to the development of dramatic characters, ideas and actions over the course of a play.

[30] Lessing, *Hamburg Dramaturgy*, p. 99.

[31] Benjamin Bennett discusses Schiller's concept in *Modern Drama and German Classicism*, p. 42, and Lenz's 'primitive theater' in *Beyond Theory: Eighteenth-Century German Literature and the Poetics of Irony* (Ithaca, New York: Cornell University Press, 1993), p. 300. For many writers the success of eighteenth-century drama as an instructive art form was directly attributable to the model of the Greeks. See Sulzer, *Allgemeine Theorie*, vol. 1, pp. 710–11.

John Gregory, for example, argues that dramatic development has a cumulative force: 'the effect of a Dramatic performance does not depend on the effect of particular passages, considered by themselves, but on that artful construction, in which one part gives strength to another, and gradually works the Mind up to those sentiments and passions, which it was the design of the author to produce'.[32] Similarly, Lessing explains that 'with the construction and elaboration of its chief personages [a play] combines larger and wider intentions; the intention to instruct us what we should do or avoid; the intention to make us acquainted with actual characteristics of good and bad, fitting and absurd'.[33] Actions, events and ideas in a play are required to follow one another in an orderly, systematic fashion, and must not be compromised by 'coups de théâtre', the 'childish curiosity' of 'surprise', or on-stage 'miracles'.[34] Diderot and Lessing explicitly ban 'miracles' from drama, Lessing claiming that they interfere with moral edification: 'We can only tolerate miracles in the physical world; in the moral everything must follow its natural course, because the theatre is to be the school of the moral world'.[35] Goethe shares Diderot's and Lessing's concerns about orderly and systematic development, prescribing 'motifs' as a means for ensuring that actions, events and ideas in plays and operas always appear rational.[36] Even the 'complication of events' ('Verwicklung der Vorstellungen') identified by Sulzer as one of the principal components of good dramatic disposition ('Anordnung') must arise from a methodical approach to action over a protracted period: 'First, the beginning of the action must necessarily be related, and the next sequence of action, forming the basis of the ensuing complication, . . . must be explained.'[37]

We first recognised in Chapter Three that Mozart's piano and orchestral 'characters' in the first movements of his concertos behave in a manner aligned with theoretical prescriptions for dramatic characters, eschewing abrupt relational transformation in favour of carefully crafted, stage-by-stage relational development and engaging listeners in challenging intellectual pursuits. Heinrich Koch's explanation of 'passionate dialogue' in the late-eighteenth-century

[32] Gregory, *A Comparative View*, pp. 116–17.

[33] Lessing, *Hamburg Dramaturgy*, pp. 99–100.

[34] For two of Diderot's numerous objections to 'coups de théâtre', see Diderot, *Selected Writings*, pp. 12, 49. Lessing dismisses 'surprise' as 'childish curiosity' in *Hamburg Dramaturgy*, p. 151.

[35] See Lessing, *Hamburg Dramaturgy*, p. 8. Diderot comments in like-minded fashion: 'dramatic art rejects miracles' in 'De la Poésie dramatique', p. 140.

[36] J. W. Goethe, *Conversations with Eckermann (1823–32)*, trans. John Oxenford (San Francisco: North Point Press, 1984), pp. 65, 69. Goethe's criticism of Rossini's opera *Moses* also appears to centre on the absence of particular 'motifs'. See *Conversations*, p. 215.

[37] Sulzer, 'Anordnung', in *Allgemeine Theorie*, vol. 1, pp. 153, 164. 'Der Anfang der Handlung muss nothwendig zuerst erzählt werden, und die nächste Folge der angefangenen Handlung, die den Grund der folgenden Verwicklung enthält, muss nothwendig eher . . . vorgetragen werden'. Bonds briefly discusses Sulzer's 'Verwicklung der Vorstellungen' (which he also translates as 'complication of events'), linking it to the Aristotelian concept of 'peripeteia', in *Wordless Rhetoric*, p. 190.

concerto supports this kind of consistent approach to interaction over the course of a multi-movement cycle – 'Now in the allegro it [the orchestra] tries to stimulate his [the soloist's] noble feelings still more; now it commiserates, now it comforts him in the adagio'[38] – an approach that is reinforced by analyses of Mozart's piano concertos in this chapter. Inter-movement consistency in dialogic organisation and development, for example, is evident in a number of concertos: K. 453/ii closely parallels the long-range relational development of K. 453/i; K. 488/i and 488/ii underscore the same progression from dialogue segues to a combination of segues and dialogued full themes; both K. 503/i and 503/ii utilise all six combinations of piano, wind and strings interlocutors, systematically delaying the same two combinations until the development and recapitulation sections respectively; and K. 459/i and 459/ii exploit similar dialogic techniques in their expositions, interpolating dialogue into their recapitulations in order to render intimate piano/orchestra relations still more intimate.

It is in Mozart's finales, however, that the full effect of systematically structured relational development is most apparent. K. 449/iii, 453/iii, 459/iii and 488/iii, although on the whole less dialogically intricate than their preceding movements, nevertheless bring procedures from earlier in the concerto together in a sophisticated fashion. By situating these procedures in a freer, less formalised co-operative setting Mozart both relaxes the piano/orchestra dialogue in general *and* intensifies specific processes. In this way, the final sections of K. 449, 453, and 459 in particular are uncannily effective at juxtaposing intricate procedural allusion with the kind of rhetorical flamboyance necessary at the concluding stage of a concerto. Systematic rigour thus co-exists with rousing climax, a potentially precarious balance negotiated by Mozart with extraordinary panache.

What has become clear is that piano/orchestra dialogue has an effect in a Mozart concerto closely akin to the effect (as envisaged by Gregory and Lessing) of dramatic construction in a play. The 'artful construction' of dialogue in Mozart's concertos, whereby allusions to procedures from earlier movements are manipulated in such a way as to '[give] strength to' the intimacy of piano/orchestra relations in some movements and the resolution of confrontation in others, ultimately conveys the message of co-operation in a considerably more powerful manner than single instances of dialogue could ever manage. The 'elaboration' of Mozart's 'chief personages', moreover, '[makes] us acquainted with [the] actual characteristic' of co-operation; musical co-operation thus becomes a representation of literal co-operation.

But what of the ideal late-eighteenth-century listener who attentively follows piano/orchestra dialogue in a Mozart concerto, and who situates it in the context of contemporary dramatic criticism?[39] Would he or she have

[38] Koch, *Introductory Essay*, p. 209.

[39] It was not uncommon for late-eighteenth-century theorists to identify ideal listeners for musical works. In the second volume of his *Introductory Essay*, for example, Koch states that a

been sufficiently engaged with the music to trace relational development in detail? The theoretical expectations of an intelligent listener to a concerto and a spectator at a play were similarly high in this respect. Goethe, Mme de Staël and Koch, for example, make comparable remarks about audience participation in plays and concertos. For Goethe, 'It is an absolute necessity that the audience be constantly engaged and not allowed to assume a position of detached contemplation.' As a result, 'actors should not . . . play to one another as if no third party were present'.[40] De Staël even equates Goethe's audiences with the Greek chorus, paying them a compliment in the process: '[they are] as patient, as intelligent, as the ancient Greek chorus, they do not expect merely to be amused . . . they contribute to their own pleasure, by analyzing and explaining what did not at first strike them'.[41] Koch identifies a similar level of active audience engagement in the concerto: 'the listener, without losing anything, is just the third person, who can take part in the passionate performance of the concerto player and the accompanying orchestra'.[42] Goethe's statement that the Greek tragedy's chorus 'had to elevate and delight the senses, emotions and mind'[43] of the audience further suggests that the chorus in Koch's scenario (that is, the orchestra) will 'stimulate . . . noble feelings' not only in the soloist but also in the actively engaged audience.

Late-eighteenth-century plays and concertos in their entirety were not designed merely to stretch the most gifted spectators and listeners; they were also contrived to appeal to the uninitiated. Writers such as Goethe readily acknowledged the different expectations of their diverse theatrical audiences: 'simple people are satisfied by seeing plenty of action, whereas a more cultured spectator will have his feelings engaged as well, and only a truly cultured person wants to reflect on a play'.[44] Thus, 'the crowd of spectators take pleasure in the spectacle' of a play like *Helena*, whereas 'the higher import will not escape the initiated'.[45] Similarly, musicians often talked of pleasing both *Kenner* and

'composition can have an effect only on those listeners whose souls and nerves are attuned to this art'. He goes on to elaborate that in ideal terms only those who 'come entirely dispassionate to the place where music will be performed, . . . merely with the intention of abandoning themselves to the pleasure which music affords them . . . can completely feel the pleasure of music'. See 'Heinrich Christoph Koch: Introductory Essay on Composition Vol. II, Part I (1787)', trans. Baker, in *Aesthetics and the Art of Composition in the German Enlightenment*, p. 146.

[40] See 'On Epic and Dramatic Poetry' (published in 1827 but written in 1797), in *Essays on Art and Literature*, ed. John Gearey, trans. Ellen von Nardroff and Ernest H. von Nardroff (New York: Suhrkamp, 1986), p. 194; and 'On Acting' (1824) in *Essays on Art and Literature*, p. 219. Diderot would have probably disagreed with Goethe on the specifics of the second remark. He argues that in order to avoid pandering to public taste, the dramatic author should 'forget' the spectator. See 'De la Poésie dramatique', p. 156.

[41] de Staël, *Germany*, pp. 314–15.

[42] Koch, *Introductory Essay*, p. 209.

[43] Goethe, 'On Greek Tetralogies', in *Essays on Art and Literature*, p. 196.

[44] Goethe, *Wilhelm Meister's Apprenticeship* (New York: Suhrkamp, 1989), p. 48.

[45] Goethe, *Conversations*, p. 130.

Liebhaber (or connoisseurs and amateurs).[46] Although the motivation for doing so was in part commercial – the *Clavier-Liebhaber* had an 'insatiable appetite' for simple piano music, for example[47] – it was also linked to the ideological aim of educating the listener. The dilettante of the Enlightenment strove to 'rationalise and understand every branch of knowledge, simplified and related through common principles of nature', an idealism encouraged by Lessing among others. Thus, a treatise written specifically to help readers pursue this goal – such as Johann Friedrich Daube's *The Musical Dilettante* (1773) – 'exemplifies the humanistic attempt "to bring enlightenment to . . . the dilettante"'.[48]

Mozart and others were well aware that late-eighteenth-century concertos should edify both *Kenner* and *Liebhaber*. The theorist Johann Adam Hiller, for example, remarks: 'At the right time and place we should bring in appropriate leaps, runs, arpeggios etc.; in the process, the unwavering approbation of all listeners, connoisseurs and musically ignorant alike, will make the composer and his work famous'.[49] The pedagogical implications of addressing the dilettante shed new light on Mozart's famous letter to Leopold (28 December 1782) about his first three Viennese piano concertos, K. 413, 414 and 415: 'These concertos are a happy medium between what is too easy and too difficult; they are very brilliant, pleasing to the ear, and natural, without being vapid. Here and there connoisseurs alone can derive satisfaction; but the music is written in such a way that the less learned cannot fail to be pleased, without knowing why.'[50] Later in the same letter, Mozart recognises the difficulties of

[46] See Komlós, *Fortepianos and their Music*, pp. 109–21. 'Originally, the differentiation referred to listeners, and to critics of music: applied to listeners, *Kenner* implied the educated and rational, *Liebhaber* the uneducated and emotional; applied to critics, the same terms distinguished between professionals and laymen' (p. 109).

[47] Ibid., p. 109.

[48] Daube, *The Musical Dilettante*, trans. Snook-Luther, p. 18.

[49] 'Abhandlung von der Nachahmung der Natur in der Musik', in *Historisch-Kritische Beiträge zur Aufnahme der Musik*, ed. Friedrich Wilhelm Marpurg (Berlin, 1754; reprint, Hildesheim: Georg Olms, 1970), vol. 1, p. 543. 'Man bringe wohlgewählte Sprünge, Läufer, Brechungen und dergleichen, an den gehörigen Orten, und in gehöriger Maasse an; so wird der ohnfehlbare Beifall aller Zuhörer, so wohl der Kunstverständigen, als derer die sie nicht verstehen, der Musik und dem Künstler zugleich Ehre machen'.

[50] Translation adapted from Anderson, *Letters*, p. 833. For the German original see Wilhelm A. Bauer, Otto Erich Deutsch, and J. H. Eibl, eds., *Mozart: Briefe und Aufzeichnungen. Gesamtausgabe* (Kassel: Bärenreiter, 1962–75), vol. 3, pp. 245–6. A reading of Mozart's correspondence immediately preceding his first Viennese piano concertos – the Mozart-Leopold letters from the beginning of Mozart's six-month stay in Paris in 1778 through the completion of *Idomeneo* in Munich in 1781 – reveals a keen interest in appealing to both amateurs and connoisseurs. On his 'Paris' Symphony, K. 297, Mozart remarks: 'I can answer for its pleasing the few intelligent French people who may be there – and as for the stupid ones, I shall not consider it a misfortune if they are not pleased. I still hope, however, that even asses will find something in it to admire'. (Anderson, *Letters*, p. 553.) Leopold, on the other hand, anxiously reminds his son not to ignore the amateur's taste: 'If you compose something which is to be engraved, make it easy, suitable for amateurs and *rather popular*' (p. 536); and 'You must remember that to every ten real connoisseurs there are a hundred ignoramuses. So do not neglect the so-called popular style, which tickles long ears' (p. 685).

gaining approbation from all quarters: 'The golden mean of truth in all things is no longer either known or appreciated. In order to win applause one must write stuff which is so inane that a coachman could sing it, or so unintelligible that it pleases precisely because no sensible man can understand it. This is not what I have been wanting to discuss with you; but I should like to write a book, a short introduction to music, illustrated by examples, but I need hardly add, not under my own name.'[51] Mozart's solution to this impasse, then, is to write a book that would educate audiences about music. Although Mozart's remarks on K. 413, 414 and 415 may have in part concerned their marketability, these remarks also acknowledged an important pedagogical responsibility – a *sine qua non* in dramatic terms – towards his diverse audience. His sense of obligation in this respect, moreover, would have been enhanced by his association in the 1780s with the freemasons, who required members to educate fellow citizens by sharing '[truth] . . . for the common good' and by '[leading] the mistaken to truth without rancor'.[52]

Further circumstantial evidence supports the idea that Mozart's piano concertos – like their counterparts in the spoken theatre – constituted a locus of pedagogy. Two of his concertos, K. 449 and 453, were dedicated to his pupil Barbara Ployer and another, K. 456, to Maria Theresia Paradis, a student of the Viennese musicians Leopold Kozeluch and Georg Friedrich Richter. The piano also fulfilled a social and broadly educative function in late-eighteenth-century Vienna. Learning the piano was considered *de rigueur* in certain social circles; as a result, piano teachers and instruction manuals were in high demand.[53] To be sure, Mozart's piano concertos did not provide learning material for budding pianists (he premiered most of them himself). Given the role of the piano in Viennese society, however, Mozart would certainly have intended his works to fulfil an edifying, and in a general sense educative, function.

From our analyses of two of Mozart's works in particular, including one of those dedicated to Ployer, we can clarify how listeners of varying aptitudes would have found these concertos equally stimulating. In K. 449, for example, the 'constantly engaged' cognizant listener – in keeping with the dramatic prescriptions of Goethe and de Staël – would have 'analyzed' and 'explained' both the veiled procedural connections among the three movements and the

[51] Anderson, *Letters*, p. 833.

[52] Joseph Holzmeister made these remarks to the 'True Concord' lodge on 11 February 1785. Quoted in Maynard Solomon, *Mozart: A Life* (New York: HarperCollins, 1995), p. 332. Mozart joined the lodge 'Beneficence' (*Zur Wohltätigkeit*) on 14 December 1784. For an informative list of secondary literature on Mozart's association with freemasonry, see Solomon, *Mozart*, pp. 601–2.

[53] See Peter Branscombe, 'The Land of the Piano: Music, Theatre and Performance in Vienna around 1800', in *Theatre and Performance in Austria*, eds. Ritchie Robertson and Edward Trimms (Edinburgh: Edinburgh University Press, 1993), pp. 3–19. See also Komlós, *Fortepianos*, pp. 122–32. Branscombe notes that 'even among the not especially musical families, a piano was part of the essential furniture of a small apartment' (p. 13).

more direct manifestation of reinforced piano/orchestra relations in the finale, as progressive reinforcements (covert and overt alike) of the prevailing message of co-operation. Similarly, the pronounced difference in the modes of piano/ orchestra discourse in each of the three movements would have allowed even the less initiated listener to make sense of relational development in the concerto as a whole. For he or she would surely have recognised the combination of intense confrontation and intimate dialogue in the first movement, the intimate dialogue in the second, and the lively, harmonious dialogue in the third, and also perceived them – albeit in a less sophisticated way than the knowledgeable listener – as a progression towards open, uninhibited co-operation. The overall relational progression from the first to the third movements of K. 459 would also have enlightened *cognoscenti* and less well-informed listeners in similar ways. While the former could have followed the finale's intricate transformation of dialogic procedures from the earlier movements (explained above) and interpreted it as evidence of a rigorous progression from refined and formalised to free and liberated co-operation, even the latter could have understood the general development from cultivated dialogue in the first and second movements to direct, brisk and bold dialogue (including the immediately recognisable *buffa*-like exchange) at the conclusion of the finale as a progression from one type of co-operative interaction to another.

At the superficial level of surprise and unpredictability in the 'plot', Mozart's continual reiterations and reinforcements of co-operation as the dominant relational message in his concertos at first seem to work against perceiving the works as dramatic. However, if, in line with classical dramatic thought, the *process* of piano/orchestra exchange across Mozart's concertos is privileged over and above the eventual outcome of the protracted exchange, the dramatic nature of the works becomes clear. Lessing clarifies that, in terms of engaging the audience, holding back the events of a play's *dénouement* is in itself insignificant: 'I rather think it would not exceed my powers to rouse the very strongest interest in the spectators even if I resolved to make a work where the *dénouement* was revealed in the first scene. Everything must be clear for the spectator, he is the confidant of every person, he knows everything that has occurred and there are hundreds of instances when we cannot do better than to tell him straight out what is going to occur.'[54] In an analogous way, the repeated reinforcement of co-operation as the dominant dialogic motivation across Mozart's concerto cycles – usually evident as early as the soloist's initial entry in the first movement, as shown in Chapter 4 – considerably *enhances* the dramatic quality of his works: the predictability of piano/ orchestra co-operation focuses a listener's attention on the *means* through which co-operation is attained, comprised and reinforced, rather than on co-operation as a simple end in itself. In fact, eighteenth-century writers on both drama and music clarify that the gradual preparation and reinforcement of ideas and emotions has an especially forceful effect on audiences. For Lessing:

[54] Lessing, *Hamburg Dramaturgy*, p. 149.

'By means of secrecy a [dramatic] poet effects a short surprise, but in what enduring disquietude could he have maintained us if he had made no secret about it! Whoever is struck down in a moment, I can only pity for a moment. But how if I expect the blow, how if I see the storm brewing and threatening for some time about my head or his?'[55] Adam Smith argues that repetition has similar force in music: 'Music frequently produces its effects by a repetition of the same idea; and the same sense expressed in the same, or nearly the same, combination of sounds, though at first it may make scarce any impression upon us, yet, by being repeated again and again, it comes at last gradually, and by little and little, to move, to agitate, and to transport us.'[56] Herein lies the essential brilliance of dramatic process in Mozart's piano concertos. By repeating and reshaping piano/orchestra co-operation over the course of a work and by continually encouraging the listener to analyse *how* it is attained, Mozart renders co-operation increasingly poignant, powerful and dramatically compelling.

Ultimately, parallels between dialogic processes in Mozart's piano concerto cycles and underpinnings of classical dramatic theory attest to the extraordinary position of Mozart's piano concertos as a medium of enlightenment in the late eighteenth century. Whereas Mozart's great operas and Lessing, Goethe and Schiller's great plays are put on a dramatic pedestal in this respect, it is high time that Mozart's piano concertos are accorded a similar status. Although Mozart's concertos, with their emphasis upon co-operation, could not have been expected to have produced direct changes in the behaviour of late-eighteenth-century audiences (Schiller makes a similar point in regard to theatrical audiences),[57] they would certainly, like their great theatrical and operatic counterparts, have led by example, provoking 'magnificent feelings, resolutions [and] passions' in their audiences and presenting 'divine ideals . . . for our emulation'.[58] As thorough workings out of the quest for harmonious, co-operative existence, Mozart's piano concertos offered exemplary models to their contemporary audiences of how to live their lives – less immediate than textual models in musical and spoken theatre perhaps, but no less powerful or enlightening.

[55] Lessing, *Hamburg Dramaturgy*, p. 149.

[56] Smith, *Essays*, p. 192.

[57] See Michael J. Sidnell's introduction to the section on Schiller in the anthology, *Sources of Dramatic Theory: 2. Voltaire to Hugo*, ed. Sidnell (Cambridge: Cambridge University Press, 1994), p. 153.

[58] Schiller, 'The Stage Considered as a Moral Institution', in *Sources of Dramatic Theory*, ed. Sidnell, p. 157.

Select Bibliography

Adams, Henry Hitch, and Baxter Hathaway, eds. *Dramatic Essays of the Neoclassic Age.* New York: Columbia University Press, 1950

Agawu, V. Kofi. *Playing with Signs: A Semiotic Interpretation of Classic Music.* Princeton: Princeton University Press, 1991

——. 'Mozart's Art of Variation: Remarks on the First Movement of K. 503'. In *Mozart's Piano Concertos: Text, Context, Interpretation,* edited by Neal Zaslaw, pp. 303–13. Ann Arbor: University of Michigan Press, 1996

Alembert, Jean le Rond d'. 'Conversation'. In *The Philosophical Dictionary or, the Opinions of Modern Philosophers on Metaphysical, Moral and Political Subjects.* Vol. 1, pp. 150–1. London: Elliot, 1786

Allanbrook, Wye Jamison. 'Comic Issues in Mozart's Piano Concertos'. In *Mozart's Piano Concertos: Text, Context, Interpretation,* edited by Neal Zaslaw, pp. 75–105. Ann Arbor: University of Michigan Press, 1996

——. *Rhythmic Gesture in Mozart: 'Le Nozze di Figaro' and 'Don Giovanni'.* Chicago: University of Chicago Press, 1983

——. 'Mozart's Tunes and the Comedy of Closure'. In *On Mozart,* edited by James M. Morris, pp. 169–86. Cambridge: Cambridge University Press, 1994

Allgemeine musikalische Zeitung, edited by Friedrich Rochlitz et al. Leipzig: Breitkopf & Härtel, 1798–1848

Allison, Henry E. *Lessing and the Enlightenment: His Philosophy of Religion and Its Relation to Eighteenth-Century Thought.* Ann Arbor: University of Michigan Press, 1966

Alth, Maria von and Gertrude Obzyna, eds. *Burgtheater 1776–1976: Aufführungen und Besetzungen von zweihundert Jahren.* Vienna: Salzer-Überreuter, 1979

Anderson, Emily, ed. *The Letters of Mozart and His Family.* 3rd edition. New York: Norton, 1985

Badura-Skoda, Eva. 'Zur Entstehung des Klavierkonzertes in B-dur KV. 456'. *Mozart-Jahrbuch 1964,* pp. 193–7

Badura-Skoda, Paul. *Kadenzen, Eingänge und Auszierungen zu Klavierkonzerten von Wolfgang Amadeus Mozarts.* Kassel: Bärenreiter, 1967

——. *Wolfgang Amadeus Mozart. Klavierkonzert C Moll KV 491.* Munich: Wilhelm Fink, 1972

Baker, Nancy Kovaleff. 'An *Ars Poetica* for Music: Reicha's System of Syntax and Structure'. In *Musical Humanism and its Legacy: Essays in Honor of Claude Palisca,* edited by Baker and Barbara Russano Hanning, pp. 419–49. Stuyvesant, New York: Pendragon, 1992

——. 'Heinrich Koch and the Theory of Melody'. *Journal of Music Theory* 20 (1976), pp. 1–48

Baker, Nancy Kovaleff. 'The Aesthetic Theories of Heinrich Christoph Koch'. *International Review of the Aesthetics and Sociology of Music* 8 (1977), pp. 183–209

——. 'Heinrich Koch's Description of the Symphony', *Studi Musicali* 9 (1980), pp. 303–16

Baker, Nancy Kovaleff and Thomas Christensen, eds. and trans. *Aesthetics and the Art of Musical Composition in the German Enlightenment: Selected Writings of Johann Georg Sulzer and Heinrich Christoph Koch*. Cambridge: Cambridge University Press, 1995

Bakhtin, Michael. *The Dialogic Imagination: Four Essays*. Edited by Michael Holquist. Translated by Caryl Emerson and Michael Holquist. Austin: University of Texas Press, 1981

Balthazar, Scott L. 'Intellectual History and Concepts of the Concerto: Some Parallels from 1750 to 1850'. *Journal of the American Musicological Society* 36 (1983), pp. 39–72

Batteux, Charles. *Les Beaux-Arts réduits à un même Principe* (1746). Edited by Jean-Rémy Mantion. Paris: Aux Amateurs de Livres, 1989

Beck, Hermann. 'Das Soloinstrument im Tutti des Konzerts der zweiten Hälfte des 18. Jahrunderts'. *Die Musikforschung* 14 (1961), pp. 427–35

Benary, Peter. 'Die Anfänge dreier Klavierkonzerte: Zur Individualisierung von Form und Gattung'. *Musica* 40 (1986), pp. 22–6

Bennett, Benjamin. *Modern Drama and German Classicism: Renaissance from Lessing to Brecht*. Ithaca, New York: Cornell University Press, 1979

——. *Beyond Theory: Eighteenth-Century German Literature and the Poetics of Irony*. Ithaca, N.Y.: Cornell University Press, 1993

Bent, Ian. 'The "Compositional Process" in Music Theory, 1713–1850', *Music Analysis* 3 (1984), pp. 29–55

Berger, Karol. 'Toward a History of Hearing: The Classic Concerto, A Sample Case'. In *Convention in Eighteenth- and Nineteenth-Century Music: Essays in Honor of Leonard Ratner*, edited by Wye Jamison Allanbrook, Janet M. Levy and William P. Mahrt, pp. 405–29. Stuyvesant, New York: Pendragon, 1992

——. 'The First-movement Punctuation Form in Mozart's Piano Concertos'. In *Mozart's Piano Concertos: Text, Context, Interpretation*, edited by Neal Zaslaw, pp. 239–59. Ann Arbor: University of Michigan Press, 1996

——. 'The Second-Movement Punctuation Form in Mozart's Piano Concertos: The Andantino of K. 449'. *Mozart-Jahrbuch 1991*, pp. 168–72

——. '*Diegesis* and *Mimesis*: The Poetic Modes and the Matter of Artistic Presentation'. *Journal of Musicology* 12 (1994), pp. 407–33

Berland, K. J. H. 'Didactic, Catecheticall, or Obstetricious? Socrates and Eighteenth-Century Dialogue'. In *Compendious Conversations: The Method of Dialogue in the Early Enlightenment*, edited by Kevin L. Cope, pp. 93–104. Frankfurt: Peter Lang, 1992

Biba, Otto. 'Grundzüge des Konzertwesens in Wien zu Mozarts Zeit'. *Mozart-Jahrbuch 1978/79*, pp. 132–43

Blackall, Eric A. *The Emergence of German as a Literary Language*. Cambridge: Cambridge University Press, 1959

Blume, Friedrich. 'The Concertos: (1) Their Sources'. In *The Mozart Companion*, edited by H. C. Robbins Landon and Donald Mitchell, pp. 200–33. New York: Norton, 1956

Bonds, Mark Evan. *Wordless Rhetoric: Musical Form and the Metaphor of the Oration*. Cambridge, Mass.: Harvard University Press, 1991

——. 'The Symphony as Pindaric Ode'. In *Haydn and His World*, edited by Elaine Sisman, pp. 131–53. Princeton: Princeton University Press, 1997

Botstein, Leon. 'The Patrons and Publics of the Quartets: Music, Culture and Society in

Beethoven's Vienna'. In *The Beethoven Quartet Companion*, edited by Robert Winter and Robert Martin, pp. 77–109. Berkeley: University of California Press, 1994

Boyle, Nicholas. *Goethe: The Poet and the Age. Vol. 1: The Poetry of Desire (1749–1790)*. Oxford: Clarendon Press, 1991

Branscombe, Peter. 'The Land of the Piano: Music, Theatre and Performance in Vienna around 1800'. In *Theatre and Performance in Austria*, edited by Ritchie Robertson and Edward Trimms, pp. 3–19. Edinburgh: Edinburgh University Press, 1993

Braunbehrens, Volkmar. *Mozart in Vienna, 1781–91*. Translated by Timothy Bell. New York: Grove, 1989

Brossard, Sebastien de. *Dictionnaire de Musique*. Paris, 1705. Reprint, The Hague: Hilversum, 1965

Brown, A. Peter. 'On the Opening Phrase of Mozart's K. 271: A Singular yet Logical Event'. *Mozart-Jahrbuch 1980–83*, pp. 310–18

Broyles, Michael. 'The Two Instrumental Styles of Classicism'. *Journal of the American Musicological Society* 36 (1983), pp. 210–42

Burney, Charles. *Music, Men and Manners in France and Italy: 1770*. Edited by H. Edmund Pools. London: Folio Society, 1969

——. *The Present State of Music in Germany, the Netherlands, and United Provinces*. 2 vols. London: T. Becket, 1775. Reprint, New York: Broude, 1969

——. *A General History of Music: From the Earliest Ages to the Present Period* (1789). 2 vols. New York: Harcourt, 1935

Cartwright, Michael. 'Diderot and the Idea of Performance and the Performer'. In *Studies in Eighteenth-Century French Literature*, edited by J. M. Fox, M. H. Waddicor, and D. A. Watts, pp. 31–42. Exeter: University of Exeter Press, 1975

Castres, Abbé Antoine Sabatier de. *Dictionnaire des passions, des vertus, et des vices*. Paris: chez Laporte, 1777

Chabanon, M. P. G. de. *De la Musique considerée en elle-même et dans les rapports avec la parole, les langues, la poésie, et le théâtre*. Paris, 1785

Charlton, David. *Grétry and the Growth of Opéra-comique*. Cambridge: Cambridge University Press, 1986

Churgin, Bathia. 'Francesco Galeazzi's Description (1796) of Sonata Form'. *Journal of the American Musicological Society* 21 (1968), pp. 131–99

Clark, Gregory. *Dialogue, Dialectic and Conversation: A Social Perspective on the Function of Writing*. Carbondale: Southern Illinois University Press, 1990

Cobin, Marian W. 'Aspects of Stylistic Evolution in Two Mozart Concertos: K. 271 and K. 482'. *Music Review* 31 (1970), pp. 1–20

Cone, Edward T. *The Composer's Voice*. Berkeley: University of California Press, 1974

Cook, Elisabeth. *Duet and Ensemble in the Early Opéra-Comique*. London: Garland, 1995

Cooper, Anthony Ashley *see* Shaftesbury, Third Earl of

Cramer, Carl Friedrich, ed. *Magazin der Musik*. 2 vols and musical supplement. Hamburg, 1783–1786. Reprint, Hildesheim: George Olms, 1971–74

Crutchfield, Richard. 'Lessing, Diderot and the Theatre'. In *Eighteenth-Century German Authors and their Aesthetic Theories: Literature and the Other Arts*, edited by Crutchfield and Wulf Koepke, pp. 11–28. Columbia, S.C.: Camden House, 1988

Czerny, Carl. *Complete Theoretical-Practical Pianoforte School*. 3 vols. London: R. Cocks, 1839

Dahlhaus, Carl. 'Der rhetorische Formbegriff H. Chr. Kochs und die Theorie der Sonataform'. *Archiv für Musikwissenschaft* 35 (1978), pp. 155–77

Daube, Johann Friedrich. *Der musikalische Dilettant. Eine Abhandlung der Komposition.*

Vienna, 1773. Translated and edited by Susan P. Snook-Luther as *The Musical Dilettante: A Treatise on Composition.* Cambridge: Cambridge University Press, 1992

Davis, Shelley. 'H. C. Koch, the Classic Concerto and the Sonata-Form Retransition'. *Journal of Musicology* 2 (1983), pp. 45–61

Derr, Ellwood. 'Some Thoughts on the Design of Mozart's Opus 4, the "Subscription Concertos" (K. 414, 413, 415)'. In *Mozart's Piano Concertos: Text, Context, Interpretation,* edited by Neal Zaslaw, pp. 187–210. Ann Arbor: University of Michigan Press, 1996

——. 'Mozart's Transfer of the Vocal "fermata sospesa" to his Piano Concerto First Movements'. *Mozart-Jahrbuch 1991,* pp. 155–62

Deutsch, Otto Erich. *Mozart: A Documentary Biography.* Translated by Eric Blom, Peter Branscombe, and Jeremy Noble. Stanford: Stanford University Press, 1965

Diderot, Denis. 'De la Poésie dramatique' (1758). In *Diderot's Writings on the Theatre,* edited by F. C. Green. Cambridge: Cambridge University Press, 1936. Reprint, New York: AMS Press, 1978

——. *Œuvres Politiques.* Edited by Paul Vernière. Paris: Garnier, 1963

——. *Selected Writings on Art and Literature.* Translated and edited by Geoffrey Bremner. New York: Penguin, 1994

——. *Rameau's Nephew and Other Works.* Translated by Jacques Barzun and Ralph H. Bowen. New York: Bobbs-Merrill, 1964

Diderot, Denis and Jean d'Alembert, eds. *Encyclopédie, ou Dictionnaire raisonné des sciences, des Arts et des Métiers, par une société de gens de lettres.* Paris 1751–72

Didier, Béatrice. 'Aspects de la Pédagogie Musicale chez Diderot'. In *Colloque International Diderot (1713–1784),* edited by Anne-Marie Chouillet, pp. 309–19. Paris: Aux Amateurs de Livres, 1985

Edwards, George. 'The Nonsense of an Ending: Closure in Haydn's String Quartets'. *Musical Quarterly* 75 (1992), pp. 227–54

Einstein, Alfred. *Mozart: His Character, His Work.* Translated by Nathan Broder and Arthur Mendel. London: Cassell, 1945

Eisley, Irving R. 'Mozart's Concertato Orchestra'. *Mozart-Jahrbuch 1976/7,* pp. 9–20

Elam, Keir. *The Semiotics of Theatre and Drama.* London: Methuen, 1980

Entick, John. *Entick's Spelling Dictionary.* New Haven, Connecticut: Sidney's Press, 1812

Feldman, Martha. 'Staging the Virtuoso: Ritornello Procedure in Mozart, from Aria to Concerto'. In *Mozart's Piano Concertos: Text, Context, Interpretation,* edited by Neal Zaslaw, pp. 149–86. Ann Arbor: University of Michigan Press, 1996

Ferguson, Linda Faye. 'Col basso and Generalbass in Mozart's Keyboard Concertos: Notation, Performance, Theory, and Practice'. Ph.D. diss., Princeton University, 1983

——. 'The Classical Keyboard Concerto: Some Thoughts on Authentic Performance'. *Early Music* 12 (1984), pp. 437–45

Finscher, Ludwig. 'Joseph Haydn–Ein Unbekannter Komponist?' *Neue Zeitschrift für Musik* 143 (1982/10), pp. 12–18

——. *Studien zur Geschichte des Streichquartetts 1: Die Entstehung des klassichen Streichquartetts: von den Vorformen zur Grundlegung durch Joseph Haydns.* Kassel: Bärenreiter, 1974

Fischer, Kurt von. 'Das Dramatische in Mozarts Klavierkonzerten 1784 mit besonderer Berücksichtigung des ersten Satzes von KV 453'. *Mozart-Jahrbuch 1986,* pp. 71–4

Flothuis, Marius. 'Bühne und Konzert'. *Mozart-Jahrbuch 1986,* pp. 45–58

Fontius, Martin. 'Mozart chez Grimm et Madame d'Epinay'. Translated from German by Sabine Cornille. In *Recherches sur Diderot et sur l'Encyclopédie,* 9 (1990), pp. 95–108

Fordyce, David. *Dialogues Concerning Education*. London, 1745

Forkel, Johann Nikolaus. *Allgemeine Geschichte der Musik*. 2 vols. Leipzig, 1788, 1801

Forman, Denis. *Mozart's Concerto Form: The First Movements of the Piano Concertos*. New York: Praeger, 1971

Framery, Nicholas Etienne, and Pierre-Louis Ginguené, eds. *Encyclopédie Méthodique, Musique*. Vol. 1. Paris: Panckoucke, 1791. Reprint, New York: Da Capo Press, 1971

Framery, Nicholas Etienne, Pierre-Louis Ginguené, and Jeŕome-Joseph de Momigny, eds. *Encyclopédie méthodique: Musique*. Vol. 2. Paris: Agasse, 1818. Reprint, New York: Da Capo Press, 1971

Fried, Michael. *Absorption and Theatricality: Painting and Beholder in the Age of Diderot*. Berkeley: University of California Press, 1980

Fubini, Enrico, ed., and Bonnie Blackburn, trans. *Music and Culture in Eighteenth-Century Europe: A Source Book*. Chicago: Chicago University Press, 1994

Fux, Johann Joseph. *Gradus ad Parnassum* (1725). Translated as *Gradus ad Parnassum: Practical Rules for Learning Composition*. London, 1768

Gallarati, Paolo. 'Mozart and Eighteenth-Century Comedy'. In *Opera Buffa in Mozart's Vienna*, edited by Mary Huner and James Webster, pp. 98–111. Cambridge: Cambridge University Press, 1997

Girdlestone, Cuthbert. *Mozart's Piano Concertos*. London, 1948. Reprinted as *Mozart and His Piano Concertos*. New York: Dover, 1964. First published in French as *W. A. Mozart et ses concertos pour piano*. Paris, 1939

Goertzen, Clifford. 'Compromises in Orchestration in Mozart's *Coronation Concerto*'. *Musical Quarterly* 75 (1991), pp. 148–73

Goethe, Johann Wolfgang von. *Essays on Art and Literature*. Edited by John Gearey. Translated by Ellen von Nardroff and Ernest H. von Nardroff. New York: Suhrkamp, 1986

——. *Verse Plays and Epics*. Edited by Cyrus Hamlin and Frank Ryder. New York: Suhrkamp, 1987

——. *Early Verse Drama and Prose Plays*. Edited by Cyrus Hamlin and Frank Ryder. New York: Suhrkamp, 1988

——. *Conversations with Eckermann (1823–1832)*. Translated by John Oxenford. San Francisco: North Point Press, 1984

——. *Wilhelm Meisters Lehrjahre*. Translated by Eric A. Blackall as *Wilhelm Meister's Apprenticeship*. New York: Suhrkamp, 1989

Grassineau, James. *A Musical Dictionary*. London, 1740. Reprint, New York: Broude Brothers, 1966

Grayson, David. *Mozart: Piano Concertos Nos. 20 and 21*. Cambridge: Cambridge University Press, 1998

Gregory, John. *A Comparative View of the State and Faculties of Man, with those of the Animal World*. 2nd edition. London: J. Dodsley, 1766

Grétry, André-Ernest-Modeste. *Mémoires, ou Essais sur la Musique*. 3 vols. Paris, 1796–7. New edition, Brussels, 1829

Habermas, Jürgen. *Theory of Communicative Action*. 2 vols. Translated by Thomas McCarthy. Boston: Beacon Press, 1984, 1987. German original, Frankfurt: Suhrkamp, 1983

Hanning, Barbara R. 'Conversation and Musical Style in the Late Eighteenth-Century Parisian Salon'. *Eighteenth-Century Studies* 22 (1988/89), pp. 512–28

Hatten, Robert S. *Musical Meaning in Beethoven: Markedness, Correlation and Interpretation*. Bloomington: Indiana University Press, 1994

Helm, Eugene. 'The "Hamlet" Fantasy and the Literary Element in C. P. E. Bach's Music'. *Musical Quarterly* 58 (1972), pp. 277–96

Hiller, Johann Adam. 'Abhandlung von der Nachahmung der Natur in der Musik'. In *Historisch-Kritische Beiträge zur Aufnahme der Musik*, edited by Friedrich Wilhelm Marpurg. Berlin, 1754. Reprint, Hildesheim: Georg Olms, 1970

Himmelfarb, Anne. 'A Mirror of Conversation: Studies in Late Seventeenth- and Eighteenth-Century English Dialogue'. Ph.D. diss., Columbia University, 1990

Hirzel, Rudolf. *Der Dialog, ein literarhistorische Versuch*. 2 vols. Leipzig, 1895

Hobson, Irmgard W. 'Goethe's *Iphigenie*: a Lacanian reading'. *Goethe Yearbook* 2 (1984), pp. 51–67

Holmes, Edward. *The Life of Mozart, including his Correspondence*. London: Chapman and Hall, 1845

Holquist, Michael, ed. *The Dialogic Imaginatin*. Trans. Caryl Emerson and Michael Holquist. Austin: University of Texas Press, 1981

Hosler, Bellamy. *Changing Aesthetic Views of Instrumental Music in 18th-Century Germany*. Ann Arbor: University of Michigan Press, 1981

Hoyle, John. *Dictionarium Musica, being a complete Dictionary or Treasury of Music*. London, 1770

Hoyt, Peter A. 'The Concept of *développement* in the Early Nineteenth Century'. In *Music Theory in the Age of Romanticism*, edited by Ian Bent, pp. 141–62. Cambridge: Cambridge University Press, 1996

Hudson, Nicholas. 'Dialogue and the Origins of Language: Linguistic and Social Evolution in Mandeville, Condillac and Rousseau'. In *Compendious Conversations: The Method of Dialogue in the Early Enlightenment*, edited by Kevin L. Cope, pp. 3–14. Frankfurt: Peter Lang, 1992

Hume, David. *Dialogues Concerning Natural Religion and the Posthumous Essays*. Edited by Richard H. Popkin. Indianapolis, Indiana: Hackett, 1990

——. *Essays: Moral, Political and Literary*. Edited by Eugene F. Miller. Indianapolis, Indiana: Liberty Classics, 1985

Hunter, Mary. *The Culture of Opera Buffa in Mozart's Vienna: A Poetics of Entertainment*. Princeton: Princeton University Press, 1999

Hunter, Mary and James Webster, eds. *Opera Buffa in Mozart's Vienna*. Cambridge: Cambridge University Press, 1997

Hurd, Richard. 'Preface: On the Manner of Writing Dialogues'. In *Moral and Political Dialogues: With Letters on Chivalry and Romance*. Vol. 1, pp. vii–lxvi. London: 1788

Hutchings, Arthur. *A Companion to Mozart's Piano Concertos*. 7th edition. Oxford: Oxford University Press, 1989

——. 'Concerto'. In *New Grove Dictionary of Music and Musicians*, edited by Stanley Sadie. Vol. 2, pp. 627–40. London: Macmillan, 1980.

Jahn, Otto. *Life of Mozart*. Translated by Pauline D. Townsend. New York: Cooper Square Publishers, 1970.

Jander, Owen. 'Romantic Form and Content in the Slow Movement of Beethoven's Violin Concerto'. *Musical Quarterly* 44 (1983), pp. 159–79

——. 'The "Kreuzer" Sonata as Dialogue'. *Early Music* 16 (1988), pp. 34–49

Johnson, Samuel. *A Dictionary of the English Language*. London, 1755. Reprint, London: Thames Books, 1979

Jones, Stephen. *Sheridan Improved. A General Pronouncing and Explanatory Dictionary of the English Language*. Wilmington, Delaware: Brynberg, 1804

Jones, Thora B. and Bernard de Bear Nicol. *Neoclassical Dramatic Criticism, 1560–1770.* Cambridge: Cambridge University Press, 1976

Jones, William. *A Treatise on the Art of Music in which the Elements of Harmony and Air are practically considered.* Colchester, 1784

Kann, Robert A. *A Study in Austrian Intellectual History: From Late Baroque to Romanticism.* New York: Praeger, 1960

Kecskeméti, Istvan. 'Opernelemente in den Klavierkonzerten Mozarts'. *Mozart-Jahrbuch 1968–70*, pp. 111–18

Keefe, Simon P. *Dialogue in the First Movements of Mozart's Viennese Piano Concertos.* Ph.D. diss., Columbia University, 1997

——. 'Dialogue and Drama: Haydn's Symphony No. 102'. *Music Research Forum* 11/1 (1996), pp. 1–21

Keller, Hans. 'K. 503: The Unity of Contrasting Themes and Movements'. *Music Review* 17 (1956), pp. 48–58, 120–9

Kennedy, Andrew K. *Dramatic Dialogue: The Duologue of Personal Encounter.* Cambridge: Cambridge University Press, 1983

Kerman, Joseph. 'Mozart's Piano Concertos and Their Audience'. In *On Mozart*, edited by James M. Morris, pp. 151–68. Cambridge: Cambridge University Press, 1994

Kinderman, William. 'Dramatic Development and Narrative Design in the First Movement of Mozart's C minor Concerto, K. 491'. In *Mozart's Piano Concertos: Text, Context, Interpretation*, edited by Neal Zaslaw, pp. 285–301. Ann Arbor: University of Michigan Press, 1996

Kirnberger, Johann Philipp. *Die Kunst des reinen Satzes in der Musik.* 2 vols. Translated by David Beach and Jürgen Thym as *The Art of Strict Musical Composition.* New Haven: Yale University Press, 1982

Knepler, Georg. *Wolgang Amadé Mozart.* Translated by J. Bradford Robinson. Cambridge: Cambridge University Press, 1994

Knigge, Baron von. *Über den Umgang mit Menschen.* Translated by P. Will as *Practical Philosophy of Social Life, or the Art of Conversing with Men.* London, 1799

Knouse, Nola Reed. 'Joseph Riepel and the Emerging Theory of Form in the Eighteenth Century'. *Current Musicology* 41 (1986), pp. 47–62

Koch, Heinrich Christoph. *Versuch einer Anleitung zur Composition.* 3 vols. Rudolstadt and Leipzig, 1782–93. Reprint, Hildesheim: Georg Olms, 1969. Translated by Nancy Kovaleff Baker as *Introductory Essay on Composition: The Mechanical Roles of Melody, Sections 3 and 4.* New Haven: Yale University Press, 1983

——. *Musikalisches Lexikon.* Frankfurt, 1802. Reprint, Hildesheim: Georg Olms, 1964

Kolb, Jocelyne. 'Presenting the Unpresentable: Goethe's Translation of *Le Neveu de Rameau*'. *Goethe Yearbook* 3 (1986), pp. 149–64

Kollmann, Augustus Frederick Christopher. *An Essay on Practical Musical Composition.* London, 1799. Reprint, New York: Da Capo, 1973

Komlós, Katalin. *Fortepianos and their Music: Germany, Austria and England, 1760–1800.* Oxford: Clarendon Press, 1995

Kronauer, Ulrich. 'Die Dramaturgie der Moral: Lessing zwischen Rousseau und Diderot'. In *Denis Diderot, oder die Ambivalenz der Aufklärung*, edited by Dietrich Harth and Martin Raether, pp. 90–103. Würzburg: Könighausen, 1987

Kross, Siegfried. 'Concerto–Concertare und Conserere'. In *Bericht über den Internationalen Kongress Musikwissenschaftlichen Leipzig 1966*, edited by Carl Dahlhaus, pp. 216–20. Kassel: Bärenreiter, 1970

Krug, William Traugott. *Allgemeines Handwörterbuch der philosophischen Wissenschaften, nebst ihrer Literatur und Geschichte.* Leipzig: Brockhaus, 1827

Kullman, Colby H. 'James Boswell and the Art of Conversation'. In *Compendious Conversations: The Method of Dialogue in the Early Enlightenment*, edited by Kevin L. Cope, pp. 80–9. Frankfurt: Peter Lang, 1992

Küster, Konrad. *Formale Aspekte des ersten Allegros in Mozarts Konzerten.* Kassel: Bärenreiter, 1991

Laborde, Jean Benjamin de. *Essai sur la musique ancienne et moderne.* 4 vols. Paris: E. Onfroy, 1780

Lacépède, Bernard Germain, Comte de. *La Poétique de la Musique.* 2 vols. Paris, 1785

Lamport, F. J. *German Classical Drama: Theatre, Humanity and Nation, 1750–1870.* Cambridge: Cambridge University Press, 1990

——. *Lessing and the Drama.* Oxford: Clarendon Press, 1981

Landmann, Ortrun. 'Einige Ueberlegungen zu den Konzerten "nebenamtlich" komponierender Dresdener Hofmusiker in der Zeit von etwa 1715 bis 1763'. In *Die Entwicklung des Solokonzertes im 18. Jahrhundert: Studien zur Aufführungspraxis und Interpretation von Instrumentalmusik des 18. Jahrhunderts*, edited by Eitelfriedrich Thom, pp. 57–73. Magdeburg: Blankenburg, 1983

Landon, H. C. Robbins. 'The Concertos: (2) Their Musical Origin and Development'. In *The Mozart Companion*, edited by Landon and Donald Mitchell, pp. 234–82. New York: Norton, 1956

Laporte, Joseph de. *Dictionnaire Dramatique, contenant l'Histoire des Théâtres, les Régles du genre Dramatique, les Observations des Maîtres les plus célebres et des Réflexions nouvelles sur les Spectacles, sur le génie et la conduite de tous les genres, avec les Notices des meilleures Piéces, le Catalogue de tous les Drames, et celui des Auteurs Dramatique.* 3 vols. Paris, 1776

Le Huray, Peter, and James Day, eds. *Music and Aesthetics in the Eighteenth and Early-Nineteenth Centuries.* Cambridge: Cambridge University Press, 1981

Lessing, Gotthold Ephrain. *Hamburgische Dramaturgie* (1769). Edited by Otto Mann. Stuttgart: Alfred Kröner, 1958. Translated by Helen Zimmern, as *Hamburg Dramaturgy.* New York: Dover, 1962

——. *Laocoön: An Essay on the Limits of Painting and Poetry* (1766). Translated by Edward Allen McCormick. New York: Bobbs-Merrill, 1962

——. *Minna von Barnhelm* (1767). Translated by Kenneth J. Northcott. Chicago: University of Chicago Press, 1972

——. 'Emilia Galotti' (1772). In *Five German Tragedies*, edited and translated by F. J. Lamport, pp. 31–103. Harmondsworth: Penguin, 1969

——. *Nathan the Wise* (1779). Translated by Bayard Quincy Morgan. Thirteenth edition. New York: Frederick Ungar, 1989

Lester, Joel. *Compositional Theory in the Eighteenth Century.* Cambridge, Massachusetts: Harvard University Press, 1992

Levin, Robert. 'Mozart's Piano Concertos'. In *The Mozart Compendium: A Guide to Mozart's Life and Music*, edited by H. C. Robbins Landon, pp. 263–4. London: Thames and Hudson, 1990

Levy, Janet Muriel. 'The "Quatuor Concertant" in Paris in the Latter Half of the Eighteenth Century'. Unpublished Ph.D. dissertation, Stanford University, 1971

——. 'Contexts and Experience: Problems and Issues'. In *Mozart's Piano Concertos: Text, Context, Interpretation*, ed. Neal Zaslaw, pp. 139–48. Ann Arbor: University of Michigan, 1996

Link, Dorothea. *The National Court Theatre in Mozart's Vienna: Sources and Documents, 1783–1792.* Oxford: Clarendon Press, 1998

Lippman, Edward. *A History of Western Musical Aesthetics.* Lincoln, Nebraska: University of Nebraska Press, 1992

Macdonald, Christie V. *The Dialogue of Writing: Essays in Eighteenth-Century French Literature.* Waterloo, Ontario: Wilfred Laurier University Press, 1984.

Maniates, Maria Rika. '"Sonate, que me veux-tu?" The Enigma of French Musical Aesthetics in the 18th Century'. *Current Musicology* 9 (1969), pp. 117–40

Marissen, Michael. *The Social and Religious Designs of J. S. Bach's Brandenburg Concertos.* Princeton: Princeton University Press, 1995

Marmontel, Jean. 'Dialogue'. In *Encyclopédie, ou Dictionnaire raisonné des sciences,des Arts et des Métiers, par une société de gens de lettres,* edited by Denis Diderot, Jean d'Alembert et al. Paris, 1751–72

Mazurowicz, Ulrich. *Das Streichduett in Wien von 1760 bis zum Tode Joseph Haydns.* Tutzing: Hans Schneider, 1982

McCarthy, John A. '"Verständigung" and "Dialectik": On Consensus Theory and the Dialectic of Enlightenment'. In *Impure Reason: Dialectic of Enlightenment in Germany,* edited by W. Daniel Wilson and Robert C. Holub, pp. 13–33. Detroit: Wayne State University Press, 1993

McClary, Susan. 'A Musical Dialectic from the Enlightenment: Mozart's *Piano Concerto in G Major, K. 453,* Movement 2'. *Cultural Critique* 5 (1986), pp. 129–69

——. 'The Blasphemy of Talking Politics During Bach Year'. In *Music and Society: The Politics of Composition, Performance and Reception,* edited by McClary and Richard Leppert, pp. 13–62. Cambridge: Cambridge University Press, 1987

Mercier, Louis Sébastien. *Du Théâtre, ou nouvel Essai sur l'Art Dramatique.* Amsterdam: Harrevelt, 1773

Merril, Elizabeth. *The Dialogue in English Literature* (1911). Reprint, New York: Burt Franklin, 1970

Meude-Monpas, J. J. O. de. *Dictionnaire de Musique.* Paris, 1787. Reprint, Geneva: Minkoff, 1981

Meyer, John A. 'Mozart's "Pathétique" Concerto'. *Music Review* 39 (1978), pp. 196–210

Milfull, John. 'The Sexual Politics of Mozart's *Magic Flute* and the Genesis of Viennese Charm'. In *Theatre and Performance in Austria,* eds. Ritchie Robertson and Edward Trimms, pp. 20–6. Edinburgh: Edinburgh University Press, 1993

Momigny, Jérome-Joseph de. *Cours complet d'harmonie et de composition.* 3 vols. Paris: Chez l'Auteur, 1803–1806

——. *La Seule Vraie Théorie de la Musique: ou le moyen le plus court pour devenir Mélodiste, Harmoniste, Contrepointiste et Compositeur.* Paris, 1821. Reprint, Geneva: Minkoff, 1980

Moore, Evelyn K. *The Passions of Rhetoric: Lessing's Theory of Argument and the German Enlightenment.* London: Kluwer Academic Publishers, 1993

Morrow, Mary Sue. *Concert Life in Haydn's Vienna: Aspects of a Developing Musical and Social Institution.* Stuyvesant, New York: Pendragon, 1989

——. *German Music Criticism in the Late 18th Century: Aesthetic Issues in Instrumental Music.* Cambridge: Cambridge University Press, 1997

Neue Zeitschrift für Musik. Edited by Robert Schumann et al. Leipzig: Breitkopf und Härtel, 1834–

Neumann, Frederick. *Ornamentation and Improvisation in Mozart.* Princeton: Princeton University Press, 1986

Niesz, Anthony J. *Dramaturgy in German Drama: From Gryphius to Goethe.* Heidelberg: Carl Winter Universitätsverlag, 1980

Oliver, Alfred Richard. *The Encyclopedists as Critics of Music.* New York: Columbia University Press, 1947

Oulibicheff, Alexandre. *Nouvelle Biographie de Mozart, suivie d'un apercu sur l'histoire générale de la musique et de l'analyse des principales œuvres de Mozart.* 3 vols. Moscow: Semen, 1843

Perry, William. *The Royal Standard English Dictionary.* Brooksfield, Massachusetts: Merriam, 1806

Pilkington, H. W. *A Musical Dictionary, Comprising the Etymology and Different Meanings of all the Terms that most frequently occur in Modern Composition.* Boston: Watson & Bangs, 1812

Platoff, John. 'Musical and Dramatic Structure in the Opera Buffa Finale'. *Journal of Musicology* 7/2 (1989), pp. 191–230

——. 'The Buffa Aria in Mozart's Vienna'. *Cambridge Opera Journal* 2/2 (1990), pp. 99–120

——. 'Tonal Organization in "Buffo" Finales and the Act II Finale of *Le nozze di Figaro*'. *Music & Letters* 72/3 (1991), pp. 387–403

——. 'How Original was Mozart? Evidence from *Opera Buffa*', *Early Music* 20/1 (1992), pp. 105–17

Powers, Harold. 'Reading Mozart's Music: Text and Topic, Syntax and Sense'. *Current Musicology* 57 (1995), pp. 5–43

Prudhoe, John. *The Theatre of Goethe and Schiller.* Oxford: Basil Blackwell, 1973

Quantz, Johann Joachim. *Versuch einer Anweisung die Flöte traversiere zu spielen.* Berlin, 1752. Translated by Edward R. Reilly as *On Playing the Flute.* New York: Schirmer, 1966

Ratner, Leonard G. *Classic Music: Expression, Form and Style.* New York: Schirmer, 1980

Reed, T. J. *The Classical Centre: Goethe and Weimar, 1775–1832.* Oxford: Oxford University Press, 1980

Reicha, Antoine. *Traité de mélodie.* Paris: Richault, 1814

——. *Traité de haute composition musicale.* 2 vols. Paris, 1824, 1826

——. *Art du compositeur dramatique, ou Cours complet de composition vocale.* Paris, 1833

Reimer, Erich. 'Concerto/Konzert'. In *Handwörterbuch der Musikalischen Terminologie,* edited by Hans Heinrich Eggebrecht. Vol. 1, pp. 1–17. Stuttgart: Fritz Steiner Verlag, 1972–

——. 'Die Polemik gegen Virtuosenkonzert im 18. Jahrhundert: Zur Vorgeschichte einer Gattung der Trivialmusik'. *Archiv für Musikwissenschaft* 30 (1973), pp. 235–44

Riepel, Joseph. *Sämtliche Schriften zur Musiktheorie. Band I: Anfangsgründe zur musikalischen Setzkunst* (1752–68). Edited by Thomas Emmerig. Vienna: Böhlau Verlag, 1996

Rochlitz, Johann Friedrich. 'Verbürgte Anekdoten aus Wolfgang Gottlieb Mozarts Leben: Ein Beitrag zur richtigern Kenntnis dieses Mannes, als Mensch und Künstler'. *Allgemeine musikalische Zeitung,* 1 (1798–99), pp. 17, 49, 81, 113, 145, 177, 289, 480, 854; 3 (1800–1), pp. 450, 493, 590

Rosen, Charles. *The Classical Style: Haydn, Beethoven, Mozart.* London: Faber, 1971; New York: Norton, 1971

——. *Sonata Forms.* New York: Norton, 1980

Rosen, David. 'The Composer's "Standard Operating Procedure" as Evidence of

Intention: The Case of a Formal Quirk in Mozart's K. 595'. *Journal of Musicology* 5 (1987), pp. 79–90
——. '"Unexpectedness" and "Inevitability" in Mozart's Piano Concertos'. In *Mozart's Piano Concertos: Text, Context, Interpretation*, edited by Neal Zaslaw, pp. 261–84. Ann Arbor: University of Michigan Press, 1996
Rousseau, Jean Jacques. *Dictionnaire de Musique.* Paris: Duchesne, 1768. Reprint, Hildesheim: Georg Olms, 1969
——. *Politics and the Arts: Letter to M. d'Alembert on the Theatre* (1758). Translated by Allan Bloom. Ithaca, New York: Cornell University Press, 1968
Ruile-Dronke, Jutta. *Ritornell und Solo in Mozarts Klavierkonzerten.* Tutzing: Hans Schneider, 1978
Schroeder, David P. *Haydn and the Enlightenment: the Late Symphonies and their Audience.* Oxford: Clarendon Press, 1990
Schwindt-Gross, Nicole. *Drama und Diskurs: Zur Beziehung zwischen Satztechnik und motivischem Prozess am Beispiel der durchbrochenen Arbeit in der Streichquartetten Mozarts und Haydns.* Laaber: Laaber-Verlag, 1989
Serwer, Howard. 'Sulzer, Johann Georg'. In *New Grove Dictionary of Music and Musicians*, edited by Stanley Sadie. Vol. 18, pp. 365–6. London: Macmillan, 1980
Shaftesbury, Third Earl of (Anthony Ashley Cooper). *Characteristics of Men, Manners, Opinions, Times.* London, 1711. Reprint, Hildesheim: Georg Olms, 1978
Sherman, Carol. *Diderot and the Art of Dialogue.* Geneva: Librairie Droz, 1976
Sidnell, Michael J., ed. *Sources of Dramatic Theory: 2. Voltaire to Hugo.* Cambridge: Cambridge University Press, 1994
Simon, Edwin J. 'The Double Exposition in the Classic Concerto'. *Journal of the American Musicological Society*, 10 (1957), pp. 111–18
——. 'Sonata into Concerto: A Study of Mozart's First Seven Concertos'. *Acta Musicologica* 31 (1959), pp. 170–85
Simon-Ingram, Julia. 'The Theatrics of Dialogue: Diderot and the Problem of Representation'. In *Compendious Conversations: The Method of Dialogue in the Early Enlightenment*, edited by Kevin L. Cope, pp. 357–67. Frankfurt: Peter Lang, 1992
Sisman, Elaine R. *Haydn and the Classical Variation.* Cambridge, Mass.: Harvard University Press, 1993
——. 'Haydn's Theater Symphonies', *Journal of the American Musicological Society* 43 (1990), pp. 292–352
——. *Mozart: The 'Jupiter' Symphony.* Cambridge: Cambridge University Press, 1993
——. 'Small and Expanded Forms: Koch's Model and Haydn's Music', *Musical Quarterly* 62 (1982), pp. 444–78
——, ed. *Haydn and His World.* Princeton: Princeton University Press, 1997
Smith, Adam. 'Of the Nature of that Imitation which takes place in what are called the Imitative Arts' (1795). In *Essays on Philosophical Subjects*, edited by W. P. D. Wightman and J. C. Bryce. Oxford: Clarendon Press, 1980
Snyder, Jon R. *Writing the Scene of Speaking: Theories of Dialogue in the Late Italian Renaissance.* Stanford: Stanford University Press, 1989
Solomon, Maynard. *Mozart: A Life.* New York: HarperCollins, 1995
——. *Beethoven.* New York: Schirmer, 1977
Sonnenfels, Joseph von. *Briefe über die Wienerische Schaubühne* (1768). Edited by Hilde Haider-Pregler. Graz: Akademische Druck- und Verlagsanstalt, 1988.

Staël-Holstein, Anne Louise Germain de. *Germany*. Translated from the French. New York: Eastburn, 1814

Stevens, Jane R. 'An 18th-Century Description of Concerto First-Movement Form'. *Journal of the American Musicological Society* 24 (1971), pp. 85–95.

——. 'Formal Design in C. P. E. Bach's Harpsichord Concertos'. *Studi Musicali* 15 (1986), pp. 257–97.

——. 'The Meanings and Uses of *Caractère* in Eighteenth-Century France'. In *French Musical Thought, 1600–1800*, edited by Georgia J. Cowart, pp. 24–52. Ann Arbor: UMI Research Press, 1989

——. 'Theme, Harmony and Texture in Classic-Romantic Descriptions of Concerto First-Movement Form'. *Journal of the American Musicological Society* 27 (1974), pp. 25–60

——. 'The "Piano Climax" in the Eighteenth-Century Concerto: An Operatic Gesture?' In *C. P. E. Bach Studies*, edited by Stephen L. Clark, pp. 245–76. Oxford: Clarendon Press, 1988

——. 'Patterns of Recapitulation in the First Movements of Mozart's Piano Concertos'. In *Musical Humanism and its Legacy: Essays in Honor of Claude Palisca*, edited by Nancy Kovaleff Baker and Barbara Russano Hanning, pp. 397–418. Stuyvesant, New York: Pendragon, 1992

——. 'The Basis of the Dramatic in Mozart's Piano Concertos'. Paper read at the Bicentenary Mozart Conference of the Royal Musical Association. London, 26–30 August 1991

——. 'The Importance of C. P. E. Bach for Mozart's Piano Concertos'. In *Mozart's Piano Concertos: Text, Context, Interpretation*, edited by Neal Zaslaw, pp. 211–36. Ann Arbor: University of Michigan Press, 1996

Strohm, Reinhard. 'Merkmale italienischer Versvertonung in Mozart's Klavierkonzerten'. *Analecta Musicologica* 18 (1978), pp. 219–36

Sulzer, Johann Georg, ed. *Allgemeine Theorie der schönen Künste*. 4 vols. Leipzig, 1771–74. Reprint, Hildesheim: Georg Olms, 1969

Swain, J. P. 'Form and Function of the Classical Cadenza'. *Journal of Musicology* 6 (1988), pp. 27–59

Swift, Jonathan. *A Complete Collection of Genteel and Ingenious Conversation* (1738). In *Swift's Polite Conversation*, edited by Eric Partridge. New York: Oxford University Press, 1963

Szondi, Peter. *Theory of the Modern Drama*. Translated and edited by Michael Hays. Minneapolis: University of Minnesota Press, 1987

Thomas, Downing A. *Music and the Origins of Language: Theories from the French Enlightenment*. Cambridge: Cambridge University Press, 1995

Till, Nicholas. *Mozart and the Enlightenment: Truth, Virtue and Beauty in Mozart's Operas*. New York: Norton, 1992

Tischler, Hans. *A Structural Analysis of Mozart's Piano Concertos*. Brooklyn, New York: Institute of Medieval Music, 1966

Tovey, Donald F. *Essays in Musical Analysis: Vol. 3, Concertos*. 7th edition. London: Oxford University Press, 1981

Triest, Johann Karl Friedrich. 'Remarks on the Development of the Art of Music in Germany in the 18th century', trans. Susan Gillespie. In *Haydn and His World*, ed. Elaine Sisman, pp. 321–94. Princeton: Princeton University Press, 1997

Türk, Daniel Gottlob. *Klavierschule, oder Anweisung zum Klavierspielen für Lehrer und Lernende*. Leipzig: Schwickert, 1789. Reprint, Kassel: Bärenreiter, 1962. Translated by

Raymond H. Haggh as *School of Clavier Playing*. Lincoln, Nebraska: University of Nebraska Press, 1982

——. *Klavierschule, oder Anweisung zum Klavierspielen für Lehrer und Lernende*. 2nd edition. Leipzig: Schwickert, 1802

Tyson, Alan. 'The Mozart Fragments in the Mozarteum, Salzburg: A Preliminary Study of Their Chronology and Their Significance'. *Journal of the American Musicological Society* 34 (1981), pp. 471–510

——. *Mozart: Studies of the Autograph Scores*. Cambridge, Mass.: Harvard University Press, 1987

——. 'Mozart's Piano Concerto Fragments'. In *Mozart's Piano Concertos: Text, Context, Interpretation*, edited by Neal Zaslaw, pp. 67–72. Ann Arbor: University of Michigan Press, 1996

Unverricht, Hubert. *Geschichte des Streichtrios*. Tutzing: Hans Schneider, 1969

Vlastos, Gregory. 'The Socratic Elenchus: Method is All'. In Vlastos, *Socratic Studies*, edited by Myles Burnyeat, pp. 1–38. Cambridge: Cambridge University Press, 1994

Wadia, Pheroze. 'Philosophy as Literature: The Case of Hume's Dialogues'. In *Compendious Conversations: The Method of Dialogue in the Early Enlightenment*, edited by Kevin L. Cope, pp. 34–53. Frankfurt: Peter Lang, 1992

Walch, Johann Georg. *Philosophisches Lexicon*. 2 vols. Leipzig, 1775. Reprint, Hildesheim: Georg Olms, 1968

Waldoff, Jessica and James Webster. 'Operatic Plotting in *Le nozze di Figaro*'. In *Wolfgang Amadè Mozart: Essays on his Life and Music*, edited by Stanley Sadie, pp. 250–95. Oxford: Clarendon Press, 1996

Walker, John. *A Critical Pronouncing Dictionary*. Philadelphia: Johnson & Warner, 1808

Walther, Johann Gottfried. *Musikalisches Lexikon*. Leipzig: Wolfgang Deer, 1732

Webster, James. *Haydn's 'Farewell Symphony' and the Idea of Classical Style: Through-Composition and Cyclic Integration in His Instrumental Music*. Cambridge: Cambridge University Press, 1991

——. 'Are Mozart's Concertos "Dramatic"? Concerto Ritornellos versus Aria Introductions in the 1780s'. In *Mozart's Piano Concertos: Text, Context, Interpretation*, edited by Neal Zaslaw, pp. 107–37. Ann Arbor: University of Michigan Press, 1996

——. 'The Analysis of Mozart's Arias'. In *Mozart Studies*, edited by Cliff Eisen, pp. 101–99. Oxford: Clarendon Press, 1991

——. 'Cone's "personae" and the Analysis of Opera'. *College Music Symposium*, 29 (1989), pp. 44–65

Webster, Noah. *A Compendious Dictionary of the English Language*. New Haven: Sidney's and Goodwin, 1806

Weimer, Eric. *'Opera Seria' and the Evolution of Classical Style, 1755–1772*. Ann Arbor: UMI Research Press, 1984

Weinsheimer, Joel. 'Afterword: The Primacy of Dialogue'. In *Compendious Conversations: The Method of Dialogue in the Early Enlightenment*, edited by Kevin L. Cope, pp. 401–5. Frankfurt: Peter Lang, 1992

Wen, Eric. 'Enharmonic Transformation in the First Movement of Mozart's Piano Concerto in C Minor, K. 491'. In *Schenker Studies*, ed. Hedi Siegel, pp. 107–24. Cambridge: Cambridge University Press, 1990

Wheelock, Gretchen A. *Haydn's Ingenious Jesting with Art: Contexts of Musical Wit and Humor*. New York: Schirmer, 1992

Will, Richard. 'When God Met the Sinner, and Other Dramatic Confrontations in Eighteenth-Century Instrumental Music'. In *Music & Letters* 78 (1997), pp. 175–209

Wolff, Christoph. 'Mozart 1784: Biographische und stilgeschichtliche Überlegungen'. *Mozart-Jahrbuch 1986*, pp. 1–10

——. 'Cadenzas and Styles of Improvisation in Mozart's Piano Concertos'. In *Perspectives on Mozart Performance*, edited by R. Larry Todd and Peter Williams, pp. 228–38. Cambridge: Cambridge University Press, 1991

Würtz, Roland. *Dialogué: Vorrevolutionäre Kammermusik in Mannheim und Paris.* Wilhelmshaven: Nötzel, 1990

——. '"Dialogué" und Mozart'. In *Mozart-Jahrbuch 1991*, pp. 71–6

Zaslaw, Neal. *Mozart's Symphonies: Context, Performance Practice, Reception.* Oxford: Clarendon Press, 1989

——, ed. *Mozart's Piano Concertos: Text, Context, Interpretation.* Ann Arbor: University of Michigan Press, 1996

Zimmer, Reinhold. *Dramatischer Dialog und Aussersprachlicher Kontext: Dialogformen in Deutschen Dramen des 17 bis 20 Jahrhunderts.* Göttingen: Vandenhoeck and Ruprecht, 1982

General Index

Index of Mozart's Works discussed in this book